Indonesia

500 km
200 miles

MALAYSIA

Sulu
Sea

Tacbolubu

Balabac

Banggi

Kudat

Kinabalu
4218m

Kanibongan

Sabah

Sandakan

Lahat Datu

**BANDAR SERI
BEGAWAN**

Tawau

Miri

Celebes
Sea

Natuna Besar
Panarik

Natuna Is.

Subi

Midai

Serasan

Datu Point

Iya

Igan

Mukah

Bintulu

Belaga

Malinau

Sesayap Lama

Tarakan

Tambalan

Sarawak

Longleju

Tanjung Selor

Sibu

Kanowit

Tanjung
Redeb

Paloh

Kuching

Sambas

Serlan

Simanggang

Kapit

Longnawan

Muaralasan

Batu Putih

Singkawang

Ngabang

Sangkulirang

Mempawah

Sintang

B o r n e o

Sanggau

Nangapinoh

Longiram

Muaramawai

Bontang

Pontianak

(Kalimantan)

Samarinda

Mt. Raya

Purukcahu

Sukadana

Muarateweh

Balikpapan

Ketapang

Palangkaraya

Tanah Grogot

Kendawangan

Kotawaringin

Pembuang

Amuntai

Sampit

Kualakapuas

Kandangan

Mamuju

Pangkalanbun

Sambar Pt.

Kumai Bay

Puting Pt.

Banjarmasin

Martapura

Kota Baru

Sulawesi

Tanjung
Pandan

Belitung

Strait

Laut

Laut Kecil Is.

Makassar Strait

Java Sea

Masalembu Is.

Makassar

Pulau Seribu
(Thousand Islands)

Bawean

Kangean Is.

Rembang

Pekalongan

Sumenep

Makassar

Bekasi
Kasikpek

Majalengka

Cirebon

Tegal

Semarang

Gresik

Madura

Bandung

Salatiga

Kudus

Surakarta

Bali Sea

Garut

Ciamis

Purwokerto

Magelang

Madiun

Kediri

Surabaya

Menjangan

Tulamben

Komodo

Cilacap

Yogyakarta

Malang

Jember

Gili Islands

Sumbawa
Besar

Pacitan

Banyu
Wangi

Bali

Mataram

Bima

a

v

a

Denpasar

Nusa Penida/
Lembongan

Padangbai

Lombok

Sumbawa

Belongas Bay

Sumb

rench

My first dives in Indonesia were in Bali in 2007 and I was immediately hooked! Since then, I have been fortunate enough to dive right across this phenomenal archipelago, experiencing some of the world's most unique marine life and wonderful people. The diving in Indonesia is truly world class with some of the best and most unspoiled reefs that I have ever encountered, and with every type of marine life imaginable, from huge pelagics to tiny critters and schooling fish. The corals in Indonesia are also amongst the most diverse in the world. With so much life around you, it is easy to understand the term 'the living reef'.

My most memorable underwater experiences have been in Indonesia, and there have been many, including diving with manta rays around Nusa Penida in Bali when an unexpected whale shark swam into the bay and circled us, seeing tasselled wobbegong sharks up close in Raja Ampat, being mesmerized by the outright bizarreness of the critters in the Lembeh Strait and experiencing unexplored and remote reefs in South Sulawesi. The sheer biomass and wilderness of areas such as Alor and Komodo are also truly amazing. Indonesia has also been a country of many firsts for me: my first whale shark sighting, my first manta rays, my first oceanic sunfish and my first Pontohi pygmy seahorse. Whether you are hoping to see big pelagics or minute critters, Indonesia does not disappoint and the diving can be surprising. Although there are no guarantees of what you will see underwater, you should always expect the unexpected in Indonesia!

The Indonesian people that I have worked with on this project have also been amongst the friendliest and most generous I could have wished for, often giving more than they have taken. Indonesian dive guides are often an exceptional source of marine information (and humor during long boat rides) and are incredibly passionate about their underwater heritage. It is this mix of extraordinary people, naturally breathtaking scenery and fantastic diving that makes Indonesia such a special place to me and one that I recommend to anyone with a taste for adventure and a love of diving.

DIVING IN
INDONESIA

The Ultimate Guide to the
World's Best Dive Spots

Sarah Ann Wormald

TUTTLE Publishing

Tokyo | Rutland, Vermont | Singapore

CONTENTS

EXPLORING THE WORLD'S LARGEST CHAIN OF ISLANDS

The Indonesian archipelago comprises approximately 17,500 islands covering an area over 5,000 kilometers long that stretches from mainland Southeast Asia in the west to Papua New Guinea in the east. Indonesia's islands are amongst some of the most stunning in the world, ranging from tiny coastal islets fringed with palm trees and white sand beaches to huge lands that support mountainous rainforests, volcanic peaks and fertile ricefields. Estimations as to the total length of Indonesia's coastline vary wildly, but even when taking a conservative estimate of 80,000 kilometers it still exceeds that of any other nation by far. The area covered by Indonesia includes over 1.9 million square kilometers of land and approximately 3.1 million square kilometers of ocean. It is hardly surprising then that the Indonesian people refer to their country as *tanah*

Left The *Shakti* liveaboard has been stationed in Raja Ampat since 2002 and offers 12 day expeditions.

Above A green sea turtle and scuba diver on a coral reef off Bunaken Island.

Below Indonesia is home to numerous species of lionfish, such as this one at Tulamben, Bali.

air kita, literally 'our land and water'. Indonesia is the world's fifteenth biggest country in terms of land area and the seventh largest in terms of land and sea combined.

Geographically, Indonesia is located in one of the world's most active and complex areas. It sits between two continental plates, the Eurasian and Australian Plates, and two oceanic plates, the Pacific and Philippine Sea Plates. This huge tectonic meeting point is subject to some of the world's greatest seismic activity. Indonesia has at least 150 active volcanoes and hundreds of dormant volcanic peaks. Earthquakes and tremors are therefore frequently felt throughout the region.

Indonesia is home to around 240 million people, which makes it the fourth most populated country in the world. The Indonesian people are made up of over 300 native ethnic groups and speak some 740 different languages and dialects. The majority of Indonesia's present-day population are descendants of Austronesian people who migrated to Southeast Asia from Taiwan around 2000 BC. Melanesians are another major group who mainly inhabit eastern Indonesia. The largest ethnic group by far are the Javanese, who make up 42 percent of the population and are both politically and culturally dominant in Indonesia today.

Indonesia's history has been shaped largely by trade since the 7th century when the Srivijaya Empire and later the Majapahit Empire traded with China and India. Trade did not just result in an increase in imported goods, but political, religious and cultural ideas were also exchanged and many were accepted and absorbed into Indonesian communities and Hindu and Buddhist kingdoms flourished. As a country with immense natural resources, Indonesia has a long history of attracting foreign interest. Islam, by far the most dominant religion, was brought to Indonesia by Muslim traders as early as the 13th century. By the 16th century, it was the established dominant religion of the land. Today, Indonesia is the world's most populous Muslim-majority nation. Christianity was similarly brought by traders, largely from Europe, who came seeking the treasures of the Spice Islands.

Contact between Indonesia and Europe did not begin properly until 1512 when the Portuguese sought to monopolize the trade in nutmeg and cloves, which were grown almost exclusively in the Malukus. The Dutch and the British were close behind the Portuguese, and once the Dutch established the Dutch East India Company (VOC) in 1602 they became the dominant European power. The VOC had enormous immediate success but finally dissolved into bankruptcy in 1800 and the government of the Netherlands established the Dutch East Indies as a nationalized colony. In many parts of Indonesia, evidence of Dutch rule is still visible in the form of forts, administrative buildings, houses and bridges. The Dutch era was finally brought to an end during the Japanese occupation of Indonesia during

A pair of honeycomb moray eels being cleaned by white banded cleaner shrimp.

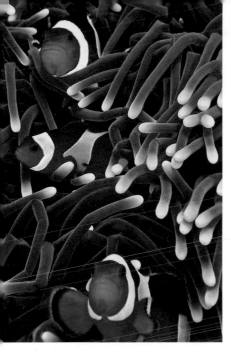

Anemonefish live in symbiosis with their host anemones, which have stinging tentacles.

provinces, each with its own administrative capital city or town and its own legislature and governor.

Indonesia has a tropical climate with two distinct seasons: the wet monsoon season and the dry monsoon season. Because Indonesia covers such a large area, the monsoon seasons vary from east to west but most of the country's annual rainfall falls over the highlands and mountains while many of the low-lying islands have very dry micro-climates. As one travels east across the archipelago, towards Australia, the climate becomes increasingly arid. Annual temperature range is minimal, varying on average between 28 and 32 degrees Centigrade, with humidity being around 80 percent.

Ideal growing conditions make Indonesia a major producer of rice, which is not only consumed domestically as the people's staple food but also exported. Indonesian cuisine also features coconut, chili, chicken and fish and draws upon influences from China, Europe, India and the Middle East. With a huge number of spices and herbs growing natively around the archipelago, Indonesian food is bursting with flavors.

the Second World War. Following the war, Indonesians, for the most part, found unity in their fight for independence, which was declared on August 17th, 1945 and eventually recognized by the Dutch in 1949.

Indonesia consists of hundreds of distinct native groups and the right to religious freedom is contained within the Indonesian Constitution. Whilst there are strong regional identities, there is a similarly strong shared national identity, which has developed with a national language called Bahasa Indonesia, religious acceptance and tolerance and a shared history of the fight for Independence. Indonesia's national motto, *Bhinneka Tunggal Ika*, meaning 'Unity in Diversity', is a true reflection of the makeup of this unique country.

Indonesia's capital city is Jakarta, home of the central government. Administratively, Indonesia is divided into 34

Farm worker on a green rice terrace, Ubud, Bali.

INDONESIA'S UNIQUE BIOGEOGRAPHY

Alfred Wallace, the Wallace Line and the Coral Triangle

ALFRED RUSSEL WALLACE

Alfred Russel Wallace (1823–1913) was a British naturalist, biologist and explorer most famous for conceiving the theory of evolution through natural selection. Wallace's paper on the evolution of species was jointly published with work from Charles Darwin, but when Darwin soon after published his book *On the Origin of Species* it was his name rather than Wallace's that became famously associated with theories of evolution.

Wallace was considered by many to be the 19th century's leading expert on the distribution of animal species and he has been referred to as the 'father of biogeography'. As well as studying the geographical distribution of species, Wallace made numerous contributions to evolutionary theory, including his pioneering work on the concept of warning coloration in animals. Unlike many other pre-eminent scientists and naturalists at the time, Wallace did not come from a wealthy family and he struggled with financial hardship throughout his lifetime. Much of his funding came from collecting specimens during his travels, which he sold to collectors back in Europe, with varying levels of success. Much of the fortune that he raised through his work as a collector he lost later in a series of bad investments leaving him to finance himself through writing numerous publications. Wallace struggled to find a permanent, long-term salaried position, and it was thanks to the efforts of Charles Darwin, amongst others, that he was eventually awarded a small government pension to support himself later in life.

Wallace documented his adventures meticulously and his reports of his explorations in Singapore, Indonesia and Malaysia are regarded by many as the best journals of scientific exploration published in the 19th century. During his travels in the Indonesian archipelago, Wallace collected over 126,000 specimens, several thousand of which were new discoveries to science. It was during his time in Indonesia that he pondered upon his theories of natural selection, which were published in 1869 in his highly acclaimed *The Malay Archipelago*, a work that was dedicated to Charles Darwin and has never gone out of print.

Wallace's theories were not met with enthusiasm from the outset as his ideas challenged not only scientific values but also religious ones. At the time in which he was writing, it was commonly believed that every species was created by God and Wallace's ideas challenged this age-old viewpoint by suggesting that species actually evolved over time as opposed to becoming extinct and that new species were not created by an almighty power.

THE WALLACE LINE AND WALLACEA

It was during his field research in Indonesia that Wallace began to notice differences between the fauna in the east and west of the archipelago. He discovered a faunal divide which split

Indonesia into two separate parts, what came to be known as the Wallace Line. He discovered that the animal species to the west of the line were all similar to or derived from species found on the Asian mainland whilst the species to the east of the line were largely of Australian descent. Along the line itself there was a mix of species, including some hybrids.

Millions of years ago, during the ice ages, sea levels were considerably lower than they are today, and Asia and Australia were joined together and formed one huge land mass on which numerous species lived, roamed and reproduced freely. This continued until the end of the ice ages when sea levels rose and plate tectonics started to take effect and pulled these land masses apart allowing water (oceans) to flood the spaces that opened up between them. As the two separate continents of Asia and Australia formed, the species that were locked into them began to evolve in different directions, making them quite specific to either continent. As time passed and isolated reproduction continued, the differences between the species, which had formerly been closely related, became much more pronounced.

The Wallace Line runs through Indonesia between Borneo and Sulawesi and down through the Lombok Strait that separates Bali and Lombok. Birds appear to mainly observe the line as many species do not fly over even narrow stretches of water and mammals are generally limited to either one side or the other. Other plant and animal groups show differing levels of observation of the line, but in general the division of species is strikingly consistent. One exception is the long-tail macaque (also known as the crab-eating macaque), which is one of only a few species of mammal found on both sides of the line.

The invisible Wallace Line is also noticeable from the geological landscape of the area, particularly when considering the continental shelf contours. The Wallace Line basically follows a deep-water channel that marks the southeastern edge of the Sunda Shelf that links Borneo, Bali, Java and Sumatra under

The soft coral crab is one of Indonesia's smallest and best disguised reef critters, Selayar, South Sulawesi.

water to the mainland of Southeast Asia. Australia is likewise connected via the shallow ocean over the Sahul Shelf to New Guinea. These geological features are indicators of the period when Asia and Australia were still one land mass.

When the two continents were formed, a number of islands and island chains were created along the Wallace Line, separated by deep water trenches from the Asian and Australian Continental Shelves. These islands are now collectively known as Wallacea and are home to a number of distinctive species. The Wallacea Islands include Sulawesi, Lombok, Sumbawa, Flores, Sumba, Timor, Halmahera, Buru and Seram and the many smaller islands

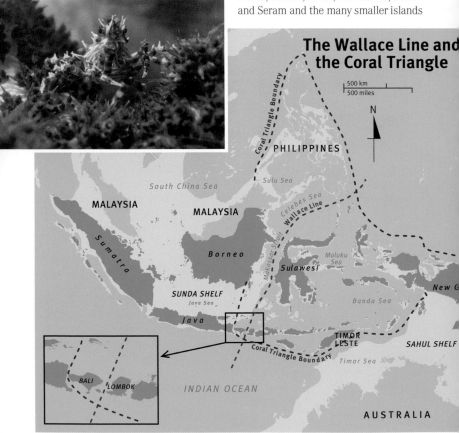

The Wallace Line and the Coral Triangle

500 km
500 miles

N

Coral Triangle Boundary

PHILIPPINES

South China Sea

Sulu Sea

MALAYSIA

MALAYSIA

Celebes Sea

Wallace Line

Sumatra

Borneo

Makassar Strait

Sulawesi

Maluku Sea

SUNDA SHELF

Java Sea

Banda Sea

New G

Java

TIMOR LESTE

SAHUL SHELF

Coral Triangle Boundary

Timor Sea

BALI   LOMBOK

INDIAN OCEAN

AUSTRALIA

that lie between Sumatra, Borneo and Java to the west and Australia and New Guinea to the south and east. In total, the Wallacea Islands encompass a land area of approximately 347,000 square kilometers and are the habitat of numerous endemic species of both plants and animals.

THE CORAL TRIANGLE

As well as straddling the Wallace Line Indonesia also sits in the heart of what is termed the 'Coral Triangle', an area

Vibrant coral reefs grow in Raja Ampat in West Papua, Indonesia. This region is at the heart of the Coral Triangle and contains more marine biodiversity than anywhere else on earth.

IC OCEAN

Coral Triangle Boundary

Bismarck Sea

PUA
W
NEA   Solomon Sea

recognized as being at the global epicenter of marine biodiversity. The Coral Triangle is a roughly triangular-shaped area covering the tropical marine waters of not just Indonesia but also Malaysia, Papua New Guinea, the Solomon Islands and East Timor.

Despite spanning only 1.6 percent of the world's oceans, the area hosts around 600 different species of reef-building corals (76 percent of the world's known coral species), 2,500 species of fish (37 percent of the world's fish species) and provides habitat for 6 species of threatened marine turtles, numerous endangered fish and cetaceans, such as tuna and blue whales. The Coral Triangle has been widely recognized as a global priority for conservation and there are numerous NGOs working on a range of conservation projects within the area focusing on the protection of vulnerable species, finding sustainable livelihoods for coastal communities and trying to reduce destructive fishing practices.

Despite the coral reefs within the triangle being of such global importance, they are amongst the most threatened in the world with almost every reef in the region being affected by overfishing. A large percentage have also suffered from destructive fishing practices. Land-based pollution and climate change and other global phenomena are also affecting coral reefs.

The extreme level of marine biodiversity in Indonesia is never more apparent than when scuba diving, and the number of species that can be seen on a single dive is truly astonishing. For an overview of the marine life that can be viewed in Indonesia's main diving areas, readers are directed to the 'What's To See?' columns in the tables on pages 14–17, which list not only marine species but also topographical features.

THE AIM OF THIS BOOK AND HOW TO USE IT

This book is designed to give an overview of the main diving destinations in Indonesia but it is by no means exhaustive. There are many, many places yet to be explored in Indonesia, but hopefully this book will guide people through the main areas that are both accessible and have diving facilities.

The aim of the book is not only to provide information to readers about diving destinations and dive sites in Indonesia but to also highlight operators who are following environmentally aware diving practices as well as safe diving practices. Readers should bear in mind that facilities across Indonesia vary greatly from east to west and therefore what operators are able to offer also varies according to location.

There are numerous operators in Indonesia who have gone above and beyond the call of duty in following environmentally aware practices and who have created marine parks and no-take zones that they patrol daily. Other operators are building schools and working with them to educate Indonesia's next generation about coral reef awareness. Some operators have even taken former shark finners under their wing and employed them in resort positions. It is this kind of commitment that really makes a difference and their continued success only means a more likely positive future for Indonesian reefs.

HOW THE BOOK IS STRUCTURED

Following introductory material on the islands of the Indonesian archipelago and their unique biogeography and marine biodiversity, an **Introduction** (pages 14–29) provides information relating to Indonesia's main diving areas (in handy table form), the variety and formation of its reefs and atolls, marine life conservation and protected areas, and general information on dive courses, equipment hire and purchase, guides and operators, and medical and insurance issues.

Seven chapters then deal with **Indonesia's Best Dive Sites** by region and subregion. At the beginning of each chapter you will find **(Name of region)**, a brief introduction and a map showing the dive sites featured in the chapter. Following on is **(Name of region) at a Glance**, which gives broad information about the region, including its geography, people, culture, food and general

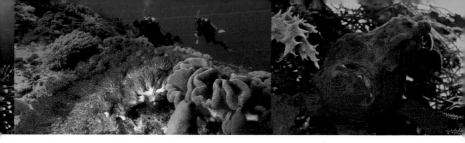

travel information, and then **Diving (Name of region)**, which gives specific diving information relating to all areas within the region and provides a list of useful contacts such as airports, dive equipment stores, hospitals and other medical centers, etc.

Each region is then broken down into individual diving areas, which all start with an overview, **Diving (Name of subregion)**, providing, first of all, general information about the geography and diving opportunities in the subregion, and then specific information on the *Difficulty Level* of the diving in that area, such as water temperature and visibility ranges, currents and conditions, *Highlights*, such as specific marine life or underwater topographical features and wrecks to look out for as well as possible marine life sightings, and *Logistics*, dealing with how to access the area.

The main part of each diving area comprises descriptions of **Best Dive Sites**, which have been selected to show a range of what is available in the area as well as the most notable sites. In some areas, sites have been described together when they have very similar conditions and topographies. The dive sites listed for each area are by no means all-inclusive, which would make this book impossibly long, but they do show a range that should offer something for all diving levels and tastes.

The **Travel Planner** section in each area is a summary of diving sites, sea conditions, packages, etc. as well as information about traveling from one area to another within the region. It also includes a section on *Recommended Operators*, including dive centers in the area that follow marine conservation practices and safe diving practices, as well as resorts or liveaboards. In some areas that are accessed by boat, transport operators have been recommended based on safety and service levels. Accommodation includes environmentally aware hotels and guest houses. In areas where the diving is not resort-based, recommended accommodation is also listed.

Accommodation has been awarded a $-$$$ rating based on the following pricing structure:

$	Less than US$50 per night
$$	US$50–$100 per night
$$$	More than US$100 per night

Each area also includes a **Marine Life Feature** that gives information about a specific fish or critter which can be seen in the area, and/or a **Conservation Feature** that provides information about conservation efforts taking place.

In the **Appendices** at the back of the book, there is additional information about *Liveaboard Diving in Indonesia*, a basic Bahasa Indonesia *Language Primer* of diving-related terms, a list of non-diving *Travel Practicalities* to consider prior to making your trip, *Dive Logs* for recording dive information and an *Index*.

Top, from left to right Exploring the USAT *Liberty* wreck; lionfish; anemonefish; coral reef; frogfish. **Far left** Reef in Lembeh, North Sulawesi.

INDONESIA'S MAIN DIVING AREAS

Region	Dive Destination	Water Temperature	Visibility	What's To See
Java	Pulau Seribu (Thousand Islands)	29–30 degrees year round.	5–10 meters average; less in rainy season, more in dry season.	*Papa Theo* wreck and an escape from Jakarta.
Bali	Nusa Penida and Nusa Lembongan	24–27 degrees July–October but thermoclines as low as 20 uncommon on the south coast; 27–29 degrees November–May.	Up to 30 meters++ June–October; from 15–20 meters November–May.	Mola July–October, year round manta rays, excellent reefs and reef life, excellent drift diving varying currents.
	Tulamben	27–29 degrees year round.	20 meters + June–October; 10 meters average November–March but substantially reduced following rain and big waves.	USAT *Liberty* shipwreck, pygmy seahorses, bump headed parrot fish, good muck diving with a range of critters.
	Padang Bai and Candidasa	Average of 28 degrees but around Tepekong, Biaha and Mimpang expect thermoclines as low as 21 degrees July–October.	Average 15 meters with less after rainfall and up to 30 meters+ in dry season (July–October).	A range of critters in Amuk Bay and Blue Lagoon, sharks, pelagics and possible mola around Tepekong and Biaha.
	Menjangan and Pemuteran	28–29 degrees year round but July–October cool thermoclines of 26 are present. See 'Other Advice'.	April–October 18–25+ meters; November–March 10–15 meters or less after rainfall.	A taste of walls, reefs and muck diving, beautiful gorgonian fans, turtles, seasonal sharks and a range of critters at Gili Manuk.
North Sulawesi	Bunaken	27–29 degrees year round.	15 meters December–February during wet season and up to 30 meters May–September in dry season.	Striking walls, green turtles, occasional passing eagle rays and sharks, good critter life and excellent marine biodiversity tropical chilled-out island resort.
	Lembeh	27–28 degrees for most of the year but July and August can be cooler, expect 26 degrees.	Year round visibility averages 10–15 meters. On very good days it may reach 20 meters.	Black sand muck diving sites with a host of critters, including numerous octopus species, flamboyant cuttlefish, rhinopias, various frogfish, eels, pipefish, seahorses and many more!
Central, South and Southeast Sulawesi	Togean Islands	Annual range of 28–32 degrees.	Average visibility 20 meters but can reach up to 40 meters March–May.	Excellent wall diving around Kadidiri, eagle rays and critters.
	Wakatobi (Tukangbesi Islands)	28–30 degrees year round but July–September temperatures can drop to 26 on occasion.	Average visibility is 20–30 meters.	Pristine reefs, stunning walls, critters, turtles, rays, sharks and picture perfect islands.

Best Time to Visit	Top Tips	Other Advice
May–September in the dry season when visibility is best.	Traveling farther from Jakarta costs more but is worth the money.	Unless you are diving with a reputable operator, take your own gear.
For mola, August, September and October are best. November has the best all round conditions, including some mola sightings, warmer water, good visibility and little rain.	Stay on Lembongan rather than diving from Bali. You will arrive at dive sites before they become crowded.	High season (June–October) has strong currents, cold water, busy dive sites and surface boat traffic. Follow the dive guide's advice.
May–October for best visibility.	Stay in Tulamben and make a sunrise dive on the *Liberty* to have it all to yourself!	July–October the wreck is very crowded with divers.
May–October for best visibility and increased chance of larger fish sightings.	Padang Bai is only a short trip from south Bali so if you don't want to move around too much day trips with Sanur operators work very well.	If planning to dive Tepekong, Biaha or Mimpang, check the swell forecast and be aware that these sites are best suited to experienced divers.
May–October during dry season for better visibility and the chance of pelagics.	This area has a mix of topographies. Try a bit of everything whilst you are here. Gili Manuk can be cold (21 degrees) so make sure you have adequate exposure protection.	Gili Manuk can be substantially colder (21 degree thermoclines) so pack a hood or vest or ask if you can hire one.
May–September is busiest for the dry season. Traveling a month either side of this period means dry conditions, good visibility and fewer divers.	Bunaken and Siladen have limited shopping facilities so pick up any essential supplies in Manado first. Listen out for turtles digging nests on the beach at night.	If your flight arrives in Manado late in the afternoon or leaves early in the morning, you may have to stay overnight in a city hotel rather than travel direct to or from Siladen or Bunaken.
Species move from time to time. For seasons, Lembeh is the same as Bunaken above.	Tell your guide from the outset what you are hoping to see. They will know which critters are at which sites at the time you visit.	Be prepared to see numerous critters but do not pin your hopes on one species too much. Things do come and go with irregularity.
March–May when visibility is best.	Dive sites near Una Una have more abundant fish life. Try snorkeling in the jellyfish lake.	Check boat schedules to and from Togean carefully. Many boats only run twice a week rather than daily.
Year round diving with little rainfall.	Diving around Tomia and its neighboring islands offers the best reefs.	If you are planning to dive with a small operator, it is advisable to bring your own gear as they may not carry a full range of sizes and fits.

Region	Dive Destination	Water Temperature	Visibility	What's To See
South Sulawesi	Selayar	28–30 degrees year round.	Up to 30 meters with an average of 20 meters.	Sharks, turtles, a range of rays, stunning coral walls with excellent macro life and beautiful island scenery, including nesting turtles. Some deep sites for more experienced divers.
Nusa Tenggara	The Gili Islands (Lombok)	29 degrees year round.	10–20 meters plus year round with less after rainfall or choppy seas.	Green and hawksbill sea turtles, white tip reef sharks.
	Belongas Bay South Lombok	26–28 degrees November–May. Thermoclines of 21–24 degrees June–October.	Average of 15 meters year round.	Schooling hammerheads and mobula rays.
	Alor	26–29 degrees but thermoclines as low as 20 degrees on occasion.	15–40+ meters. Reduced visibility at some sandy sites after rainfall.	Dolphins, pelagics, pristine reefs, abundant marine life and racing currents.
	Komodo	May–October 28 degrees in the north of the park. December–March operators dive the south which can be 20–24 degrees.	Best June–October with 25–35 meters in the north. December–March around 15 meters in the south.	Manta rays, reef sharks, unique topographies, excellent reef life with abundant fish and adrenaline-pumping currents.
	Kupang (Timor)	Year round 26–29 degrees.	Year round 10–20 meters, less after rainfall and choppy seas.	Stingrays and freshwater caves.
Maluku	Ambon Bay	27–29 degrees year round.	5–20 meters depending on weather and proximity to the monsoon season (July–September).	Wide-ranging critter life, including numerous species of frogfish, cuttle-fish, octopus, nudibranch, leaf scorpionfish, shrimps and crabs. *Duke of Sparta* wreck.
	Halmahera (Weda Bay)	28–30 degrees year round.	15 meters at worst after rainfall, up to 40+ meters during dry periods.	Breathtaking, immense coral walls, atoll reefs, sharks at deeper dive sites, no other boats, stunning terrestrial landscapes and birds of paradise.
Raja Ampat, West Papua	Misool	28–30 degrees year round.	15–25 meters average.	World-class soft corals, various reef sharks, epaulettes and wobbegongs, turtles, numerous rays inc. mantas, pygmy seahorses and critters. Extreme biomass in the MER no-take zone.
	Kri	27–30 degrees year round.	10–25 meters+ July–September is at the lower end due to winds.	Exceptional biomass, large schools of fish, a range of sharks and rays, turtles, critters and decent currents at some sites.

Best Time to Visit	Top tips	Other Advice
October–April when the seas are calmest.	Try fluoro diving at Selayar Dive Resort, an experience not to miss.	Selayar Dive Resort does not operate April–October.
April–October when sea conditions are calmest and there is least rainfall.	Choose your island carefully. They vary from offering very lively night scenes to remote getaways.	Seas can be choppy in the wet season November–March and boats are occasionally cancelled.
Late June–Late October for hammerheads. August and September are best for schooling mobula rays.	The area is very remote so pack a good book and enjoy the peace and quiet.	Some sites are for experienced divers only. Make sure you meet the requirements for diving here.
Diving all year but some operators close January–March for the rainy season.	Book well in advance. There are limited operators and places fill up fast.	Currents in Alor can be strong. Divers should have some experience in drift diving.
Excellent diving all year as operators switch from the north to the south seasonally.	If choosing a shore-based operator in Labuan Bajo, opt for one with speedboats that access all areas of the park.	There are strong currents in the marine park so diving is best suited to those with experience of drift diving.
Diving available all year but visibility is better during dry season months March–November.	There is only one operator so book in advance.	If diving the caves, make sure you have the appropriate experience and ability.
Diving is closed from around July– September (check with your operator). March–June has best visibility.	Let your guide know from the outset what you want to see. Critters move around and guides will know which sites offer the best sightings.	Diving immediately after the monsoon season (July–September) means lower visibility and more debris in the water. Carry a DSMB as there can be boat traffic overhead in the bay.
Diving is closed June–September (check with your operator).	Take time to join a rainforest trek or bird watching trip whilst you are here. Let your operator know in advance if you need gear hire.	This is a very remote area so pack everything you need and don't rely on being able to make purchases in the area.
Most operators close July–September. Diving around full moon or new moon means more current.	Bring your own exposure suit as many operators insist on this and a long 3 mm is recommended. Book as long a trip as time and finances allow as it is worth it.	This area is very remote and phone signal is limited to non-existent. Dive within limits and with a computer.
Pelagics are more common November–May. Visibility is best June–October.	Bring your own gear and if you don't like currents avoid full moon and new moon.	As with Misool, this area is very remote and phone signal can be limited. Dive within limits and with a computer.

INTRODUCING THE ULTIMATE DIVE DESTINATION

For many years Indonesia was just too far off the map for many divers to visit. It was viewed as an intimidatingly large country which could be incredibly difficult to travel through with poor transportation links, little infrastructure, unreliable communications and limited emergency services. Now, it is more accessible than ever before, particularly the western parts of the archipelago which have undergone vast changes and boomed with tourism in the last decade. Bali is the classic example where you can experience five-star hotels, luxury living and a lively bar and nightclub scene. This boom in tourist facilities is still fairly localized, though, and for those wanting peaceful, tranquil diving holidays it is easy to base yourself outside the tourist hotspots whilst benefiting from a wide choice of accommodation and dive operators. Transport across the archipelago does become a little more sporadic as you venture further east and some areas, such as Raja Ampat, are still very remote and the diving is still largely by liveaboards, but divers now have a choice in how remote they want to go. Arguably, there is nothing quite

like diving in an area where you are the only dive boat for miles around, but for those who do not want to venture quite so far east there is excellent diving with reputable operators right across the archipelago.

INDONESIAN REEFS

Indonesia is unique in that it boasts all types of reefs—fringing reefs, barrier reefs and atolls—on which to dive across the archipelago. Difficulty levels vary enormously from shallow, clear lagoons with little current to deep, open sea pinnacles with crashing waves and powerful currents. Indonesian reefs boast over 500 species of corals, 10,000 species of invertebrates and sea plants and over 3,000 species of fish. They are home to 6 out of 7 of the world's turtle species and more than one-third of all whale and dolphin species, and form part of the migratory routes of over 30 species of marine mammals. Indonesian reefs support the most varied and abundant marine life on earth.

FRINGING REEFS

The majority of reefs in Indonesia explored by divers are fringing reefs where the coral grows right up to the edge of the island. Fringing reefs in Indonesia are usually characterized by a reef 'flat' which can sit at anywhere between 1 and 10 meters before it 'drops off', either into a sloping reef or, in other areas, a vertical wall. Reef flats tend to have a limited range of coral species, usually robust branching corals and some soft species. There is generally

A scuba diver approaches a sea fan on a coral reef around Bunaken Island, North Sulawesi.

a high percentage of damaged coral and coral rubble resulting from wave action in the shallow waters and at several meters below the reef crest. Some fringing reefs also have a back reef or boat channel which is a little deeper and calmer than the reef flat itself and is usually more of a sandy area. Fringing, sloping reefs and walls provide for excellent diving as these are the areas where deeper dwelling marine species will come closest to the surface. Fringing reefs are usually subject to varying degrees of current as the water moves around the associated island. The currents bring nutrients to the reef in the form of plankton and quite often cooler water from the open sea. Fringing reefs are often the best place to see visiting pelagics, such as sharks, rays and even mola, as they visit the reef to either feed or be cleaned by the large numbers of smaller reef fishes. Fringing reefs are seen all around Indonesia and are usually accessed by boat or from shore.

BARRIER REEFS

A barrier reef is basically a fringing reef where the back reef or boat channel has become a large lagoon. The Great Barrier Reef in Australia is the most famous example and measures 2,000 kilometers in length and, in places, the lagoon is as much as 100 kilometers wide. An island can have several barrier reefs which extend outward around the island in a ripple-like formation and the lagoon between the barrier reef and the island can also harbor smaller patchy reef areas. Charles Darwin in his publication *The Structure and Distribution of Coral Reefs* theorized that all barrier reefs were at one stage fringing reefs which had then grown outward leaving a lagoon behind them and forming a barrier reef further out from the island. He went on to suggest that if, over time, the island subsided what would be left would be an atoll (see diagrams 1–3, page 22).

ATOLLS

Atolls–circular rings of coral growth with centralized lagoons rising up from the deep–are perhaps the most visually stunning of reef structures. The largest atoll in Indonesia is Taka Bone Rata Atoll

Left The Lembeh Strait in North Sulawesi is famed for critters but it also boasts a range of soft corals.

Below The crater rim of the stratovolcano Mount Agung is the highest point in Bali.

The *Aurora* liveaboard has eight guest cabins and makes expeditions across Indonesia.

in South Sulawesi (Flores Sea) and it is actually the largest atoll in Southeast Asia and the third largest atoll in the world. Taka Bone Rate is 72 kilometers by 36 kilometers and encompasses more than 20 small islands and numerous reefs. Atoll lagoons contain water that is considerably richer than the waters surrounding the atoll because, as deep ocean water filters through the walls of the atoll it collects nutrients that were previously locked away in the reef. The water inside the lagoon is completely cut off from the open ocean so this highly concentrated nutrient-rich water remains undiluted. This isolation of the water also means that is it unaffected by problems stemming from land, such as run-off containing pollutants. The effect is that atoll lagoons can support a much higher concentration of life than other lagoons, such as those that form behind barrier reefs.

Atoll formation has been examined in more recent times, and whilst Darwin's theory does make sense there are some areas where geological evidence does not entirely support his hypothesis. The 'Karstic Saucers' explanation also takes in to account the rise in sea levels following the ice age, a factor which Darwin did not consider. This alternate theory is based on the notion that exposed limestone, for example, an island, will be acted on by the weak acid contained in acid rain and will slowly erode in the center. Given that sea levels have risen

approximately 120 meters since the last ice age, the increase in water level means that as the center of the island erodes and the surrounding sea rises, only a rim will be left at the surface on which coral will form. The process of erosion in the center continues, making the island virtually hollow itself out into what we now see as a deep saucer shape–an atoll (see diagrams 4–6, opposite).

MARINE LIFE CONSERVATION AND MARINE PROTECTED AREAS

Coral reef habitats across the globe are facing a tremendous range of issues and pressures and Indonesian reefs are no exception. In parts of the archipelago, overfishing has and continues to be a major issue, with fish being caught for subsistence, domestic sale and international export. Sadly, destructive fishing practices, such as cyanide fishing and dynamite fishing, are also evident in some regions. Irresponsible tourism has led to some areas where corals have been broken, and anchor damage is also visible on numerous reefs. In the past, in some parts of Indonesia entire bays

Local children fish directly from the beach at sunset, Bali, Indonesia.

The Formation of Barrier Reefs

1 A fringing reef forms around an island.

2 The island sinks and the fringing reef grows into a barrier reef.

3 The island sinks below the surface, and only an atoll remains. (After Darwin, 1842)

The Formation of Atolls

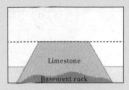  

4 Limestone is exposed by geological forces.

5 Rainfall erodes exposed limestone.

6 Water level rises and eroded limestone is colonized by coral. (After Purdy, 1974)

were dredged and the coral was almost entirely removed to be used as building material. During the rainy season, when there is run-off from the island land masses, large amounts of both natural and unnatural debris, a large portion of which is plastic, is washed into the waters. Many of these issues are not unique to Indonesia but are problems that affect reefs worldwide. Indonesia has innumerable pristine reefs but divers should be aware that from time to time, and depending on where and when you visit in Indonesia, they are likely to see some of these issues or at least their effects. When booking a dive trip in Indonesia, try to opt for operators who operate environmental dive practices and are active in reef and marine life conservation efforts. The recommended operators in this book have been selected on the basis of both their safe diving and marine conservation practices.

There are numerous marine parks (MPAs) across the archipelago and more are being created as education regarding the importance of reefs for both the

Blue sea stars are a common sight in Indonesia, particularly on shallow reef tops, Bunaken, North Sulawesi.

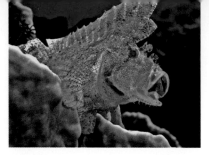

Leaf scorpionfish, such as the white one pictured here, can be difficult to spot amongst the corals.

environment and the economy becomes more widespread. The majority of marine parks are total no-take zones, which means no fishing, no harvesting of turtles eggs and no shell collecting. Other parks are divided into zones using similar titles. Whilst the parks are a big step forward, the main problem they face is enforcement of the regulations. In some areas, such as the Misool Eco Resort no-take zone in Raja Ampat and the Selayar Dive Resort in South Sulawesi, boats are used to patrol park waters and this seems to be effective. In other marine parks without patrols, there are still instances of destructive fishing practices and illegal fishing within the boundaries. One of the best ways to support a marine park is to dive there as many of the established parks have systems in place for divers to purchase park entry tags of varying duration and the fees fund the running of the park and its projects.

In addition to marine parks, there are numerous independent marine conservation projects all over Indonesia, ranging from turtle hatcheries and manta ray identification databases to artificial reefs and coral reef monitoring. The majority of these projects are worthwhile and help to increase awareness of various issues facing Indonesia's coral reefs and their inhabitants. Check with chosen operators(s) for conservation projects in the areas you are visiting which can be very interesting and informative. Often the operators welcome help.

ADDITIONAL CONSIDERATIONS

These are some additional points to consider when making a dive trip to Indonesia but this is not intended to be a comprehensive list:

Dangerous Marine Life

Although Indonesia is home to a number of venomous marine species, there are very, very few that will attack divers unprovoked. Most cases of marine injuries tend to be coral cuts, minor jellyfish stings and injuries caused by standing on marine creatures such as sea urchins and occasionally stonefish. The following is a brief listing of the most commonly found, potentially hazardous marine inhabitants of Indonesia:

- *Stinging marine creatures* Cone shells, stingrays, box jellyfish.
- *Stinging corals* Hydroids, fire coral.
- *Venomous marine creatures* Lionfish, stonefish, sea snakes (both olive and banded), crown of thorns sea star, sea urchins, blue ringed octopus.
- *Marine predators* Great barracuda: Usually will not attack but there have been reported bites when divers have approached too closely and too quickly. Wobbegong sharks: The same as for the barracuda above. Wobbegongs are bottom dwellers and bites have been reported following people standing on them. Titan triggerfish: Can be aggressive during nesting periods when they are known to charge at divers and bite on occasion.

Discounts

Discounts for diving are often available for professional-level divers (Divemaster level and above), expatriates living and working in Indonesia and Indonesian nationals. Large group bookings, divers making longer stays and large numbers of dives may also qualify for discounts depending on your operator's policies.

Check at the time of booking. Also see 'Bargaining' in the Travel Practicalities section, page 281.

Dive Boats

Across the archipelago a number of different boat types and styles are used for diving but most are small to medium sized speedboats with outboard engines that have been fitted out with tank rack holders and entry points and exit ladders for divers. Few traditional boats remain but the traditional *jukung* (a wooden boat with two outriggers) is still used in some parts of Bali, and whilst their numbers are dwindling in favor of fiberglass there is nothing that beats sailing on a large *jukung* for stability, space, comfort and a true feeling of being in Indonesia. The majority of liveaboards are either converted from original Indonesian *phinisi* schooners or have been purpose-built as liveaboards in the same style and using the same age-old building techniques. (See 'Liveaboard Diving in Indonesia', page 272.) Most larger operators own their own boats whilst smaller dive centers may use a range of charter boats and it is not entirely uncommon to find yourself on a very narrow fishing boat with the tanks laid at your feet. Facilities on

board day trip dive boats can vary from having nothing other than the boat and its captain to having a bathroom on board, dry areas, sun decks, GPS, prepared lunches, snacks, drinks and fresh water tanks for cameras. As a bare minimum, choose operators who carry first aid kits, oxygen, flotation devices and some form of communication equipment, which can range from marine radios to basic cell phones.

DIVE COURSES
Recreational Courses

Dive courses are widely available around Indonesia, from beginner courses to Divemaster training and above (see 'Professional Level Courses' overleaf). The majority of courses taught in Indonesia are PADI courses although in recent years SSI have increased their market share and other certifications are available through select operators, such as BSAC and CMAS. If you are hoping to take a dive course during your trip, it is advisable to book it in advance, especially if you are traveling at peak times. If you are traveling further east of Bali or

Above Balinese *jukung* boats, such as the one operated by World Diving Lembongan, offer very comfortable diving.

Left Although small, the blue ring octopus is one of Indonesia's most deadly marine creatures.

if you are taking a liveaboard, then it is imperative to book courses ahead of time to ensure that there is an instructor and materials available. On the whole, standards of training in Indonesia are amongst the highest in Southeast Asia but it is still worth spending a little time selecting the dive center that best suits your needs. Operators listed in this book are recommended for both fun diving and courses.

Professional Level Courses

Indonesia has undergone a boom in recent years in the number of professional level courses being taught, though most are conducted in Bali through major dive centers in Sanur. Instructor level courses vary from operator to operator and can be from two to six weeks and prices are similarly wide-ranging. Check to see what is included. Accommodation, course fees, exam fees, materials and registration costs may or may not be covered depending on the dive center. Instructor courses are also regularly offered in the Gili Islands, Bunaken and Nusa Lembongan. Instructor level courses are carefully scheduled by operators to coincide with the timing of Instructor Examinations so be aware that you will need to fit into operators' schedules unlike with recreational level courses which can be conducted at any time. Divemaster courses and other professional internships are widely offered and are similarly varied from operator to operator.

Recommended Operators for Professional Training

- *Bali*

Bali Scuba PADI 5 Star CDC Based in Sanur with purpose-built classrooms, training pool, range of boats, equipment hire, professional and friendly service. www.baliscuba.com. Tel: +62 (0) 361288 610. Email: letsdive@baliscuba.com.
Crystal Divers www.crystal-divers.com. Email: info@crystal-divers.com.
Blue Season Bali www.baliocean.com. Email: info@baliocean.com.

- *Nusa Lembongan*

World Diving Lembongan Well-established and reputable PADI center with training pool, range of boats and equipment hire. www.world-diving.com. Email: info@world-diving.com.
Blue Corner Dive www.balidivetraining. com. Email: info@bluecornerdive.com.

- *Gili Islands, Nusa Tenggara*

Trawangan Dive www.idc-gili.com. Email: idc@trawangandive.com.
Oceans 5 Dive ww.oceans5dive.com. Email: info@oceans5dive.com.

- *Bunaken Island, North Sulawesi*

Two Fish Divers www.twofishdivers. com. Email: info@twofishdivers.com.

Technical Diving Courses

Technical diving courses are available in Indonesia but they are not particularly widespread. The majority of operators offering technical diving courses are based in Bali although they are also available in other areas with select operators.

Opposite Large dive centers like Bali Scuba offer a range of facilities and professional level training.

DAN (Divers Alert Network)

DAN (Divers Alert Network) is the diving industry's largest safety association and they provide emergency assistance and medical information to recreational scuba divers. They also offer dive insurance, which is highly recommended. Some operators in Indonesia actually insist on a DAN policy (check with your operator). In the event of a dive incident in Indonesia, it is recommended that you call DAN Australia (the nearest branch) as well as your insurance company if you do not have DAN cover: DAN Australia: Tel +61 (0) 882129242 (English only).

EQUIPMENT HIRE AND PURCHASE

Equipment hire is readily available in areas such as Bali, Lombok, Komodo, North Sulawesi and South Sulawesi. However, as you travel east of these areas the choice and availability of gear for hire becomes increasingly limited. Most operators purchase their rental

gear from Bali or Jakarta, which takes time to be delivered, and because of shipping costs and often limited storage facilities they do not carry huge selections. Liveaboards and some resorts in Raja Ampat will require you to have at least the basics, such as a mask, fins and exposure suit, as they do not carry a large stock or range of sizes of hire gear. For diving in these areas, it is strongly recommended that you bring your own equipment. If you opt to hire gear, make sure you let operators know that this is your intention in advance and supply them with size requirements. Make sure you are aware of any items that you are required to bring with you.

Purchasing equipment in Indonesia can save you money depending on your home country. For example, buying gear in Indonesia is substantially cheaper than in Australia where equipment prices are considerably higher. Do your research before you come and try to order in advance. Bali has a number of dive equipment stores which supply Aqualung (also available in Jakarta), Mares and Scubapro brands. See below:

- *Master Selam* Aqualung supplier with retail outlets in both Bali and Jakarta. Also stocks Apeks, Trident, Suunto, Underwater Kinetics, Sea and Sea, Intova, Light and Motion, Ikelite, Bauer compressors and Luxfer cylinders. Orders can be placed in advance by

Master Selam have well-stocked equipment stores in both Bali and Jakarta and advance ordering is possible.

Manta rays are one of the largest and most majestic marine rays found in Indonesia.

email so that stock is ready for collection when you arrive. Aqualung service and repairs also carried out. www.master-selam.com. Email: enquiries sales@masterselam.com

- **Bali Branch** Jalan By Pass Ngurah Rai No. 314 Sanur, Denpasar 80228. Tel: +62 (0) 361283138. Fax: +62 (0) 21285736.
- **Jakarta Branch** Jalan Bangka Raya No. 39A Pela Mampang, 12720. Tel: +62 (0) 217199045. Fax: +62 (0) 217198974.
- **Dive Sport Bali** Jalan By Pass Ngurah Rai No. 25 B. ScubaPro supplier based in Sanur, Bali. Also stocks Uwatec, BARE, Sub Gear and GoPro. Tel: +62 (0) 361283463. www.divesportbali.com. Email: info@divesportbali.com.
- **Ocean King** Jalan By Pass Ngurah Rai No. 19. Mares supplier based in Sanur, Bali. Tel: +62 (0) 361710990. www.okdiveshop.com. Email: sales@okdive-shop.com.

Many operators have small retail facilities which stock smaller items such as masks, snorkels, clips and slates, but with the exception of some of the major diving facilities in Bali buying larger items of gear such as regulators and BCD's means a visit to a dive store.

GUIDES

Indonesia is home to some fantastic guides with keen eyes and exceptional local knowledge but it is also home to some difficult diving conditions and strong currents. It is strongly recommended that divers choose reputable operators with certified guides. A certified dive guide (Divemaster) will be trained to handle emergencies. Some

Below Frogfish, such as the one pictured here, are efficient hunters and use a lure to entice prey.

Bottom A traditional fishing boat (*jukung*) in the Komodo National Park, a paradise for diving and exploring and home to the famous Komodo Dragon, Nusa Tenggara.

insurance policies require divers to be diving with a properly certified and 'in date' dive guide. Many operators display their guides' certifications in their dive centers. If you are unsure of the level of training of the guide, check with your operator when booking.

Experienced dive guides based at reputable resorts tend to have reasonable English and some will be able to speak the basics of other European languages, most notably French and German.

INSURANCE FOR DIVING

Diving insurance is strongly recommended for anyone diving in Indonesia. Some operators, particularly those operating liveaboards and those in more remote parts of the country, will insist on seeing a copy of your policy when you arrive at the dive center or vessel. Whilst many operators do not require divers to have insurance, divers are urged to take out policies regardless. Hyperbaric chamber fees can be very expensive and not all areas where diving is available have a chamber nearby, so any policy should cover the policyholder for medi-vac. (Depending on the type of plane and destination medi-vac alone can cost US$25,000–30,000.) Check your insurance documents carefully and make sure you are aware of any depth restrictions on the policy. Ideally, it should cover you to 40 meters. Most policies will NOT cover divers who are decompression diving or diving to depths which are in excess of their certification level so make sure that you are staying within recreational dive limits and within the limits of your training. Some policies also require divers to be accompanied by a certified dive guide. See 'Guides' on page 26. Dive insurance through DAN (Divers Alert Network) is highly recommended (see page 25).

MEDICAL CLEARANCE

Learning to Dive When enrolling in dive courses you will be asked to complete a medical questionnaire to ensure your fitness to dive. If you have any pre-existing medical conditions you will need medical clearance from a doctor. A minor medical examination may also be necessary. Your examining doctor will need to provide you with a medical clearance letter which states that you are fit for diving. Examinations can be done in Indonesia but it is strongly recommended that if you have any known conditions, particularly those that affect the lungs, heart, sinuses, ears or may cause blackouts or convulsions, you seek medical guidance and clearance from your own doctor prior to making the trip. If in doubt about any medical issues ask your operator to email you a medical questionnaire in advance and seek professional medical guidance.

CERTIFIED DIVERS

When signing up for diving you may also be asked to complete a medical questionnaire. If you have any pre-existing conditions or conditions that have developed since your last dive training, a medical clearance letter should also be sought.

This hyperbaric chamber, located in Bali, is one of Indonesia's two internationally recognized recompression facilities.

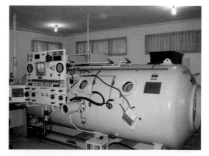

Stunning, colorful soft corals decorate the reefs around Siladen Island, North Sulawesi.

NITROX/ENRICHED AIR

Nitrox is widely available in Indonesia, particularly on liveaboards where many operators actually require you to have a nitrox certification. Some areas that have strong currents do not use nitrox due to concerns that divers will exceed the safe diving depths for the specific gas blend. In many areas where nitrox is offered, it is free of charge but in other areas you should expect to pay a surcharge. Check with your operator.

RECOMPRESSION CHAMBERS

Indonesia has a number of recompression chambers in a mixture of public hospitals, petroleum company facilities and naval and military hospitals. If you suspect Decompression Illness (DCI), the first step is to contact your insurance provider. (Many policies that cover you for recompression treatment state that you have to attend the chamber of their choice, not your own.) Depending on where you are in Indonesia, the reliability of the nearest chamber and the severity of your symptoms you may be advised to go to the nearest chamber or you may be transported by medi-vac to one in a different region or even overseas (both Darwin and Singapore are close options for some areas of Indonesia). Out of the numerous chambers in Indonesia, only those in Bali and North Sulawesi are internationally recognized hyperbaric facilities:

BALI RSUP Sanglah, Jalan Diponegoro, Denpasar, Bali. Emergency Tel: +62 (0) 361226363 or for the switchboard operator +62 (0) 361227911 or 227915.

NORTH SULAWESI RS Prof Dr R. D. Kandou, Jalan Malalayang, Manado, North Sulawesi. Tel: +62 (0) 431853191.

Other chambers have been listed in regional sections of this book but divers are strongly urged to contact DAN (Divers Alert Network, page 25) and their insurers first to check their procedures for dealing with DCI cases in the area you are visiting.

SAFETY CONSIDERATIONS
Recommended Equipment

Whilst basic equipment is available for hire in most areas of Indonesia, it is recommended that divers invest in some basic safety essentials. The following list of equipment is strongly recommended for all divers:

- *Dive computer* This is the most reliable method of ensuring you do not exceed no-decompression limits. Make sure you are familiar with the computer's settings and functions prior to diving.
- *An SMB* (Surface Marker Buoy) and for those that know how to use them, a DSMB (Delayed SMB) is preferable. These are by far the best visual signaling aids. A DSMB that can be put up from at least 5 meters (preferably from 30 meters with a reel), allowing you to send the SMB up in advance of surfacing.
- *An audible signaling device* such as a whistle.
- *A secondary visual signaling device* such as a torch or signaling mirror.
- *Underwater torch*
- *Reef hooks* for those who have experience with them.
- *A tank banger* or other means of making noise underwater. Tank bangers

in the form of pointer sticks also work well for stabilizing yourself in current.

Note: Some operators require you to carry an SMB and other signaling devices. Check for any requirements with your operator when booking.

Single Divers

If you are traveling alone, reputable operators usually group you with divers of the same experience and certification level and provide you with a buddy in the form of another guest or the dive guide.

Hotels in some areas will charge a single supplement, whilst in others discounts are given for having only one person in a room. Check the operator's policy on single travelers when booking.

Liveaboards will often charge hefty single supplements if you want your own cabin but if you are happy to bunk in with another single traveler usually the supplements do not apply. A couple of dive resorts also operate this policy with their rooms. Some of the more exclusive live aboards now also offer single cabins at their standard rate.

Technical Diving and Rebreathers

Technical diving and rebreather facilities are available throughout Indonesia but on a substantially smaller scale than recreational diving due to limited access to gas mixes. Check with your chosen operator when booking to see what they can cater for.

TIPPING DIVE STAFF

Check with your operator for their policy on tipping staff. If you would like to reward an individual guide or instructor directly, ask them if it is okay to do so. In general a rate of US$5-$10 per day is suggested by many operators for guides and instructors. (See also 'Tipping' in Travel Practicalities, page 284.)

WORKING IN DIVING IN INDONESIA

Working in Indonesia on a tourist visa is strictly prohibited and immigration officers do regular checks on dive centers in major tourist areas. Being caught out can come with hefty implications for the individual and the company involved. If you are coming to Indonesia to work, it is best to secure a position before you arrive. Reputable companies will include in the salary package a working visa, called a KITAS, and a work permit. Generally, the KITAS and work permit are valid for one year but it is possible to purchase six month permits too. If you are planning to arrive in Indonesia and then secure a position, you will need to leave the county (usually to Singapore) to attend the Indonesian Embassy for processing of the KITAS. Usually the logistics of this will be taken care of by your employer. Check the visa situation you are being offered by any potential employer before accepting a position.

KITAS and work permits are available for instructors but generally not for Divemasters as this is considered a position that can be filled by Indonesian nationals so most companies will require an instructor level certification.

Frogfish colors vary. This picture from Padang Bai, Bali, shows both blue with red and grey specimens.

INDONESIA'S BEST DIVE SITES

The Welcome Monument, one of Jakarta's most iconic monuments, is situated near the Grand Hyatt roundabout.

Jakarta, Indonesia's Main Entry Point

Jakarta, the capital city of Indonesia, is situated on the northwest coast of Java. The international airport, Soekarno-Hatta, is the largest in Indonesia and many travelers find themselves transiting here on their way to other parts of Indonesia. For those who are new to Asia, the culture shock can be startling. Jakarta is a city of enormous proportions. With an estimated population of 10.3 million in 2011, it is the most populous city in Southeast Asia. It has immediately apparent drawbacks. It is polluted, disorganized, subject to flooding, overcrowded, humid, chaotic and at times nothing short of bewildering. Despite this, it is a major up and coming city and if you have enough time to explore and ample patience there are luxurious shopping malls, five-star hotels, vibrant night life, a rich mix of cultures and a hip and cosmopolitan outlook. Jakarta is a city of contrasts where gleaming modern skyscrapers tower over shanty slums and where street food stalls trade for less than a dollar a dish outside of the city's most decadent restaurants. Depending on how long you are here for (and how brave you are) you can choose to embrace the city or steer clear of it!

On arrival at Soekarno-Hatta airport there is a USD35 Visa on Arrival fee (unless traveling from an exempt country). If you do not have cash, you will be escorted to an ATM.

For overnight layovers there are some reasonable airport hotels. The FM7 Resort Hotel (www.fm7hotel.com); Reservations +62 (0) 2155912525) and the Sheraton Bandara Hotel (www.sheraton.com/bandara); Reservations +62 (0) 215597777) both offer shuttle buses to and from the airport. For those staying longer than 12 hours, the city can be explored relatively easily but allow plenty of time for traffic jams and unexpected delays, especially in the rainy season! The airport has three terminals; T1 for domestic flights, T2 for international and T3 (the newest and most pleasant) for low-cost carriers.

Blue Bird Taxis are the most reputable and are found widely across the capital. From the airport to Merdeka Square in Central Jakarta it takes approximately one hour. Places of interest include the National Monument (Monas), Kota Batavia (the old Dutch colonial part of Jakarta), Istiqlal Mosque (the largest mosque in Southeast Asia) and for shopping lovers there is no shortage of malls. Try Grand Indonesia and Plaza Indonesia near the Welcome Monument or to really splash out Senayan City and Plaza Senayan.

If your layover is less than six hours, it's not worth venturing out and your best option is to stay either in the airport or check into a nearby hotel and make the most of the facilities.

Diving Pulau Seribu
A Small Island Chain Just to the North of Jakarta

Unlike what its name (Thousand Islands) suggests, there are only 110 islands in the Pulau Seribu archipelago, which stretches 45 kilometers north of Jakarta. By government decree, only 36 islands are designated for recreational use and of these only 11 have resorts and 2 are historic parks. Twenty-three of the islands are privately owned and the remainder are either uninhabited or support small fishing communities.

Historically, the islands were used by the Dutch as part of their defense of Jakarta and Onrust Island became a naval base in 1610 under the VOC. Today, it is protected as an historical site. Administratively, the Thousand Islands fall under the province of Jakarta. They are, in fact, the only regency of Jakarta with Pramuka Island being the capital.

The islands closest to Jakarta suffer from heavy pollution resulting from the poor living conditions of those resident on the coast of Jakarta and from industrial pollution and waste water from the city. But as you move progressively away from the Jakarta end of the archipelago,

Above One of the Thousand Islands, known locally as Pulau Seribu, Indonesia.

water clarity improves dramatically.

The northern part of the Thousand Islands' chain is now a National Marine Park and there are numerous conservation projects in place there, including protected mangrove areas and a hawksbill turtle rehabilitation and breeding program on Pramuka Island.

The best time to visit the Thousand Islands is from May to September during the dry season. From November to March, the rainy season results in even lower visibility and there can be large quantities of rubbish in the water as a result of run-off from Java. Heavy rainfall and stormy conditions also mean boat crossings are less comfortable.

Accommodation on the Thousand Islands is basic and many resorts appear shabby. If you are looking for luxury, take a longer trip and head down to Bali. Seasonally, there can be a lot of mosquitoes around the islands, so pack repellent.

Pulau Seribu Islands

Dua Barat I.

Dua Timur I.

Penjaliran Timur I.

Gosong Rengit I.

Peteloran Kecil I.

Penjaliran Barat I.

Penjaliran Timur I.

Pabelokan I.

Jagung I.

Rengit I.

Nyamplung I.

Sebaru Besar I.

Bundar I.

Kapas I.

Sebaru Kecil I.

Lipan I.

Pantara Timur I.

Pantara Barat I.

Laga I.

Iyu Kecil I.

Iyu Besar I.

Saktu I.

Kayu Angin Melintang I.

Kelor Barat I.

Kelor Timur I.

Semut Besar I.

Jukung I.

Cina I.

Sepa Timur I.

Melinjo I.

Sepa House Reef

Melintang Besar I.

Perak I.

Sepa Barat I.

Tondan Timur I.

Putri House Reef

Pelangi I.

Papa Theo Wreck

Melintang Kecil I.

Tongkeng I.

Putri Timur I.

Tondan Barat I.

Panjang Bawah I.

Putri Gundul I.

Putri Barat I.

Kayu Angin Putri I.

Kayu Angin Bira I.

Belanda I.

Macan Kecil I.

Matahari I.

Bira I.

Genteng Besar I.

Kuburan Cina I.

Genteng Kecil I.

Bira Kecil I.

Bulat I.

Kayu Angin Genteng

Pamegaran I.

Panjang Kecil I.

Panjang Besar I.

Kelapa I.

Harapan I.

Kaliage Besar I.

Semut Kecil I.

Opak Besar I.

Kaliage Kecil I.

Opak Kecil I.

Kotok I.

Kotok House Reef

Peniki

J a v a   S e a

Karya I.

Panggang I.

Pramuka I.

Karang Beras I.

Ayer I.

from Marina Ancol by spee

from Muara Angke

Tidung Besar I.

Tidung Kecil I.

from Marina Ancol by

from Muara Ang

Payung Besar I.

Kudus Lempeng I.

Karang Kudus I.

Tengah I.

Biawak I.

Kongsi I.

Pari I.

Tikus I.

from Marina Ancol by

from Muara Angke

Burung I.

from Marina Ancol by speed boat,

from Muara Angke by ferry, 2.5 hrs

Lancang Besar I.

Lancang Kecil I.

Bokor I.

Laki I.

PULAU SERIBU ISLANDS

20 km
10 miles

Java Sea

Tanjung Pasir

Muara Baru

Muara Angke

Marina Ancol

JAKARTA

PULAU SERIBU'S BEST DIVE SITES

Looking out over the ocean from one of Pulau Seribu's many white sand beaches, it is hard to imagine that Jakarta is only a relatively short boat ride away. The islands are good for weekend escapes, and whilst the diving does not compare to that found in other parts of the archipelago there are a handful of reasonable sites with a mix of marine fishes and creatures. Pulau Seribu is worth a visit when you don't have the time to travel farther afield, and it is a practical option for those based in Jakarta who want to learn to dive before exploring some of Indonesia's better known areas.

PAPA THEO WRECK

The *Papa Theo* wreck lies on a sandy slope to the east of Papa Theo Island at between 15 and 30 meters. The wreck was a small cargo ship that sank in 1981, and despite being under water in an area with currents for over 30 years it is still reasonably intact and now forms the base of a mini reef system. Visibility around the wreck is only around 5 meters on average and there can be currents. To go round the entire wreck involves diving to just over 30 meters. It is therefore not a recommended site for inexperienced divers. Access to the site is by boat and the entry point is directly over the wreck. If currents are running fast, then enter up current and a negative entry may be required. Whilst fish life around the wreck is mediocre at best, the wreck has

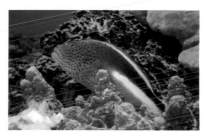
Brightly colored hawkfish are often seen perched on hard corals, Indonesia.

developed a reasonable coverage of hard and soft corals. Plate corals cover much of the structure, with soft colorful tubers, small fans and groups of sea whips decorating the sides and deck of the vessel. Bushy feather stars are found on most boulder coral formations and there are several small barrel sponges and branching formations scattered around. The wreck provides habitat for several shade-dwelling species such as pinnate batfish, lionfish and occasional blue spotted stingrays. Numerous species of reef fish are found on the wreck, albeit not in vast numbers: butterfly fish, angelfish, damsels and wrasse all swim in and out of the structure and moray eels and scorpionfish are amongst some of the more interesting residents.

The *Papa Theo* is certainly not in the same league as the USAT *Liberty* in Bali (pages 68–9), but it is a pleasant enough wreck dive if you are in the area and not put off by the low visibility.

This honeycomb moray eel's mouth and teeth are being cleaned by a white banded cleaner shrimp.

Moray Eels *Muraenidae*

There are numerous genera of moray eel that collectively cover around 200 different species, all of which fall into the Muraenidae family. Moray eels range in size from the smallest barely stretching to 12 cm to the largest being in excess of 2 meters.

Moray eels are found in warm and temperate waters worldwide and they are commonly seen on both deep and shallow water reefs. All genera have numerous physical traits in common, including long, elongated bodies, slightly flattened tails and large mouths which house numerous sharp and pointed fang-like teeth which work in tandem with a second set of 'teeth' in their throats.

During the daytime, it is unusual to see a moray eel out in the open and the most common sightings are of moray eel heads peering out of crevices. To breath, the moray eel opens and closes its mouth to suck in water, which passes over the gills and exits through the vented openings on the back of the moray's head. This mouth action is sometimes misinterpreted as threatening behavior.

Although moray eels appear to be shy and secretive, they are serious carnivorous

Fimbriated moray eels are also known as spot-face moray eels due to their black markings.

predators whose diet consists of reef fish, molluscs and shrimps. They are one of the only species of fish that have been noted to engage in interspecies hunting, whereby two or more eels will work together to force prey from its shelter. Moray eels have few predators themselves, only some sharks, barracuda and large groupers.

Moray eels are frequently thought to be a dangerous reef inhabitant but evidence shows that their natural instinct is to hide and not fight. However, there have been reports in the past of moray eels biting divers, but in almost all instances the eels were provoked. Moray eels have relatively poor vision and rely on their sense of smell (using their tube-like nostrils), and most bites have stemmed from feeding incidents when the eel has mistaken fingers as part of the food being offered. It is worth noting that moray eels have a strong bite which cannot be released, so any bite means the jaws of the eel must be literally pried off— a good reason not to feed them!

Some of the commonly seen species in Indonesia include the giant moray eel, yellow margin moray eel, fimbriated moray eel, white mouth moray eel, white eyed moray eel, honeycomb moray eel, zebra moray eel and the snowflake moray eel. Moray eels have beautifully patterned bodies and different species have different markings ranging from fine stripes to spots and patches.

Moray eels usually hide amongst the corals during the day rather than swim, like this fimbriated moray.

KOTOK HOUSE REEF (KOTOK JETTY)

An easy jetty dive featuring an artificial reef, reasonable fish life but visibility can be limited and coral damage is evident.

Starting from the jetty on the north side of Pulau Kotok, at around 5 meters, head directly out (north) and down to 20 meters where the artificial reef (and toilet!) is positioned. Once you have explored the deeper area, head east making your way back up the sloping reef to the shallows. Finish by swimming back along the top of the reef to the jetty. The site can be dived in reverse if the currents are running from east to west. Aside from the artificial reef there are some pleasant patchy coral areas between 10 and 15 meters to the east of the jetty. As with most dive sites in Pulau Seribu, fish life is mediocre and damage to the reef is visible, especially in the shallows where the predominant bottom composition is coral rubble. Fish life is best around the artificial reef where it is possible to see angelfish, butterfly-fish, Moorish idols, wrasse, lionfish and schools of damselfish hovering over branching corals, making for a pretty reef scene. On good days, schooling fusiliers also pass over the reef. Do not cast aside the rubble areas without having a look first as they frequently harbor some interesting bottom dwellers. Nudibranchs, moray eels and gobies are often spotted and blue spotted stingrays are not unusual.

Kotok House Reef is often used as a training site for dive courses as it provides easy conditions, a gentle slope and enough of a range of marine life to satisfy beginners.

SEPA HOUSE REEF AND JETTY

A sloping coral reef which starts from the jetty on the west side of Pulau Sepa, which is characterized by medium density hard and soft coral, and whilst fish

Despite being brightly colored, lizardfish blend in well with their reef environments.

life is not abundant this site does have a reasonable variety and on occasions turtles have been spotted here.

Visibility at Sepa House Reef averages 5 to 10 meters but this is a shallow site and conditions are usually mild, which makes it suitable for all levels.

From the jetty, make your way down the sloping reef which peters out to a sand bottom at around 20 meters. The dive is to the south of the jetty following the shoreline of the island. Make your way progressively shallower until reaching the reef crest at 5 meters. The reef displays some patches of healthy corals, mainly branching, plate and boulders, with soft corals interspersed, and in the 15 meter range there is a selection of gorgonian fans that are worth investigating. On the sandy bottom, blue spotted stingrays are often seen along with flounders lying camouflaged. The reef offers mediocre fish numbers but Moorish idols flit about the reef, angels and butterfly fish add color to the scene, moray eels nestle into the reef and boxfish, puffer-fish, triggerfish and porcupinefish are all seen with regularity.

This is not a dive that will take your breath away, but if you are in Jakarta and desperate to dive, the sites in Pulau Seribu are at least something to dip your fins into!

PULAU SERIBU
TRAVEL PLANNER

The Thousand Islands offer year round warm water of 29 to 30 degrees and most operators hire 3 mm short suits as standard. If you have booked through a Jakarta dive center, they will take care of equipment requirements for you, but if booking direct with one of the resorts you will need to arrange this with them. Equipment standards vary from resort to resort but generally equipment maintenance standards appear to be at the low end. If you have your own gear, it is worth taking.

As visibility averages 5 to10 meters, an underwater signaling device—a tank banger or rattle—is recommended. Most sites are dived relatively shallow but there are some deeper dives, such as the *Papa Theo* wreck which, at the lowest point, reaches 32 meters.

Operators from Jakarta carry first aid kits and oxygen. Medical supplies in resorts vary from resort to resort. The nearest recompression chamber is in Jakarta.

Dive sites offer medium density coral and fish numbers, and in many areas the reef is badly damaged from destructive fishing practices. That said, there are some pleasant dives with a range of marine species and relatively easy diving conditions.

Pulau Seribu's popularity is increasing as more and more Jakartans are looking for weekend getaways. Hopefully, increased tourism here will see an improvement in standards, which are not unacceptable but are generally basic at the time of writing.

Difficulty Level

Many Jakarta operators use Pulau Seribu sites for dive training as they are generally easy with little current, shallow reefs and warm water. However, visibility averages 5 to 10 meters and can be less after rainfall.
HIGHLIGHTS Warm water, blue spotted stingrays at many sites and occasional turtles and the *Papa Theo* wreck.
LOGISTICS Getting to the Thousand Islands is relatively simple. If you are booking through a Jakarta-based dive operator, most will include transport from Ancol Marina (north Jakarta) as part of the package price. If you are booking diving and accommodation directly through one of the resorts on the islands, they also include transport in the package. Boat travel time varies depending on which island you are staying on. The closest islands, such as Ayer and Bidadari, are around 30 minutes by fast boat, but if you are traveling to one of the northern islands, such as Sepa or Putri, it takes around two hours by fast boat depending on the sea conditions.

Most operators offer weekend diving packages which include an early morning departure from Ancol on a Saturday morning followed by two dives in the afternoon, an overnight stay, two dives on Sunday morning and a return boat to Ancol on Sunday afternoon.

Sepa Island is one of the islands of the Thousand Island chain near Jakarta, Java.

Weekend Getaways

The diving in Pulau Seribu does not lend itself particularly well to long stays as there is a limited number of sites, but it is ideal for those living and working in Jakarta who want to make short weekend trips as it does not involve flights. The following is an itinerary for a weekend break to the islands:

SATURDAY Early morning departure from Ancol Marina to the island of your choice (note that the islands further from Jakarta offer better conditions). Arrive mid-morning in time for lunch and two afternoon dives. Overnight in Pulau Seribu.

SUNDAY Two morning dives followed by lunch and then return boat transfer back to Ancol Marina.

Boat transfers are included in the weekend package prices offered by operators.

Island Hopping

It is possible to travel from one island to another without transiting back through Ancol, but you will need to let operators know in advance and it can be quite expensive and also depends on the time of year.

Tips for your trip

▶ Make sure you allow enough time on Saturday morning to reach Ancol Marina as traffic starts building up early on a weekend. If you need to cross the city, set off early.

▶ Check with your operator in advance which pier your boat will depart from as there are numerous piers and it can be confusing.

▶ Take a taxi to Ancol as it will be able to take you closer to the pier than the car park, which means less distance to carry gear. It can also be quite difficult and expensive finding a parking space.

▶ Pre-book your taxi to pick you up from the pier on Sunday afternoon.

This white mouth moray eel is one of the more shy and solitary species of moray eel found in Indonesia.

▶ If you are able to stay longer than a weekend, it is possible to extend your stay. Check with your operator if you are considering this.

Jakarta Dive Centers and Pulau Seribu Dive Trip Operators

Master Selam Jalan Bangka Raya, No. 39A Pela Mampang, Jakarta 12720. Tel: +62 (0) 217199045. www.masterselam.com.

Bubbles Dive Center Jalan Guru Mughni No. 18, Jakarta. Tel: +62 (0) 2152922233. www.bubblesdivecenter.com.

Kristal Klear Dive Hotel Kristal, Jalan Tarogong Raya, Cilandak Barat, Jakarta Selatan 12430. Tel: +62 (0) 2175818025. www.kristalkleardive.com.

Pulau Seribu Resorts

Alam Kotok All inclusive resort on Kotok Island. Tel: +62 (0) 215356958. www.alam-kotok.co.id.

Sepa Island Beach Resort All inclusive resort on Sepa Island. Tel: (agent) +62 (0) 216827 4005. www.sepaisland.com.

BALI

Bali is known as the Island of the Gods, and with swirling colors, breathtaking landscapes, lively dances, almost daily ceremonies, rich culture and tradition it certainly lives up to its name. Bali also offers some incredible dive sites without being as remote as other areas in Indonesia. There is a range of accommodation options, from five-star hotels to backpacker guest houses, making it possible for all budgets and tastes. Bali gives you a flavor of Indonesia but you don't necessarily have to forget about your home comforts, unless you want to, in which case it is still easy to lose yourself in the rice fields

SEE MENJANGAN AND PEMUTERAN MAP

Bali Sea

Pasir Cape   Menjangan I.
                        Teluk Antrima Bay
Ketapang
            West Bali
            National Park   Banyupoh   Gondol Beach
                        Pejarakan   Lovina Beach
                        Pemuteran   Banyuwangi   Penyabangan
Gilimanuk   Jayaprana   Hot   Natural Gas   64
            Grave Site   Spring   Mount   Pura Pulaki   Musi   Gerokgak   Kalisada   Seririt   Temukus
            Pura Bakungan   Sangiang   Pura Melanting   12
Banyuwangi   Historic   1004m   Brahma Arama
            Site   Mount   Mount Bajra   Vihara
            Protestant   Blimbing Sari   Merebuk   1077m   Busung Biu   Views
            Community   1394m
    Melaya   Eka Sari   Catholic   Mount   Sepang
                        Community   Pakukajang
            Warna Sari   1288m
    Candi Kesuma   Manis Tutu   Munduk
    Pabuahan Cape   31   Tista   Temu
    Munduk Ranti   Baler Bale Agung   Manggis Sari   Kebon Padangar
    Banyu Biru   Negara   Yeh Embang   Bunut Lobang
    Buffalo Races   8   Kauh   Asahduren   Pangeragoan   Mundeh
    Pangambengan   Mendoyo   Medewi   Kangin
                Dangin Tukad   Pekutatan   Mundeh
    Pengambengan   Yeh Kuning   Pura Rambut   Gumbrih
    Cape   Siwi   Mundeh
                                Medewi Surfing   Lumbu
                                Beach   Lalang Linggah
                                            Soka Beach   Bajera
                                            Enjung Menalo
                                            Pasut Beach

INDIAN OCEAN

away from the hubbub of the tourist areas. The diving around Bali covers a range of sites: walls and easy conditions in Menjangan, critter-laden black sands in Padang Bai and Tulamben and vibrant reefs and adrenaline-pumping currents around Nusa Penida. Macro life is abundant off the mainland as the islands of Nusa Penida and Lembongan attract bigger fish, including manta rays and mola. Padang Bai also offers some challenging dives and good opportunities to see sharks. Tulamben boasts the US *Liberty* shipwreck and good critter life. In short, there is little that Bali does not deliver!

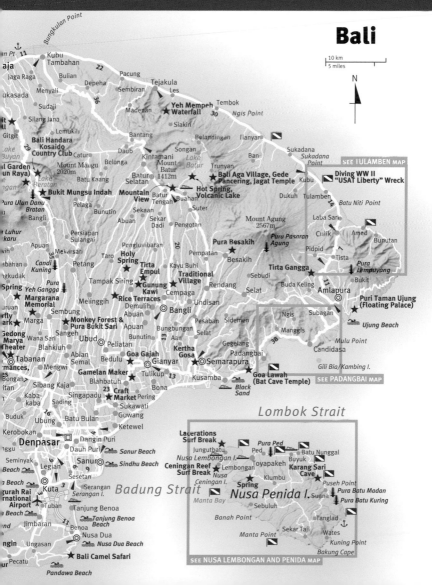

Bali

10 km
5 miles

N

Bali at a Glance
The Paradise Island of the Gods

At just under 6,000 square kilometers, Bali is only a small part of Indonesia but it has undoubtedly one of the biggest personalities. From lively, colorful dance displays to peaceful and serene meditation there is something about Bali which will inspire everyone. Bali is approximately 153 kilometers from east to west and approximately 112 kilometers from north to south, but within that area it boasts a wealth of natural beauty, from dramatic volcanoes to picture postcard white sand beaches.

Bali is home to over 4,000,000 people, over 90 percent of whom are Hindu. The Balinese way of life has been inspired by numerous cultures, including Indian, Chinese, Hindu and Buddhist. This rich mix can be traced back through Balinese history to when the Javanese Hindu Majapahit Empire, of which Bali became a colony in 1365, declined in the 15th century, resulting in an exodus of some of the most highly regarded intellectuals, artists, musicians and religious heads from Java to Bali.

Young dancers perform a welcome dance in a full moon ceremony in Bedulu village, Ubud, Bali.

BALINESE HINDUISM

Balinese Hinduism stems from both Indian Hinduism and Buddhism and provides a complete belief system incorporating philosophy, mythology, theology, animism, ancestor worship and even magic. It forms part of everyday life, from making numerous daily offerings to dealing with the death of a loved one. For all major (and most minor) events, there are ceremonies to be held, procedures to be followed and practices to be carried out, all of which are done with incredible attention to detail, enthusiasm and pride.

The prevalent feature of the Balinese Hinduism religion is one of 'balance'. For all good there must be equal evil, and the majority of the ceremonies are based on restoring and maintaining this balance. The legendary stories of good versus evil are often displayed through the many Balinese dances that are definitely worth watching with their swirling colors, rhythmic sounds and limitless energy! The dances range from surprisingly formal to seemingly unchoreographed leaping and crouching. The most famous Balinese dances are the Kecak and Legong, of which there are displays throughout the year. The traditional music for Balinese dances is played on the Gamelan, an instrument similar to the xylophone but accompanied by a range of cymbals and gongs. The music is entirely percussion with the musicians becoming as animated as the dancers.

ARTS AND CRAFTS

Balinese painting, sculpture and wood carving are famous the world over and pieces can be seen and purchased all over the island. Look out for Balinese masks and kites in particular.

TOURISM

Western tourism began in Bali as far back as the 1930s when the island was portrayed as a spiritual land with a harmonious population at peace with themselves and nature. Tourism had early setbacks at the time of the Sukarno presidency but several events led to a turnaround. In 1963, Mount Agung erupted, killing thousands, and this was followed by a change in government. Indonesian relations with Western countries were re-established and the paradise island image was restored.

The tourism industry in Bali has had to face more recent problems following both the 2002 and 2005 Bali bombings in which many tourists, largely Australians, were killed. Despite these tragic events, however, tourism numbers have now returned to the pre-bombing levels. Western governments have lowered travel advice warnings for Indonesia and most areas are considered 'safe' places to visit. There are currently a number of Western tourists in custody in Bali for drugs-related offences for which Indonesia has a zero tolerance approach.

GETTING IN AND AROUND

Bali's main airport, Ngurah Rai International Airport, also known as Denpasar International Airport, is situated 13 kilometers south of Denpasar, approximately a one-hour drive from

Some of the most dramatic and spectacular rice terraces in Bali can be seen near the village of Tegallalang, Ubud, Bali.

both Sanur and Kuta depending on traffic. Most major international airlines and almost all Indonesian domestic airlines fly into Ngurah Rai on a regular basis. Taxis are widely available from the airport. It is best to choose one that operates on a fixed pricing system rather than trying to 'agree' a price with the driver. Taxi drivers in Bali are well used to Western travelers and most speak basic English.

The Bali Bombing Memorial in Kuta commemorates those who lost their lives in the 2002 bombing.

Diving Bali
A Small Island With Huge Variety

The diving around Bali is every bit as diverse as the island itself. Dive sites vary from warm, turquoise water in tranquil bays to sites in front of harsh rocky cliff faces with chilling thermoclines, powerful surges and ferocious currents. There is something for every level of diver here, from the beginner to the seasoned expert. The diversity of marine life is exceptional also. Bali provides one of the few opportunities for divers to see the mighty mola or sunfish (see Marine Life Feature for Nusa Penida and Nusa Lembongan, pages 58-9), manta rays and other large pelagics. But diving in Bali is not only for big fish enthusiasts. Macro divers have a selection of treats awaiting them, too, such as pygmy seahorses, orangutan crabs and ghost pipefish to name but a few, all of which can all be found on Bali's fringing coral reefs. In short, it would be a tough challenge to find a diver who would not be happy with diving in Bali!

Tulamben in Bali is home to a large school of bumphead parrotfish, pictured here with a diver observing them.

In recent years, the diving industry has developed rapidly, with many more dive centers offering a wider range of dive sites and dive courses at more competitive prices. As the number of foreign divers has increased, there has been a subsequent increase in facilities for divers. Dive equipment stores have opened up; there is an internationally recognized recompression chamber; dive operations have opened up in different locations within the region making multi-region trips easy to organize; nitrox is now widely available as are professional level courses in a range of languages; a growing number of dive centers focus on technical diving and there has also been a noticeable improvement in general dive practices and environmental awareness. Gone are the days when throwing an anchor from the dive boat was deemed acceptable. As a result of numerous mooring buoy projects in the early 2000s, most sites now have mooring buoys specifically for dive boats. Since these changes came into play, coral has regenerated in areas that were previously suffering from anchor damage. Various environmental and conservation projects are in action all over Bali, from collecting marine debris to protecting sharks, and turtle hatcheries have resulted in the once depleting number of turtles around the island making a healthy recovery.

Dive areas that were previously only accessed by long boat trips or laborious car journeys have now developed into diving hubs with new accommodation,

Top The ornate ghost pipefish is one of the six known species of ghost pipefish.

Above Manta rays such as this one often feed on plankton close to the surface, creating incredible silhouettes.

restaurants and other facilities opening up. This means that divers are no longer holed up in South Bali but are able to stay in the regions where they wish to dive. Whilst it is entirely possible to dive all regions of Bali from one of the main tourist areas in the south, it is no longer necessary and this eliminates long traveling times each day which, in turn, means more time under the water!

Each dive area in Bali has numerous operators to choose from (see individual regions for recommendations), most of which are able to cater for divers of all experience levels, and offer spectacular reefs and an incredible range of marine life. From muck diving to the mighty mola, Bali has it all!

USEFUL CONTACTS

Medical Centers

Bali International Medical Center
Jalan Bypass, Kuta, Denpasar.
Tel: +62 (0) 361761263.

SOS Medical Center Jalan Ngurah Rai
Bypass, Denpasar. Tel: +62 (0) 361
720100. www.sosindonesia.com.

Recompression Chamber

Sanglah Rumah Sakit Jalan Diponegoro,
Denpasar. Tel: +62 (0) 361227911.
www.sanglahhospitalbali.com.

Dive Stores

Master Selam Jalan Ngyrah Rai Bypass,
Sanur. Aqualung (Suunto and Apeks) dive
equipment supplier with a good selection of new equipment and spares. Also
able to service and repair Aqualung
equipment on site. Tel: +62 (0)
361283138. www.masterselam.com.
Email: sales@masterselam.com.

Dive Sport Jalan Ngyrah Rai Bypass,
Sanur. Scubapro dive equipment supplier
with selection of new gear and spare
parts, minor repairs and maintenance
can be carried out on site. Tel: +62 (0)
361766888 (Kuta) or +62 (0) 361283463
(Sanur). www.bali-divesport.com.

Ocean King Jalan Ngyrah Rai Bypass
No. 19, Sanur (100 meters from Lotte
Mart traffic lights). Mares dive equipment
supplier with large selection of new
equipment and spare parts. Servicing
and maintenance also offered. Tel: +62
(0) 361710990. www.okdiveshop.com.

Others

DPS (Ngyrah Rai) International Airport
Tuban, Kuta, Denpasar.
Tel: +62 (0) 361751011.

Directory Enquiries 108

BALI TRAVEL PLANNER

Bali is not a large island but the diving regions are spread out and range from the most northwestern corner to the small islands off the east coast. Fortunately, travel around Bali is relatively simple and many operators will help with logistics if these are booked in advance. Below are a number of itineraries of various duration, including 1 day trips, 5 to 6 day tours for those on week-long holidays, 7 day adventures and a complete 12 day itinerary taking you to the best of the diving regions that Bali has to offer.

Day Trips From a Central Base

Whilst Bali offers a range of diving areas spread out along its coastline and offshore islands, for those traveling with children or non-diving family members moving from place to place is not always practical or desirable. If you are based in one of the tourist regions in the south, there are numerous operators based in Sanur who offer daily fun diving trips to all areas around the island, including Menjangan (usually an overnight trip), Tulamben, Padang Bai, Amed and Nusa Penida. Operators provide hotel pick-ups in the morning, road or boat transport to your destination of choice, 2 to 3 shore or boat dives and lunch before having you back in your hotel by mid to late afternoon. Not only is this easier than moving your group around, it means you can enjoy the tourist facilities in the south whilst experiencing diving on remote reefs at the same time. With all of the logistics taken care of for you, it is a stress-free way of diving numerous spots around Bali while being able to enjoy other activities.

Recommended Operators

Diving

Bali Scuba (Author's Choice) Jalan Danau Poso 46, Sanur. Friendly, organized and professional 5 Star PADI Dive Center and Career Development Center, full range of courses from children to professionals, purpose-built pool, daily fun diving trips to all areas of Bali and Penida, hotel pick-ups and drop-offs, all vehicles with AC, equipment hire, nitrox, retail store. Tailor-made safaris are also an option. Tel: +62 (0) 361288610. www.baliscuba.com. Email: letsdive@bali-scuba.com.

Other operators in the Sanur area include:
Crystal Divers www.crystal-divers.com.
Aquamarine Diving Bali www.aqua-marinediving.com.
Blue Season Bali www.baliocean.com.
Atlantis www.atlantis-bali-diving.com.
Bali Diving Academy Operations in Tulamben, Pemuteran, Lembongan and Sanur. www.scubali.com.
D-Scuba Club www.d-scubaclub.com.

Mainland Bali 5–6 Day Itinerary: Wrecks, Reefs, Critters and Walls

A 5 to 6 day itinerary for Menjangan, Padang Bai and Tulamben. This is a fairly fast-paced tour focusing on areas which do not require numerous dives to see the best of what there is on offer. It is suitable for all levels of divers with an additional sixth day of diving for more experienced divers.

Day 1 Arrive at DPS airport and transfer to Pemuteran. Book your dive center in advance and they should be able to organize an airport pick-up and driver for you. Arrive in Pemuteran (where there is a possibility of an afternoon dive depending on arrival time) and overnight there.

Day 2 Two morning dives on Menjangan Island or Secret Bay and one afternoon dive or night dive in Pemuteran. Overnight in Pemuteran.

Day 3 Either a morning dive in Pemuteran and then transfer to Tulamben or an early morning departure to Tulamben and one afternoon dive in Tulamben. Transit time from Menjangan to Tulamben is approximately four hours. Overnight in Tulamben.

Day 4 Early morning dive on US *Liberty* wreck plus 1 to 2 more day dives. Night dive on *Liberty* wreck. Overnight in Tulamben.

Day 5 Diving in Padang Bai (possible to use Tulemben operator or transit to Padang Bai operator; approx. 2.5 hours by car. Two day dives in Padang Bai around Amuk Bay and Blue Lagoon. Overnight in Padang Bai.

Day 6 (optional for experienced divers) Morning dives at Gili Biaha, Tepekong or Mimpang. Return to South Bali area for an overnight prior to departure the next day (allow 24 hours after last dive prior to flying).

Best of Bali 7 Day Itinerary: Mantas, Mola and Wrecks

A 7 day itinerary for Penida and Tulamben combined. If you are hoping to see mola, the best time for this itinerary is from August to October. The manta rays are year round but sightings are less frequent in November. This tour allows for a longer time in Nusa Lembongan to increase the chances of a mola sighting and the opportunity to visit a manta site, though both are dependent on good conditions.

Day 1 Arrive at DPS airport and transfer by car and speedboat to Nusa Lembongan (last boat to the island leaves Sanur at around 5 pm); if arriving on a later flight, an overnight in Sanur will be required). Operators on Lembongan can arrange transfers or you can book direct (see transport operators in Nusa Penida section). Overnight in Lembongan.

Days 2–4 Morning 2 dive trip, third afternoon dive dependent on your operator and conditions. Overnight in Lembongan.

Day 5 Morning 2 dive trip followed by afternoon transfer back to Sanur (30 minutes) and transit to Tulamben (3.5 hours). Overnight in Tulamben.

Day 6 Early morning wreck dive on US *Liberty* followed by two more day dives or possible night dive on the *Liberty* (recommended).

Day 7 Early morning wreck dive followed by optional second dive. Return to South Bali area for an overnight prior to departure the next day, allowing 24 hours after last dive prior to flying.

Full Circle 12 Day Bali Itinerary

A 12 day itinerary covering everything: Nusa Penida, Tulamben, Padang Bai, Menjangan. This tour takes in the best of Bali diving, allowing for extra time in Penida for spotting manta and mola (July–October) and additional dives in Padang Bai for experienced divers.

Days 1–4 Same as for 5 day Mainland Bali Itinerary (page 46).

Day 5 Diving in Tulamben, 2 to 3 day dives, plus possible night dive on the US *Liberty* wreck. Overnight Tulamben.

Day 6 Transit to Padang Bai, approximately 2.5 hours by car. Afternoon dives in Padang Bai around Amuk Bay or Blue Lagoon. Overnight in Padang Bai.

Day 7 Diving Padang Bai, 2 to 3 day dives, plus possible night dive. Overnight in Padang Bai.

Day 8 Experienced divers: morning diving at Gili Tepekong, Biaha or Mimpang followed by transfer to Sanur and last boat to Lembongan. (Check Rocky Fast Cruise online at www.rockyfastcruise.com for latest departure time.) Less experienced divers: morning transfer to Sanur and boat to Lembongan. Afternoon dive in Lembongan. Overnight Lembongan.

Days 9–11 Day diving around Nusa Penida and Lembongan, 2 to 3 dives per day and possible night dive (depending on conditions). Overnight in Lembongan on Day 11 or return to Sanur for overnight stay.

Day 12 Departure day from either Lembongan or Sanur. First boat to leave Lembongan arrives in Sanur at around 9.30 am. Allow at least one hour to travel from Sanur harbor to the airport.

Diving Nusa Penida and Nusa Lembongan
Drift Diving, Pelagics and Vibrant Reefs

Nusa Penida offers divers stunning vibrant reefs, abundant marine life, manta rays, sharks, seasonal mola sightings, turtles and some exhilarating drift dives. The majority of dive centers are based on nearby Nusa Lembongan, which is a relaxed and easy-going island with world-class sunsets and a strong sense of Balinese tradition. A number of the dive sites around Lembongan and Penida are better suited to experienced divers but there are many sites suitable for all levels, and operators time dives with the tides to minimize the strength of the currents. The diving around these islands is amongst the best in Bali, and if you are hoping to catch sight of some of Bali's larger fish then this is the place to be. On shore, Nusa Lembongan offers a range of places to stay, from backpacker guest houses to private villas, and there are numerous restaurants which cater for a similar range of budgets. All in all, if you are looking for big fish and great currents mixed in with a relaxing island break, Lembongan should definitely be on your list of places to visit.

Nusa Lembongan lies 12 kilometers across the Badung Strait to the east of Bali. Accommodation on the island ranges from backpacker rooms to luxury hotels and private villas.

Lembongan is often described as being comparable to Bali 20 years ago. There is a laid-back atmosphere, beautiful scenery and a slow pace of life. Traditionally, seaweed farming provided a major source of income, and seaweed farmers can still be seen hauling in their heavily laden baskets at low tide. Tourism now provides an income for many but the island's strong sense of local tradition

Above The view over Jungutbatu Bay, Nusa Lembongan, with Mount Agung on Bali visible in the distance.

does not seem to have been lost with the recent boom in tourist visitors.

Lembongan has a range of local convenience stores and a hospital with a doctor's clinic which caters for basic medical problems and has a supply of oxygen. Transport on Lembongan is mainly by motorcycle. It is possible to rent both motorbikes and bicycles from most hotels and homestays. Some hotels and restaurants operate pick-up trucks to collect guests upon request from around the island.

DIFFICULTY LEVEL Fast drifts and some-times unpredictable conditions make for some adrenalin-charged diving. There are a number of calmer sites suitable for beginners, and most sites can be timed to minimize currents for those who prefer a more relaxed pace.

HIGHLIGHTS Manta ray dive sites (No. 2), mola from late July to late October, exhilarating drifts over vibrant reefs, abundant fish life and passing pelagics.

LOGISTICS Whilst most of the dive sites are situated around Nusa Penida, almost all dive centers, accommodation and restaurants are on Nusa Lembongan. It is possible to make day trips here from Bali but dive boats leaving from Lembongan usually arrive at the sites first and have more flexible schedules to accommodate conditions and tides.

There are numerous boat services from Sanur to Lembongan and many Lembongan operators will arrange transfers if you book in advance.

PENIDA AND LEMBONGAN'S BEST DIVE SITES

NUSA PENIDA: TOYAPAKEH BAY
☆**AUTHOR'S TOP CHOICE**

Toyapakeh truly embodies the term 'The Living Reef' as everything is alive and vibrant: abundant, healthy corals, schooling fish in the blue, clouds of antheas glimmering in the sun's rays as they dance over rolling staghorn corals and brightly colored basslets darting over bommies. Pelagics are often seen here, including tuna, marbled stingrays, reef sharks and mola. Macro photography lovers will not be disappointed either by this fascinating underwater garden.

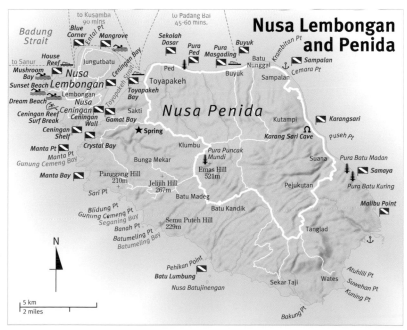

Toyapakeh is a drift dive site around Toyapakeh Bay. The prevailing current runs from south to north and entry is made in front of the steep-sided banks of Nusa Penida with the exit being in the region of the pontoon. The initial descent is down a stunning coral wall to a shelf at around 10 meters, which then gives way to a sloping reef. If the current is from north to south, enter between the permanent pontoon and the jetty and drift south to the wall.

Topographically, Toyapakeh is a predominantly hard coral slope with a range of bommies. The best coral can be found between 15 and 20 meters where there is a mix of bommies, dugouts, shelves and ledges. Scorpionfish lie disguised on the coral-encrusted slope, marbled stingrays are often spotted and giant moray eels, ribbon eels, octopus, nudibranchs and mantis shrimp can all be found amongst the rich mix of corals. Make your way back up the reef, which can be surprisingly tough when the current is pushing out from the bay, and the safety stop is usually in the region of the permanently moored pontoon. Staghorn corals dominate the shallows and provide habitat for schools of colorful antheas and giant trevally. Jackfish are known to school to the north side of the pontoon. When drifting north of the pontoon, stay close to the reef as the currents here are often strong and unpredictable.

NORTH COAST NUSA PENIDA: BUYUK, PURA MASGADING, PURA PED, SEKOLAH DASAR

The north coast of Nusa Penida is one long stretch of sloping reef which makes for some excellent drift diving. The four dive site names refer to the entry points and the stretch of reef immediately to the west of them. Realistically, one can drop in at any point and cover more than one

dive site in one dive depending on the current. Buyuk is the most easterly and is named after the small local harbor there. Pura Masgading (also referred to as Sental) is next, followed by Pura Ped, which takes its name from the second most important temple in Bali located on the shore. Sekolah Dasar is the most westerly site before swinging around the corner into Toyapakeh. Current strengths are variable on the north coast but generally pick up as you near the channel. The far end of Sekolah Dasar can be a roller

Mola, also known as oceanic sunfish, are seen around Nusa Penida from June through to October.

LUCKY DIP Mola are seen seasonally at many of Penida's dive sites so it is well worth looking out into the blue. There are also several whale shark sightings each year around Nusa Penida and these mostly tend to be along the north coast sites.

coaster! Currents at Buyuk are usually mildest but the bay area can be subject to up and down currents, especially near low tide. Conditions and visibility are generally better on a rising tide across all four sites. There is a healthy mix of soft and hard corals, with a higher percentage of soft coral at the Buyuk end of the stretch and more hard coral at the Sekolah Dasar end. Turtles and large pelagics are more frequently spotted around Buyuk, whereas Sekolah Dasar provides for more abundant reef life and colorful coral. Pura Ped and Pura Masgading are also well known for mola sightings in the season.

Reef cuttlefish, also referred to as sepia, are found across Indonesia, this one was pictured in Bali.

For all dives along the north coast, enter the water just out from the seaweed farm in the shallows. The drop-off begins at around 10 meters at a 45 degree angle. The dive sites are incredibly deep, with the slopes going down to over 100 meters. The best coral coverage is around 20 meters and at most sites it begins to peter out just below 40 meters. There is a good variety of coral species, huge sponges, tables and big bommies of boulder and brain corals, all interspersed with soft coral species and sea whips. One of the most spectacular sights is the rolling meadows of staghorn coral at the end of Sekolah Dasar drifting west in between 5 and 10 meters. Schooling grey and pastel blue antheas can be found in droves in the shallow water sunlight.

Regardless of where you drop in on the north coast, the fish life is varied and there are opportunities to see everything you would expect to find on a healthy reef. Look out for larger pelagics in the blue, especially during the cooler water months of July to October.

CRYSTAL BAY AND BAT CAVE

On the south end of the channel that runs between Nusa Penida and Nusa Ceningan, Crystal Bay offers phenomenal visibility, beautiful coral, abundant and varied marine life, pelagics and some interesting currents. The main sloping reef is along the side of the island that sits in the bay, but it is also possible to dive along the top of the sloping reef where there is a beautiful shallow (10 meters) coral garden that is more suitable for less experienced divers.

The sloping reef features some interesting overhangs and an abundance of staghorn corals, and as you near the front of Nusa Cenginan island there is a drop-off with stunning coral coverage. Scorpionfish, frogfish, cuttlefish, nudibranchs, mantis shrimps and banded sea snakes are all regularly seen here as well as larger species, such as giant trevally, tuna, reef sharks and turtles. The drop off is incredibly deep and currents can be unpredictable, making it an area for experienced divers only. It is at the drop-off that divers wait for glimpses of the

Sea whips, or whip corals, such as this one can grow to more than several meters in length.

mola as it comes up to be cleaned. Mola can also be seen from the coral garden on top of the reef.

If there is little current, it is possible to continue the dive from the front of the island by heading back along the other side towards the Bat Cave. There are two channels starting at around 7 meters. Follow the western channel which leads into a tunnel taking you up into the cave. It is also possible to drop in from the boat between the island and the mainland directly in front of the underwater tunnel to the cave. The view is spectacular as you emerge through the darkness and look up into the shimmering pool of light. The bottom of the bat cave is exactly 5 meters, so it is also a great place to make your safety stop. Do not try and enter the cave when the currents are strong as getting back into the bay can be very challenging!

MANTA POINT AND MANTA BAY (MANTA POINT I AND II)

There are two manta ray dive sites along the south coast of Nusa Penida which provide stunning scenery, rugged underwater topographies featuring swim-throughs, drop-offs, walls and slopes, crashing waves and, of course, the opportunity to dive with one of the most majestic and graceful marine creatures of the ocean planet. (See Reef Manta Rays feature, Nusa Tenggara, page 184.)

Both sites are located in front of steep limestone cliffs and are best dived when conditions are flat and calm. Big swells or strong winds can cause crashing waves that result in strong surges underwater that can move divers back and forth 10 meters at a time! The bottom composition of these sites is mainly rock covered with close-cropped corals as the surge makes it difficult for upward growth. Both sites have white sandy channels and large underwater boulders which have fallen from the cliffs over time and these makes excellent swim-throughs and hiding places for lobsters, resting bamboo sharks and small stingrays.

Manta Point (also known as Manta 1 or Batu Lumbung) is situated on the southeasterly point of Nusa Penida. The scenery here is incredible: staggering limestone cliffs with waves beating at their feet, small white sand coves and rock pinnacles. The entry point for the dive is up against the cliffs in a small bay, slightly west of the outcropping of two large rocks, the most southerly looking like a shoe. Divers enter the water close to the cliffs and descend to around 8 meters where there is a huge boulder which forms a natural cleaning station for the mantas. These amazing creatures will literally wait in line for their turn to swim up the rock and then hover above it whilst the cleaner fish go to work. On days when there are many mantas here for cleaning, divers need not venture any further than this one spot (see guidelines on diving with Mantas and Mola, page 59). For a deeper dive, or if there are no mantas at the cleaning station, pick one of the sandy channels and follow it away from the cliffs. The site slopes down to around 18 meters and then very gradually continues down to a large sandy patch at 40 meters. On the sand there are frequently large numbers of blue spotted stingrays. Another option is to drop in on the westerly side of the bay where there is a drop-off to 30 meters. Manta Point is home to the larger, more mature mantas, and on days when the water is plankton-rich the mantas will be on the surface feeding with their cephalic fins rolled down, making their mouths seem like enormous caverns swimming towards you. These animals are harmless, though, and will come incredibly close if you remain still and calm. Chasing them for a closer look is counterproductive as they will leave the area.

Manta Bay (Manta II or Telaga Sakti) is also situated in the south coast of Penida but not as far east as Manta I. The site is actually three large bays which get progressively deeper from west to east (from

PAY ATTENTION
Keep a close eye on your tank pressure and head up to your safety stop early at around 70 bar (not the usual 50 bar). If there are down currents, you may find that you need a bit extra in reserve.

The lizardfish is a bottom dwelling species that is well camouflaged against coral rubble and reef.

5 meters to 20 meters). The coral coverage here is predominantly hard coral and in the deeper areas there are interesting coral formations, bommies growing upwards and patches of staghorn coral. Navigation is simple as it is just a case of following the cliffs around the bays. The mantas here tend to be smaller juveniles keeping to the shallows and feeding on the surface. Manta sightings here can be sporadic and less reliable than at Manta Point.

Being on the south side of Penida, both of these sites are prone to cooler water temperatures from July to October.

NUSA LEMBONGAN: MANGROVE (JACKFISH POINT)

With its bright colors, passing pelagics, undulating terrain, abundant marine life and exhilarating drifts, Mangrove, along with Toyapakeh, is a diver's favorite site. The reef is steeply sloping at the east end, and as you drift west it levels out into wide sweeping, stepped plateaus that round the north side of Lembongan Island. Coral is vibrant with a healthy mix of soft and hard species.

Mangrove is named after the mangrove forest on the north side of Lembongan and it is famed for its fast-paced drifts. From 10 meters upward there is a stretch of staghorn corals that houses schools of antheas and many juvenile fish. From 10 meters to around 25 meters is a series of stepped plateaus and below 25 meters is a steep drop-off which should be avoided due to strong currents. Diving the plateaus gives you a sensation of flying through the water whilst watching the reef speed by below. Currents here can range from 0 to 4 knots and you can cover some serious ground in an hour. The best coral coverage and fish life is at 15 to 20 meters. In the shallower water the site is also

Above Manta rays have enormous mouths which they open wide during feeding in plankton-rich waters.

Right Manta rays have spot patterns on their undersides which are like fingerprints and are unique to each individual.

Far right The coloration of black manta rays, such as this one, is known as the 'melanistic morph'.

Below right If divers passively observe manta rays and avoid chasing them, they will come very close of their own accord.

popular with snorkelers which can mean busy boat activity on the surface so a DSMB is recommended. Due to the stepped topography of the reef, it can be suitable for novice divers who can experience a good drift by sticking to one of the shallower levels. Avoid diving here when there is a steep drop in tide as this is when currents are at their strongest and visibility can be reduced.

Look out for bigger pelagics, including eagle rays, barracuda and sharks passing through, and if the currents are not running fast then critter and macro life is easy to find on this vibrant reef.

NUSA LEMBONGAN: BLUE CORNER (JURASSIC POINT)

Porcelain crabs live in and under many different species of anemones found across Indonesia.

Phenomenal currents, chilling thermoclines, mola, sharks, eagle rays, marbled stingrays, sailfish and exhilarating diving, this site is not for the inexperienced diver. The site starts just out from the lighthouse situated on the northeast corner of Nusa Lembongan. When diving Blue Corner, enter further out from the reef and descend straight down to around 30 meters. If the currents are running fast, then the descent needs to be appropriately paced so that you hit the reef rather than being swept out. The site itself is fairly small and if you miss the descent it can be difficult to get back on track against the currents.

Blue Corner is a steep reef with big boulder-like formations which form three 'corners' in a row. The main dive area is along the three corners. There is a drop-off down to a shelf at 30 meters with various bommies and formations and also some great natural hollows which can be used for avoiding currents.

From 30 meters, the reef slopes down again and it eventually bottoms out at around 50 meters. The bottom composition is almost all rocky with thin and flat hard coral coverage due to the strong currents preventing upward growth, but this is a site for looking away from the reef and into the blue for big fish. The site is subject to fast drifts and strong up and down currents if not timed right. Slack high tide is when there is least current, and diving a couple of hours before gives manageable currents and more chance of seeing bigger pelagics. A fast fall in tide should be avoided. The currents not only bring out the bigger fish but also some seriously cold thermoclines, especially from July to October, which is also a good time to spot mola. On good days, it is not unheard of to see six or seven. As this site is for experienced divers only, you often find you are the only group of divers here.

Just Going With the Flow....

Most of the diving around Nusa Penida (and in many parts of Indonesia) is drift diving and the currents can vary from almost nothing to drifts where divers cover 2 kilometers of shoreline in just 40 minutes! Whilst some divers love the exhilarating thrill of 'flying' along the reef, others find it a daunting and nerve-racking experience. Here are some general guidelines which can help make diving in currents both safer and more enjoyable.

Follow the directions of your guide and only enter the water when instructed to do so.

During the dive, stay behind the guide.

Stay close to the reef or the bottom as currents here will be weaker.

● Secure all dangling equipment.

● Control your buoyancy and let the current move you along.

● Use reef formations as shelter if you want to take a breather.

● Do not fight the current as it is easy to become overexerted.

● To determine current direction, look at indicators such as soft coral and reef fish, which generally swim head on into the current.

● Carry a delayed surface marker buoy (DSMB) and make sure you are familiar with how to inflate it.

● If you become separated from your group, look around for one minute. If you don't find them, go up and you should be reunited on the surface.

● If you cannot see your boat upon surfacing or if you have any doubt about whether your boat has seen you, do NOT wait in strong surface currents. Swim across the current, towards the shore if possible.

Tidal currents vary according to the time of the tide because the vertical rise and fall of the tides also creates a horizontal movement of water moving either from the open ocean towards the shore on a rising tide or from the shoreline to the open ocean on a falling tide. There are also periods at high tide or low tide when the horizontal movement of water is minimal or non-existent and this is termed 'slack high' or 'slack low'. As a general rule, diving on slack high is preferable as visibility is usually much better. On days when there is a large tidal range, such as close to a new moon or full moon, currents can be expected to be faster as there is a greater horizontal movement of water. When there is only a minimal range (neap tides), currents are least ferocious. Neap tides occur twice a month in the first and third quarter of the moon.

Time your dives with the tides, remember the general guidelines and go with the flow!

Look at the small fish over the reef for indications of current changes. They swim head first into the current.

The Mola or Sunfish *Mola ramsayi*

The sunfish is one of the strangest looking fish in the ocean and yet one that divers often place highly on their list of things to see. As the heaviest known bony fish in the world and weighing in at over 2,250 kilograms, the mola has two dorsal fins making it as tall as it is long. The most distinguishing feature of the mola is its main body area—of which there is very little—and which is flattened laterally. This strange shaping explains the German name for the fish, *schwimmender kopf*, which translates as 'swimming head'. The word mola comes from the Latin and means 'millstone', perhaps in reference to either the shape or the marbled coloration of the fish, which is very typical in the *Mola ramsayi* species commonly seen around Nusa Penida.

Mola live on a diet of nutritionally poor jellyfish, and in order to maintain their body weight they consume huge quantities of it. Ordinarily, they are deep water fish but they are seen around Nusa Penida from July to October as they drift up the reefs on the cold thermoclines, making their way into the shallower waters. Year round mola carry an incredibly heavy parasitic load, and thus these giant fish rely on some of the reefs' smallest inhabitants to unburden them through cleaning.

Mola cleaning is an incredible sight as this huge fish, which averages around two meters, cruises up the reef hoping to attract the attention of the smaller reef fish. Bannerfish are one of the great mola cleaning fish and can be seen literally leaving the reef in swarms as they flock to the mola. Other cleaner fish include cleaner wrasse, which mostly clean around the gills and mouth, butterfly fish, which focus on the eyes, and even emperor angelfish have been seen cleaning the dorsal fins. Another means by which the mola is thought to rid itself of parasites is by 'jumping', a phenomenon often witnessed by fishermen and during surface intervals. The mola will break through the surface and then crash back down, creating an almighty splash which is thought

Mola are the heaviest of all known bony fish and can weigh up to 2,250 kilograms.

Passively observe mola to ensure longer and less invasive interactions. Here, the author watches a mola in Crystal Bay, Nusa Penida.

to break off parasites in the process.

They are a truly Jurassic-looking fish which, as a member of the order Tetra-odontiformes, are closely related to pufferfish, porcu-pinefish and triggerfish. The mola is also referred to as the Balinese sunfish (or moonfish to the French—*poisson lune*). The name sunfish is thought to come from its habit of sunbathing on the surface of the water.

GUIDELINES FOR DIVING WITH MANTA RAYS AND MOLA IN BALI

The following Code of Conduct has been disseminated across operators in Bali and its aim is to allow divers to witness these amazing creatures without interfering with or disturbing their natural behavior.

• Always stay close to the reef. Never approach the mola from above. If you wait, it will slowly swim up the reef as it is being cleaned.

• If manta rays or mola are just entering a cleaning station, do not approach until the cleaning has begun and the fish have been stationary for at least a minute. Once the cleaning begins, the fish will relax and are less likely to be startled.

• Do not get too close. Stay at least 3 to 5 meters from manta rays and mola.

• If manta rays and mola are swimming or approaching a cleaning station, stay at least 10 meters away to give them a chance to settle.

• Do not touch manta rays or mola. Their skin's surface is covered with a mucus membrane to protect against infection. Touching the fish removes parts of the membrane.

• Do not swim under or behind mola as this startles them.

• Do not block a manta or mola's exit from a cleaning station. Never crowd either fish as they will become startled and flee.

• If manta rays are cleaning, remain passive and observe them from the bottom of the cleaning station. Do not swim to the top of it.

• If a manta ray or mola approaches you, remain still and calm. Jerky movements will startle the fish. Neither mola nor manta rays are harmful.

• Do not use flash photography as this disturbs the fish.

• Do not use personal underwater motorized propulsion vehicles or make loud noises.

• Be courteous to other divers and re-strict your interaction time to 5 minutes when other groups are present.

• Dive with companies who follow the Code of Conduct and always follow your dive guide's directions.

NUSA LEMBONGAN TRAVEL PLANNER

There are numerous operators on Nusa Lembongan offering fun diving and courses. The standard daily package is a two-dive trip. Equipment hire is widely available, groups usually comprise a maximum of 4 guests, dives tend to be limited to 25 to 30 meters and 60 minutes. As most dives are drift dives, an SMB or other signaling device is recommended. From November to May, water temperatures on average are 28 to 29 degrees. From June to October, the temperature drops to 2 to 27 degrees on the north and thermoclines as cool as 20 degrees are not uncommon on the southern sites. Most operators hire long 5 mm wetsuits.

Visibility ranges from a low of 10 to 15 meters during the wet season and can reach 40 meters in the dry season. Whilst Nusa Penida is renowned for its pelagics, mantas and molas, there is a wealth of critter life, too. Frogfish, ghost pipefish, orangutan crabs and numerous other species can be found at almost all of the dive sites.

The north coasts of Nusa Lembongan and Nusa Penida are sloping reef drift dives with abundant fish life, healthy, colorful coral coverage and passing pelagics. South coast sites can be difficult to access when there is a big swell but this is where Penida's manta rays gather for feeding and cleaning in front of towering vertical limestone cliffs. Nusa Penida offers stunning topographies both above and underwater.

Left Bali is famous for its traditional outrigger boats known locally as *jukung*.

Below Jungutbatu village on Nusa Lembongan has a pretty sand beach and no shortage of places to stay.

Recommended Operators

Diving

World Diving Lembongan (Authors Choice). A reputable and upmarket British-owned PADI 5 Star dive center offering full service and daily fun diving trips and PADI courses from beginner to professional levels. It operates the only large *jukung* (traditional outrigger boat) on the island plus smaller speedboats, and provides equipment hire. It has a good reputation for its professional service, experienced guides, small dive groups and safety consciousness. Dive and stay packages are available using local accommodation ranging from budget to upmarket. Excellent booking and email communications. This operator will also organize airport pick-ups and transfers to the island. Tel: +62 (0) 8123900686. www.world-diving.com.

Blue Corner Dive The main operation is based to the north of Jungutbatu village. This full service PADI 5 Star IDC Center offers the full range of PADI courses up to instructor level plus daily fun diving, bungalow and dormitory accommodation and a lively bar. Blue Corner also has operations in Mushroom Bay catering for courses and fun diving trips, as well as being based at NusaBay Resorts in both Nusa Lembongan and Pemuteran. Their NusaBay operations—NusaBay Lembongan and NusaBay Menjangan in Pemuteran—offer upmarket accommodation and diving packages. Multi-destination trips are available. Tel: +62 (0) 87761377718/+62 (0) 82341308480. www.bluecornerdive.com.

Other reputable dive operators based on Nusa Lembongan offering daily fun diving and dive courses include:

Two Fish Divers PADI 5 Star IDC facility offering accommodation at Villa Jepun. Two Fish also has operations in North Sulawesi (Bunaken and Lembeh) and in Lombok. www.twofishdivers.com.

Big Fish Diving offers accommodation at Secret Garden Bungalows and yoga at the Yoga Shack. www.bigfishdiving.com.

Lembongan Dive Center www.lembongan-divecenter.com.

Bali Diving Academy is based at No. 7 Bungalows. It also has operations in Pemuteran. www.scubali.com.

Accommodation

Pondok Baruna Lembongan Well established with a range of rooms from budget to mid-range with a swimming pool, bar and popular restaurant serving excellent Balinese and Western cuisine. $–$$. www.world-diving.com/www.pondokbaruna.com.

Batu Karang Luxury resort with views over Jungutbatu Bay and Mount Agung. Offers rooms, suites and villas, swimming pools, restaurant, bar, spa and massage service. $$$. www.batukaranglembongan.com.

Tiger Lilly's Stylish bungalows in a pretty garden. Swimming pool, restaurant and bar. $$. www.tigerlillys-lembongan.com.

There is no shortage of bungalows, homestays and guest houses on Nusa Lembongan, and outside of the high season it can be arranged once you are on the island. From mid-July to early October, however, booking in advance is recommended.

Transport

Rocky Fast Cruise Provides a 30 minute speedboat service from Sanur to Lembongan. Hotel/airport pick-ups and drop-offs provided. www.rockyfastcruise.com.

Other

Aquatic Alliance An NGO based on Lembongan involved in numerous marine conservation projects and monitoring manta ray sightings. Free marine life and manta ray talks (recommended) on Tuesday and Thursday evenings at the Yoga Shack. www.aquaticalliance.org.

Diving Tulamben and Amed
Critters, Calm Conditions and Bali's Most Famous Wreck

The USTA *Liberty* shipwreck is the crowning glory of diving in Tulamben (see pages 68–9 for its history). It is an easy wreck to navigate and is thus suitable for all levels of divers. It has grown into a reef system that attracts marine life like bees to a honey pot. It is colorful, bold, full of history and gives rise to incredible night dives. The surrounding area boasts black sand slopes littered with critters and macro life, and there is also a coral wall site for those seeking more fish activity. Tulamben offers very easy diving, mostly from the shore, and there is a range of operators to suit all budgets.

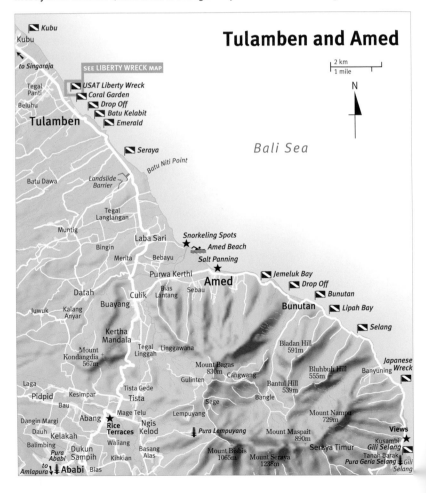

Tulamben and Amed

Kubu
Kubu
to Singaraja
Tegal Panti
Beluhu
Tulamben
SEE LIBERTY WRECK MAP
USAT Liberty Wreck
Coral Garden
Drop Off
Batu Kelabit
Emerald
Seraya
Batu Niti Point
Batu Dawa
Landslide Barrier
Tegal Langlangan
Muntig
Bingin
Merita
Laba Sari
Bebayu
Purwa Kerthi
Snorkeling Spots
Amed Beach
Salt Panning
Amed
Bali Sea

2 km
1 mile
N

Datah
Culik
Bias Lantang
Sebau
Jemeluk Bay
Drop Off
Bunutan
Bunutan
Lipah Bay
Juwuk
Kalang Anyar
Buayang
Selang
Kertha Mandala
Biadan Hill 591m
Mount Kondangdia 567m
Tegal Linggah
Linggawana
Mount Bagas 830m
Cangwang
Bluhbuh Hill 555m
Banyuning
Japanese Wreck
Laga
Kesimpar
Tista Gede
Gulinten
Bantul Hill 539m
Pidpid
Bau
Tista
Sege
Bangle
Dangin Margi
Abang
Mage Telu
Lempuyang
Mount Nampu 729m
Views
Dauh
Kelakah
Rice Terraces
Ngis
Kelod
Pura Lempuyang
Mount Maspait 890m
Seraya Timur
Kusambi
Gili Selang
Balimbing
Waliang
Basang
Alas
Mount Bisbis 1065m
Mount Seraya 1238m
Pura Geria Selang
Gili Selang
to Amlapura
Pura Ababi
Dukun
Sampih
Kihkian
Ababi
Bias
Tanah Barak

Tulamben is a small fishing village situated on the northeast coast of Bali. The village has retained its small size with the main drag being only around 500 meters long running inland from the *Liberty* wreck to the drop-off.

Tulamben's tourism industry is based on diving and the *Liberty* wreck, as most locals draw a living from the dive industry in some way or another. Night life in Tulamben is limited to dive resort bars and local *warung* (food stalls), which generally close around 10 pm. This is the perfect place for a diving getaway with no hustle or bustle and a leisurely pace.

Tulamben's 'beach' is formed from round black rocks resulting from Mount Agung's 1963 eruption. When there is a strong wind or a big swell, these black beaches with their crashing waves appear quite harsh in contrast to the rest of Bali's placid sandy coastline. Tulamben has been blessed with astonishing views: open ocean to the east with amazing sunrises, Lombok in the distance and, if you look inland, Mount Agung towering above you.

Tulamben has a handful of local convenience stores selling snacks, drinks, toiletries and local produce. Everything in Tulamben is within walking distance up and down the main road. There is a clinic in the nearby town of Kubu with a doctor on call.

DIFFICULTY LEVEL Tulamben diving is relatively shallow. With little current and warm water, it is ideal for every level of diver.

HIGHLIGHTS The USAT *Liberty* shipwreck is a must. Night dives here are incredible and are not to be missed. Tulamben also offers resident schooling bumpheads, muck diving and critters, excellent macro life and passing pelagics.

LOGISTICS It is recommended that you stay in Tulamben itself so that you can

Shipwrecks have always fascinated divers and the USAT *Liberty* is no exception.

access the sites early. It gets busy here, especially from July to October. Whilst Tulamben has not developed greatly in terms of tourism, there are a number of dive operators as well as several excellent dive resorts (see recommended operators below), accommodation (backpacker to luxury) and a selection of *warung* and restaurants. Everything in Tulamben is situated along a short stretch of main road which runs between the ocean and the foothills of Mount Agung. Most Tulamben-based dive resorts offer pick-up services for guests who are coming from other parts of Bali. From the airport and from Sanur and Kuta, the drive is around three hours. Whether you travel to Tulamben in the dry season or rainy season, the landscape is awe-inspiring, either rugged, barren and dry or lush, green and fertile. At either time, the view of Mount Agung towering over this small fishing town is spectacular.

TULAMBEN'S BEST DIVE SITES

USAT LIBERTY WRECK

The USAT *Liberty* is not only a great wreck dive but it has become a truly living reef in its own right as a vibrant and healthy mix of brightly colored corals have encrusted the entire structure. Marine life flocks to the wreck, to feed, take shelter in its many crevices and exist in symbiosis with this colorful jewel which stands out against the somewhat desolate black sandy slopes on which it has come to rest.

The wreck is accessed via a stony beach entry which turns to a sparse collection of corals extending to around 10 meters where they peter out into a black sand slope. Approaching slightly from the south side of the wreck at 18 meters, you hit the point where the keel sits on the sand. The super structure stretches up to around 5 meters at the shallowest part. Start by covering the deepest side of the wreck first and then work your way back up. As you round the seaward edge of the wreck, the masthead is visible at 22 meters lying outwards from the wreck towards the open sea. One of the guns can be seen clearly protruding out at 25 to 26 meters and is now the base for some stunning soft corals and fans. As you work your way back up the wreck at around 15 meters, it is possible to swim through certain areas. This is not a penetration wreck as the structure is now so broken down that it is all open, but when you look out through the ships ribs, facing the ocean, you do experience the sensation of being inside the body of the ship. The anchor lies within the wreck at approximately 20 meters and is visible against the ship's broken remains. Look for the captain's wheel at 16 meters.

Take your time on the wreck as there is a huge amount of macro life. The soft corals and fans are littered with various

Diver with schooling jackfish at the site of the USAT *Liberty* wreck in Tulamben, Bali.

This great barracuda was pictured inside the body of the USAT *Liberty* wreck in Tulamben.

types of shrimps and pygmy seahorses are seen here too. (This is where a guide who knows what to look for really pays off.) Don't forget to keep glancing upwards as schooling fish gather above the wreck and occasionally larger, solitary pelagics such as barracuda and sharks are spotted here. If you get out early, it is a great site for bumphead parrotfish sightings. Early dives also mean fewer divers. If you are diving this site after 9.30 am, be prepared to be following a line of other groups around the wreck. The wreck is breaking down, so be careful with your buoyancy when swimming around the structure so as not to make contact with it. The surrounding black sand is very fine, and if it is disturbed it takes time to settle and reduces visibility. This is a spectacular dive and suitable for all levels. There is plenty to look at for experienced divers and photographers and a great introduction to wreck diving for beginners.

USAT LIBERTY WRECK BY NIGHT

It is recommended that you dive the *Liberty* in daylight hours first to get a feel for its layout. However, this is not a tricky night dive if you follow a basic route of starting at the middle of the wreck and working your way up. As a night dive, it does not need to be a deep dive and 15 meters gives you good coverage of the main structure and plenty of no decompression time.

Diving the wreck at night is all about the marine life and is an opportunity not to be missed. Larger predatory fish such as groupers can be seen inside the structure and they are not afraid of weaving in and out of your fins! The wreck itself, with its bright colored corals, provides excellent camouflage for a range of crab species: decorators, hermits and spider crabs on fans. Lobsters peer out of crevices, extravagant looking nudibranchs do a poor job of blending in on the black sand-covered surfaces and brittle feather stars are abundant. Look inside branching corals and watch them retracting away from the torchlight. Around the base of the wreck, check for its daytime residents hunkered down for the night, such as parrotfish in their cocoons and smaller

reef fish tucked away out of site of the evening's predators.

As with any night dive, the trick is to go slow and use a good LED torch that really shows the true colors of the corals which look even more magnificent when cast against a dark background. Huge bumphead parrotfish are often seen settling down inside the wreck. Remember they are getting ready to sleep so be considerate with your flashlight!

The USAT *Liberty* wreck lists to one side. This image shows the angle of some of the main supports.

THE DROP OFF (TULAMBEN WALL)

The Drop Off is another of Tulamben's beach entry sites and is situated 400 to 500 meters south of the *Liberty*. The Coral Garden site sits in between the two. Entry is from a small black stone beach where traditional fishing boats are harbored. The beach is known locally as Pantai Drop Off, *pantai* meaning 'beach' in Indonesian. As you look out

Bumphead parrotfish are best observed at night or at dawn. This school was pictured at dawn in Tulamben.

to sea from the beach, there is a rocky outcrop jutting out from the mainland slightly to the south, and it is beneath this that the Drop Off is situated. As with most of Tulamben's sites, the black rocks give way to a 45 degree black fine sandy slope at around 12 meters. The sandy approach to the Drop Off is a good place to look for bottom dwellers, particularly as you near the wall and coral coverage starts to increase. Continue south as you meet the reef and then the wall, which drops down almost vertically in places with a good healthy mix of hard and soft corals characterized by huge sponges and impressive gorgonian fans. When diving on the wall, keep an eye out to the blue and above for schooling trevally and passing bigger fish. The reef and wall are mainly a rock and hard coral base which are colorful despite the black sand surrounds. Soft corals grow out of the wall and there are many crevices and small overhangs which are worth looking into

Bumphead parrotfish such as this one can grow up to 1.3 meters in length and weigh up to 50 kilos.

for crabs, lobsters and shrimps. The Drop Off is not one of the most stunning walls in Indonesia but it does provide a nice variation from Tulamben's black sandy slopes. Visibility at the Drop Off is variable and is reduced after rainfall. Watch your fins and your buoyancy as the fine sand particles take a long time to settle. The Drop Off is often dived later in the day, so tends to be busy. Despite being a wall dive this site is suitable for all levels.

SERAYA

With numerous shrimps, nudibranchs and all manner of critters, this is a muck diving fanatic's 'must see' site. Seraya is a 45 degree black sand slope around a 20 minute boat ride south of Pantai Drop Off. The entry point is just in front of the Markisa Resort. The slope starts at 8 meters with sporadic rocks, hard corals and anemones but the coverage is 95 percent sand. Do not let this put you off

Harlequin shrimps are a very shy species that have exquisite markings. This one was photographed near the *Liberty* wreck in Tulamben.

A Brief History of the USAT Liberty

The USAT *Liberty* (United States Army Transport) shipwreck is one of the main reasons why divers flock to Tulamben as it lies in relatively shallow, calm water just 30 meters out from the beach. The *Liberty* was built as a 120-meter-long cargo ship equipped with two guns during the Second World War. In January 1942, the ship was torpedoed by a Japanese submarine whilst anchored off the Lombok coast. Incredibly, no one was hurt but the ship was badly damaged. The US Navy towed the ship to northern Bali to the harbor of Singaraja. However, the plan fell short as the harbor was already fully occupied, leaving the US no option but to ground the ship on the beach of Tulamben for unloading. The ship was stripped bare and left to be returned to Singaraja when the harbor became available. The war, however, diverted attention away from the damaged ship. In 1963, it was still grounded on the beach at Tulamben when Mount Agung erupted. The lava flow from the volcano pushed the ship off the beach and back into the sea to its current resting

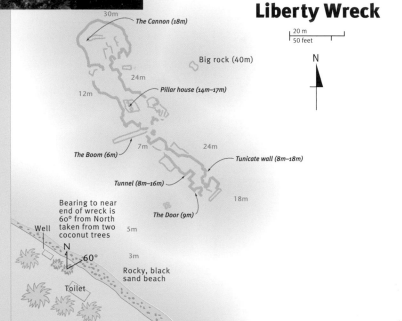

Liberty Wreck

30m — The Cannon (18m)

20 m
50 feet

N

Big rock (40m)

24m

Pillar house (14m–17m)

12m

7m   24m

The Boom (6m)

Tunicate wall (8m–18m)

Tunnel (8m–16m)

18m

Bearing to near
end of wreck is
60° from North   The Door (9m)
Well   taken from two
coconut trees   5m

N
60°   3m

Rocky, black
sand beach

Toilet

place. The ship lies parallel to the beach. As it slipped into the water, it listed onto its side and lies with the deck facing the open ocean, the starboard side underneath and the port side facing up to the surface. The shallowest part of the wreck is only around 5 meters where the superstructure stretches upwards. The deepest part is around 28 to 30 meters where the bow has settled into the sand. If you approach directly from the shore, the main bulk of the wreck starts at around 10 to 12 meters.

For a detailed dive site description, see Tulamben's Best Dive Sites, USAT Liberty Wreck, pages 64–5.

Top Coral growth on the USAT *Liberty* wreck, Tulamben, Bali.

Above Exceptional corals have grown on the wreck of the *Liberty*, which attracts a wide variety of marine life.

Opposite The *Liberty* wreck is shallow enough for both snorkelers and free divers to enjoy.

though as critters of all types can be found here, from harlequin shrimps, different species of lionfish, leaf scorpionfish and an abundance of nudibranch species. There are a couple of concrete blocks on the slope which are worth investigating as they have formed mini cleaning stations. Dive this site by heading down to around 25 meters and then slowly zigzagging back up. There can be mild currents here, so having a pointer stick can be handy to hold yourself steady on the sand, particularly if making a photography dive. At the reef crest there are the remains of two broken down artificial reefs, one dome-shaped, one airplane-shaped. Despite their poor condition, they are worth taking a look at for a range of hiding critters. Swim along the rocky reef crest looking out for pipefish, ghost pipefish and occasional eels of different varieties. This is not a stunning dive site, but for macro lovers and photographers with a keen eye it can be rewarding.

Lionfish have venomous spines and should be treated with caution. This one was photographed at Seraya, Tulamben.

CORAL GARDEN

Another black sand slope which is situated in between the *Liberty* wreck and the Drop Off site, directly in front of the Tauch Terminal Tulamben Dive Resort, is the Coral Garden, which is accessed directly from the beach. Starting at a depth of 2 to 15 meters, this is a great site for muck diving but there is not much to see in terms of coral coverage. Be patient, though, and scour around every rocky formation as there is a wide range of nudibranchs here and many other critters that are common to the area, many of which have excellent camouflage. This site does have one major draw: juvenile black tip reef sharks can be spotted in the shallows. As the site is so close to the beach, it is best dived when the sea is calm. When there are big waves, there can be quite a strong surge underwater and visibility drops substantially. This is an easy dive that can be dived shallow and has minimal current, making it suitable for all levels.

This dorid nudibranch is from the Chromodorididae order of nudibranchs and was photographed in Tulamben.

EMERALD

Emerald dive site is around a 10 to 15 minute boat ride south from Pantai Drop Off. The site is a sandy black slope down to around 10 meters where the coral reef starts and drops off quite steeply. On the way down, look out for hundreds of garden eels sticking out of the sand. The reef itself is characterized by huge

sponges and a good mix of hard and soft corals, not dissimilar to the Drop Off. At 25 meters reef fish school slightly out in the blue and on the reef itself there is a good overall selection of marine life: lionfish, fire dart gobies, porcupinefish and ribbon eels on the sand. As with the Drop Off, this site makes a welcome change from the black sand slopes if you are not much of a muck diving fan. Bumphead parrotfish are seen here as is evidence of their presence—teeth marks on the hard corals! This is a nice dive site for beginners and provides a mix of muck diving and reef diving.

Left Thorny oysters such as this one usually snap shut when approached by divers.

Below These dancing shrimps have distinctive green eyes and are commonly found in shady areas under rocks.

The Bumphead Parrotfish *Bolbometopon muricatum*

The bumphead parrotfish, also known as the humphead parrotfish or green hump-head parrotfish, grows up to a length of 1.3 meters and can weigh up to 46 kilograms, which makes it both the largest and heaviest of all parrotfish species. Its growth process is slow and it can live up to 40 years. Sexual maturity is reached late in life for the bumpheads and so their replenishment rates are low. Despite this, they are not yet listed as endangered. Adult members of the species develop a bulbous forehead, from which their name is taken, and their beak-like front teeth are almost fully exposed as they are only partly covered by their lips. These two characteristics give the bumpheads an almost science fiction appearance. They generally live in small aggregations but group numbers as large as 75 have been recorded.

Juveniles are often found in shallow lagoons and sea grass beds whereas adults tend to be in outer lagoons or on sea reefs above 30 meters. They are often found sleeping in caves or on shipwrecks during the night.

Bumpheads survive on a diet of benthic algae and live coral, and they contribute substantially to both reef degradation and maintenance. During the feeding process, the bumpheads will ram their heads against hard corals to break them down into smaller, more easily digestible pieces, and in one year a mature bumphead will consume over 5 tons of structural reef carbonates, much of which is passed out in the faeces. As such, bumpheads form an important part of the reef ecosystem. Due to the bumpheads' extraordinary dental arrangement, their teeth marks are easily identifiable on coral reefs.

Below Schooling bumphead parrotfish, Tulamben.

Inset Visible on this hard coral are the teeth marks of a bumphead parrotfish.

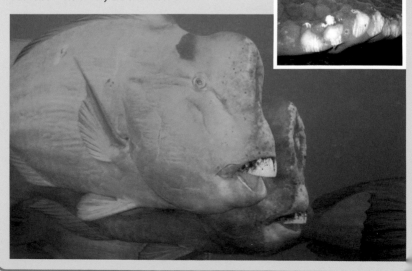

TULAMBEN TRAVEL PLANNER

Annual water temperature range is from 27 to 30 degrees and most operators hire a mix of 3 mm short and long suits. Visibility ranges from 10 to 25 meters year round. After heavy rain or big waves, it can drop substantially. Currents here are minimal.

Most dive operators offer diving on a sliding price scale depending on the number of dives you make. Expect to pay a surcharge for night dives, boat dives, early morning dives and equipment rental.

The three main shore dives (the Liberty Wreck, Drop Off and Coral Garden) are dived daily and are scheduled with the first dive of the day on the wreck and then 2 to 3 more dives elsewhere scheduled for later on in the day, with night wreck dives also available. Group sizes vary. Budget operators tend to have larger groups of up to eight divers.

Beach entries in Tulamben are tricky. The large, rounded black stones on the beach can be slippery and loose underfoot so booties are essential. Traditional narrow outrigger *jukung* are used to access the sites outside of walking distance. For nearby sites, divers walk along the beach whilst their assembled gear is transported by motorbike or carried on a local woman's head, which is quite a sight!

Recommended Operators

Diving

Tauch Terminal Tulamben Dive Resort (Author's Choice) Well situated on the beach directly in front of the Coral Garden dive site. SSI Platinum Resort offering beginner to instructor level courses. PADI courses also available. Daily fun diving in Tulamben and day trip boat safaris to Amed, Padang Bai, Nusa Penida and Menjangan. Two swimming pools, accommodation (dive and stay packages available), restaurant, bar, spa, equipment hire and nitrox available. Pick-up and drop-off service. Professional operation, based in a beautiful resort, small groups and experienced guides. Tel: +62 (0) 361774504. www.tulamben.com.

Villa Markisa An upmarket dive resort based on the outskirts of Tulamben providing quiet, relaxing surroundings and high-end accommodation with swimming pool, spa facilities and restaurant. The resort offers excellent access to dive sites, including the Liberty Wreck. The house reef here is Seraya, which is located directly in front of the resort. Dive and stay packages are available. Tel: +62 (0) 81337141 550. www.villa-markisa.com.

Tulamben Wreck Divers PADI Dive center with a range of accommodation and swimming pool. PADI courses and daily fun diving at Tulamben sites and day trips to further afield around Bali. Tel :+62 (0) 36323400. www.tulambenwreckdivers.com.

Traditional fishing boats are used for transporting divers in Tulamben, Bali.

Diving Menjangan and Pemuteran
Pretty Dive Sites in Bali Barat National Park

From sandy slopes and vertical walls around Menjangan and one of Indonesia's most successful bio-rock projects in Pemuteran to critter diving in Gilimanuk, this northwest corner of Bali offers diverse topographies set within and around the Bali Barat National Park. This area of natural beauty may be slightly off the beaten track, and whilst Pemuteran village is quiet, it is laid back and has everything you need for a relaxing and peaceful break away from the hustle and bustle of Bali's busier tourist areas, perfect for those who want easy diving and time to appreciate the stunning natural surroundings.

Pemuteran is a relatively small and sleepy coastal town which attracts tourists wishing to visit the Menjangan National Park (Bali Barat National Park). The majority of local people, who are mainly Hindu and some Muslim, are fishermen or farmers growing sweet corn and keeping livestock,. Some are also involved in the tourism industry and in construction. Pemuteran is still considered an off the beaten track part of Bali and as such the choice of restaurants and places to stay is more limited than in major tourist areas in the south of Bali. There is a range of hotels along the Pemuteran beach which tend to be mainly upmarket resorts, and there are mid-range and budget homestays along

the main road and just set back from it. For eating out, there are numerous cheap local *warung* and more high-end hotel restaurants. The National Park area is one of stunning natural beauty: green forests bordered by black sand beaches that open up onto clear tropical waters.

Tourists have been visiting the Menjangan Park and diving in the area for decades and the locals speak reasonable English as well as numerous phrases in a handful of other European languages.

For medical emergencies, there is a local medical clinic 30 minutes away in

Green turtles are often found resting amongst corals on the reef, like the one pictured here.

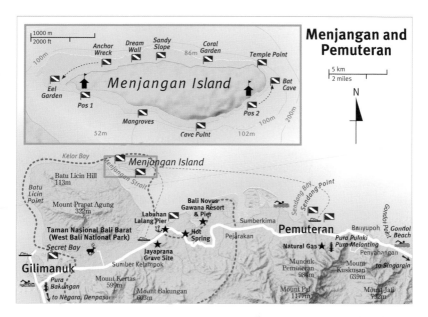

Gerokgak and a number of hospitals in Singaraja. The nearest recompression chamber is in Sanglah Hospital, Denpasar.

DIFFICULTY LEVEL Very easy year round diving with minimal currents, warm waters and sites that can be dived either shallow or deep to suit experience level.

HIGHLIGHTS Menjangan offers very easy diving with a little bit of everything available: walls, slopes, critters and muck. If you are in Bali and looking to relax and get away from it all in an area of natural beauty, then Menjangan is a good option. Turtles are often seen here and sharks sightings are frequent from July to October.

LOGISTICS Diving around Menjangan is based around the small coastal town of Pemuteran, which is approximately a four-hour drive from Denpasar Airport, Sanur and Kuta. Most operators will provide airport pick-ups for a surcharge or included in the package price. There are numerous operators in the area and

Schooling yellow snappers are a common sight around Menjangan Island.

many of them are based in higher end beachfront hotels with which they offer dive and stay packages. It is entirely possible to dive with a center based at one resort and stay elsewhere, particularly if you are looking for more budget accommodation.

MENJANGAN AND PEMUTERAN'S BEST DIVE SITES

MENJANGAN ISLAND: CAVE II (CAVE POINT)
☆AUTHOR'S CHOICE

Cave II is a wall site on the south of the east coast of Menjangan, which offers some interesting vertical rifts and faults, one of which forms a narrow but tall cavern that stretches back into the wall some 3 to 5 meters and can be entered. Entry to the site is made in front of the banks of the island where you drop in over the crest of the wall which sits at around 5 meters. The wall itself is a mix of hard and soft corals with the latter

being more notable. Large gorgonian sea fans of varying colors and wild looking bushes of black corals adorn the wall, and on days with good visibility the underwater reefscape is really quite impressive. The wall stretches down to 35 meters where the corals peter out to white sand. The site can be dived in either direction depending on current. The cave is a narrow, vertical opening at around 12 meters, which you can swim into, and there is enough space inside to turn around and peer out to the black coral bordered blue. Only one diver can enter at a time, and it is not ideal for those who do not like confined spaces. Shortly after the cave, there is a small L-shaped swim-through which also offers nice views out. Fish life here is mediocre in terms of abundance but batfish are frequently spotted, lionfish cling to the wall, occasional small schools of yellow back fusiliers and schooling

Looking out to the blue from inside of Cave II, Menjangan.

This soft coral has the delicate arm of a brittle star trailing across it.

Above These yellow snappers are schooling in front of the bio-rock structures in Pemuteran.

Left Gilimanuk is home to many species of frogfish, such as this green painted variety.

basslets. As depth increases, so does the coral density, and heading east the reef has medium to good coverahe with some interspersed sandy patches and rubble in between the sponges and leather, plate and stone corals. There are also a number of small fans and whips. Reef fish abundance is medium and Moorish idols, nudibranchs, lionfish, angelfish and parrotfish swim around the reef. Anemones are worth checking out for commensal shrimps and porcelain crabs.

Highlights here include moray eels hiding amongst the corals, blue spotted stingrays on the sandy areas and, from July to October, when temperatures tend to be a little lower, black tip reef sharks and eagle rays are seen along with numerous turtles which nest on the north coast beach of Menjangan Island.

GILIMANUK: SECRET BAY
Secret Bay is a shallow black sand muck diving site situated close to Gilimanuk harbour. The site reaches a little over 9 meters, and because of the fine sandy bottom visibility here can be very low. Always try and dive on high tide or

bannerfish are seen, and in the shallows towards the jetty there are good numbers of sergeant majors, chromis and damsels. An easy wall dive with some interesting topographical features.

MENJANGAN ISLAND: SANDY SLOPE
Sandy Slope is along the northern coastine of Mengjangan and is a pretty coral reef despite what its name suggests. Entry is made next to the mooring over the shallow sand bottom. The slope drops away from around 5 meters at almost a 45 degree angle and small branching corals and soft coral formations come into view immediately, with small aggregations of damsels and

Smashing Mantis Shrimps *Odontodactylidae*

Mantis shrimps are members of the Stomatopoda order of crustaceans. Some species can grow to up to 30 cm long. The smashers are so-called because of their blunt raptorial appendages which they use to literally smash open shells for food. These small shrimps really do pack a punch with a strike speed that has been measured at 23 meters per second from a standing start, approximately the same acceleration speed as a .22 caliber bullet leaving a gun barrel. Even if the mantis shrimp misses its prey, with a strike of this power the resulting shock wave through the water can be enough to stun or even kill smaller victims. Mantis shrimps range in coloration. Among the most common are the peacock mantis shrimp (below) and the smaller pink-eared mantis.

Mantis shrimps spend much of their time in solitude hiding under rocks and ledges or in tunnels in sand and rubble. They venture out from their burrows to hunt for snails, molluscs, crabs and oysters. Despite their power, mantis shrimps can be quite shy creatures and will often duck under cover when approached by divers although some individuals also display curiosity.

Along with their striking speed, mantis shrimps are equipped with what are considered to be the most complex of eyes in the entire animal kingdom. The eyes, which are mounted on stalks, are able to move independently of each other, giving these small shrimps an incredibly wide field of vision. The mantis shrimps' eyes enable them to view both polarized light and multispectral images, making them exceptionally accurate when hunting.

During mating rituals, the male will fluoresce to attract a female (which are only fertile at certain times of the tidal cycle). After mating, some species will lay eggs in their burrows whilst in other species the female will carry the eggs under her tail. Mantis shrimps tend to favor shallow reefs and sandy areas, which perhaps explains why the female's reproductive cycle is so interlinked with that of the tides. In a life time, a mantis shrimp may breed between 20 and 30 times.

The peacock species below was photographed in Lembeh but mantis shrimps, particularly the peacock variety, are seen on reefs all over Indonesia.

The peacock species of mantis shrimp packs one of the most powerful punches of the animal kingdom.

These bicycles form part of the Pemuteran Bio-Rock Project. A batfish can be seen swimming above.

before it but avoid diving here when the tide is going out or when there are big waves. There is little here in terms of coral as this is a true muck diving site: black sand with sporadic sponges and small coral formations, natural debris and trash. Whilst these are randomly distributed, they attract all kinds of critters and every piece is worth exploring thoroughly. The range of species that can be seen here is wide and changes from season to season, but frequently spotted species include frogfish, ghost pipefish, dragonets, nudibranchs and stonefish. The mimic octopus and Ambon scorpionfish are sometimes seen here also. There are numerous diadema sea urchins, and this is one of only a few places that the rare and endangered Banggai cardinal-fish can be seen, often hiding amongst the urchins' spines.

Diving here is very much a case of swimming around the sandy bottom and looking for outcroppings or places that could provide shelter for critters. Following a back and forth pattern allows for maximum bottom coverage.

Because Secret Bay receives water from the Bali Strait, the temperature here can be surprisingly cool compared to the Pemuteran and Menjangan sites and it can be as low as 23 degrees. A long 5 mm wetsuit is advised, particularly as dives here can be longer than usual owing to the shallow depth of the site.

PEMUTERAN: BIO-ROCK PROJECT

The Bio-Rock Project is situated in front of the Werner Lau dive center at Pondok Sari Hotel on Pemuteran beach, thus entry to this shallow site is via the shore. The name Bio-Rock suggests only one feature but there are, in fact, around 12 to 14 major structures ranging from

Organisation. Historically, the reefs around Pemuteran were badly damaged through destructive fishing practises. Both dynamite and cyanide were being used, and the local villagers saw the need to improve the reefs for both tourism purposes and to increase fish numbers. Today, the people of Pemuteran village have taken action to prevent the use of destructive fishing practices, which are also banned in the Menjangan Park area. The project is supported through donations from individuals and a number of dive resorts, while hotels donate electricity, staff and additional funding.

The project attracts large numbers of chromis and damselfish. Batfish are frequently seen and schools of yellow snapper often gather around the structures as well as occasional passing barracuda and an assortment of other reef fish. Whilst this is not a challenging site or a stunning natural reef, it is certainly interesting, and as the conditions here are very easy it is suitable for all. Besides, it is also a worthwhile cause operated by local villagers and donations are welcomed. The project is on the sand flat, but a little further out there is also a steeper sloping reef which has medium coral density and a range of reef fish.

dome shapes and bicycles to Balinese statues and arches as well as numerous smaller ones. The structures are made from iron and use electrolytic mineral accretion technology. Basically, a low-voltage DC current is passed through the structures, increasing their growth rate. This allows the corals to support dense fish populations and to be more resilient to environmental stresses. The site and the structures are very shallow, ranging from 3 to 7 meters, and they follow a rough trail, so navigating from one to the next is not a problem.

The project was put in place in 2000 by the local village people and Yos Diving Center (which is no longer operating). Today, the project is managed by the local village which has formed a Biorock

MENJANGAN AND PEMUTERAN
TRAVEL PLANNER

The area offers a range of walls around Menjangan Island, slopes off Pemuteran's outer reef and macro and muck diving at Secret Bay to the northwest of the island. Menjangan offers divers in Bali a taste of many different topographies but it has limited sites of each type, so if you are looking for a serious wall diving holiday you may well be better placed in Sulawesi. Similarly, if you want a muck diving holiday, then the Lembeh Strait or Ambon Bay may be a better choice. However, if you want to try a few different things and to relax and enjoy the beauty of the Bali Barat Park, then Menjangan/Pemuteran is the perfect destination.

Annual water temperatures range from 28 to 29 degrees but cooler thermoclines of 26 degrees can be present from July to October. The best visibility is from April to October when it averages 18 to 25 meters plus. During the wetter months of November to March, the range is from 5 meters after rainfall to around 15 meters. The peak season is June to October and this is when more pelagics are seen passing through the area.

Most operators offer various diving options, from individual dives to 2 or 3 dive days. Nitrox, equipment hire and dive courses are widely available. When diving around Menjangan Island, which is within the National Park, there is a ticket fee payable which most operators either build into their prices or add on as a small surcharge. The tickets are two Euros at the time of writing. The National Park area is a no-take, no-fishing, no hunting, no collecting and no anchoring zone.

As the area is remote, operators limit dives to 60 minutes and depths are usually a maximum of 30 meters. Most sites are accessed by boat. From Pemuteran beach it is a 20 minute boat ride to Menjangan Island.

Recommended Operators

Diving

Werner Lau (Author's Choice) Dive centers based at both Pondok Sari and Matahari Beach Resort and Spa. Both centers offer nitrox, equipment hire, courses, fun diving within the Menjangan Park and Pemuteran and dive and stay packages. Staying outside of the two resorts in local accommodation is also an option. Local hotel pick-ups provided. Services in English, German and Indonesian. $$. www.wernerlau.com. Email: bali@wernerlau.com.

Blue Corner Dive Located at Nusa Bay Menjangan Resort. Daily fun diving, PADI courses, dive and stay packages. Also with operations in Nusa Lembongan. Tel: +62 (0) 87761377718. www.bluecornerdive.com. Email: info@bluecornerdive.com.

Bali Diving Academy Based on Pemuteran Beach. Daily fun diving, courses, equipment hire and dive and stay packages at either Taman Sari or Amertha Villas. Also with dive centers in Nusa Lembongan, Tulamben, Sanur and on Gili Trawangan. $$. Tel: +62 (0) 361270252. www.scubali.com. Email: info@scubali.com.

Accommodation

Pondok Sari Beach Resort International standard hotel based in central location on Pemuteran beach, range of rooms and bungalows, restaurant, swimming pool. $$. Tel: +62 (0) 36294738. www.pondoksari.com. Email: info@pondoksari.com.

Pondok Lebih Homestay Jl Raya Pemuteran. Small locally owned guest house with comfortable rooms, AC, hot water set back from the main street. $. Tel: +62 (0) 81239316777. www.pondoklebih.com. Email: pondoklebih-pemuteran@gmail.com.

Diving Padang Bai and Candidasa
A Variety of Sites Along Bali's East Coast

The bustling port of Padang Bai offers easy critter diving in both the Amuk Bay area and Blue Lagoon where frogfish, ghost pipefish, nudibranchs and a wide range of macro life abound. It's not all black sand though. There are coral reefs, abundant marine life and some exhilarating current diving off the rocky pinnacles of Batu Mimpang, Gili Tepekong and Gili Biaha. Sharks are regularly spotted here along with other pelagics and occasional mola in the season. These advanced sites boast stunning corals, wild topographies and anything is possible out in the blue!

Padang Bai is traditionally a harbor and fishing town and the public boats heading to Gili and Lombok all depart from here as well as boats which have come from further east in Indonesia. The town is small with everything located on the

Above Beautiful Indonesian countryside at Candidasa.

Below Padang Bai is not just home to critters as many species of reef fish such as these abound.

small main road that follows the path of the beach around the harbor. Thus, everything in Padang Bai is within walking distance. Being the main public boat terminal out of Bali, Padang Bai attracts a large number of backpackers looking for cheap transport to other islands. The restaurants and majority of homestays in the area cater for this market. There are a few more mid-range options and a couple of upmarket hotels but high-end options are more limited here than in South Bali.

DIFFICULTY LEVEL Diving Padang Bai ranges in difficulty level. The critter dives around Amuk Bay and Blue Lagoon are suitable for all levels whilst Batu Mimpang, Gili Tepekong and Gili Biaha offer sites only advisable for advanced divers who have experience of diving deep and in strong currents.

HIGHLIGHTS A range of critters in Amuk

Bay, including nudibranchs, stingrays, waspfish, frogfish and many more. Wild and untamed conditions around the 'Gili Pinnacles', which feature interesting topographies, white tip and black tip reef sharks and occasional rays and a host of reef life.

LOGISTICS There are two main options for diving around Padang Bai: stay in Padang Bai or Candidasa or dive the area by making day trips from one of the main operators in South Bali. If you are working your way up Bali's east coast or planning to head over to Lombok or the Gili Islands, then staying in Padang Bai works well. However, if you are looking to make a handful of dives during your holiday to Bali, Padang Bai is not the most ideal holiday destination. Therefore, using a day trip operator from the south is recommended. Operators in Sanur provide hotel pick-ups from the south of

the island and Padang Bai is an hour by car. This is followed by two or three dives with lunch included and then an hour's drive back to the South. If you are making two dives, it is possible to be back at your hotel by 3 pm in the afternoon.

Padang Bai is home to some very small and intriguing critters.

PADANG BAI AND CANDIDASA'S BEST DIVE SITES

CRITTER DIVING IN PADANG BAI: BLUE LAGOON AND JEPUN

These are both critter dive sites which are great for spotting macro life. They are easily dived from Padang Bai, just a 5 to 10 minute boat ride from the main harbor. Both sites attract small reef fish as well as critters but not in abundance and there is only medium variety. For critters, however, these sites make great introductions to muck diving. Unlike some other sites in the area, they are suitable for divers of all levels of experience.

Blue Lagoon is a small bay to the north of the main Padang Bai harbor, with a shallow white sand and rubble flat area at just 3 to 6 meters which then drops in

the form of a slope to 30 to 35 meters. The flat has sporadic coral patches and bommies and scorpionfish lie camouflaged on the rubble, blue spotted stingrays rest on the bottom, razorfish dramatically dive into the sand if you get too close, and seahorses are sometimes spotted here too along with a range of nudibranch species. The entry is in the bay over the flat, then make your way down the slope. Heading north along the slope there is a coral wall along the front of the edge of the bay which is a mix of hard and soft corals and an excellent place for spotting critters. Check amongst the feather stars for ornate ghost pipefish and ribbon eels, moray eels and for lionfish amongst the corals.

Night dives are also possible in Blue Lagoon when the conditions are good.

The venomous spines of this juvenile lionfish are clearly visible in this picture taken in Padang Bai.

It makes an excellent site by torchlight for Spanish dancers, frogfish and a range of crabs and shrimps.

Jepun is on the south side of the larger Amuk Bay to the north of Blue Lagoon, but unlike Blue Lagoon with its white sand Jepun is a dark sandy slope which has been subject to some artificial reef projects. The sand slope drops away from

Scorpionfish are closely related to the lionfish family and like them bear venomous spines.

5 meters and there are only occasional coral formations: anemones, branching corals and sponges. This is more of a true muck diving site. Along the slope there is a range of man-made structures placed to attract critters, fish and general marine life. It is also worth noting that there is a small wreck here, too, which is approximately 8 meters in length and which attracts fish. Occasionally, schooling yellow snapper are seen here along with damselfish, chromis and Moorish idols. More interesting critters seen on the slope include spiny devilfish, nudibranchs, including chromodoris and nembrotha, reef octopus, ribbon eels, oriental ghost pipefish and cockatoo waspfish. The critter species change from season to season and anything is possible!

This small wreck at Jepun, Padang Bai, attracts both reef fish and critters to the sandy slopes.

The Ribbon Eel *Rhinomuraena quaesita*

Ribbon eels are a smaller species of eel which lead fascinating life cycles not only involving three completely different phases of coloration but also complete changes in gender. Ribbon eels begin life as juveniles, when they are easily recognized by the bright yellow dorsal fin that runs the length of their dark black bodies. As the eel matures, the black changes to a bright electric blue with an equally vivid yellow dorsal fin. This marks the male stage of its life. The eel continues to grow, and at approximately 1.3 meters its color changes again, this time to yellow, and the eel enters its female stage, whereupon it is able to lay eggs.

Ribbon eels are found predominantly on healthy coral reefs but they also seem to do well on damaged reefs where they favor sand and rubble areas. They are frequently found hiding under rocks and ledges or buried in the sand with just their heads and upper body visible. It is quite a rare sight to see the entire length of a ribbon eel at any stage of its life cycle. The have long protruding nostrils which are almost seahorse-like in appearance and are used to sense vibrations in the water. As with moray eels, divers often mistake ribbon eels as being aggressive as they are commonly seen with their mouths widely opening and closing in what could be interpreted as a threatening manner when they are, in fact, just breathing.

Despite their slender bodies, ribbon eels have an incredible lifespan of up to 20 years and can grow to over a meter in length. Ribbon eels are carnivores and their diets consist of shrimps and small fish.

Ribbon eels do not appear to be seasonal and can be seen throughout the Indonesian archipelago.

Above This male stage ribbon eel has its mouth open for breathing. Note the flared nostrils.

Left It is unusual to see ribbon eels swimming such as here. This specimen is in the yellow-blue male phase.

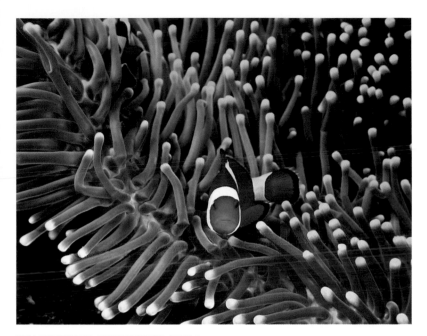

GILI TEPEKONG: THE CANYON, WALL AND SLOPE

Gili Tepekong is the larger rock that sits to the east of Gili Mimpang. The site is around a 20 minute boat ride from Padang Bai and needs to be dived when conditions are good. Whereas Amuk Bay offers easy diving, Gili Tepekong is for more experienced divers only as currents can be quite strong. For those who have the ability, Tepekong can be an adrenaline-fueled dive with pelagics, schooling fish and challenging conditions! Whilst the rock is only around 50 meters long, there are two different areas for diving here.

The Canyon is situated on the southwestern corner of Tepekong and is exactly as the name suggests, a canyon. The sides of the canyon are formed of black rock which offers a stunning contrast to the soft and hard corals that grow over it. As Tepekong is surrounded by deep waters, it is prone to cold

False anemonefish such as this one are commonly found on anemones around Padang Bai.

thermoclines which not only keep the coral healthy but also mean it is a good place to see larger pelagics. Keep an eye out to the blue for passing sharks, rays, tuna and occasionally larger schools of fish. From August to October, mola are occasionally seen. Entry is close to the tip of the island and the site direction is dependant on the current. Check it first and be ready for it to change during the dive!

General reef fish life here is healthy and moray eels, parrotfish, sweetlips and angelfish are abundant. In the shallows, especially, there are large numbers of butterfly fish, damsels and basslets which all add splashes of color to the unique topography.

On the south and east of Gili Tepekong is a wall and a slope which are deep sites and are also recommended for

White tip reef sharks are a sociable species of shark. This pair were pictured in a small cave.

advanced divers due to currents. This area can also be dived heading in either direction depending on the direction of the water movement. The wall starts at around 14 meters and drops down to 40 meters and offers schools of unicornfish hovering over the reef, schooling bannerfish in the blue and a good chance of passing pelagics. The slope offers more reef fish. Schooling sweetlips, a full range of triggerfish, angelfish, butterfly fish and damsels all add color and vibrancy to the reef. Turtles and barracuda can also be seen here.

GILI BIAHA

This site is on the most northern of the three rocks and outcroppings to the north of Amuk Bay. Biaha Rock is surrounded by deep waters and can be very subject to surge so diving here is best when sea conditions are relatively flat. Even then, this is a site for advanced divers only. Stay in close to the reef and get ready for an exhilarating drift! The east side of the rock offers a mix of walls and steep slopes from 5 meters down to 40 meters which are covered with a mixture of short-cropped hard and soft corals. The currents here have prevented huge outward growth but there are a

number of gorgonian fans and black corals that add to the look of wilderness which makes Biaha an unforgettable dive site. In the middle of the crescent-shaped east coast of Biaha, at 12 meters, is a cave which opens up to around 4 to 5 meters from bottom to top and which is often home to white tip reef sharks and lobsters. It is possible to enter the cave but only recommended for those with suitable experience and on dives where there is minimal surge. On good days, the view looking out from the cave into the blue is stunning.

The side of Biaha which faces the mainland is also diveable and offers a rock and coral slope at around a 45 degree angle. The slope extends down to almost 60 meters and can be a great place for spotting sharks and banded sea snakes. Both diving areas also provide for a wide range of marine life amongst the coral, not just pelagics out in the blue, for the reef is alive with scorpionfish, cuttlefish, a range of nudibranchs, aggregations of cardinalfish amongst the corals, leaf scorionfish and all manner of more common reef fishes.

PADANG BAI AND CANDIDASA TRAVEL PLANNER

Whether you decide to stay in Padang Bai or if you decide to choose to make a day trip from the south of Bali, most operators offer equipment hire, fun diving packages and courses. Dives are all boat dives which depart from the main harbor beach in Padang Bai and journey times range from 5 minutes to 30 minutes depending on the site and boat type. The sites in Padang Bai can be dived all year round but in the wet season visibility is reduced and strong winds creating big waves can make sites around Gili Tepekong, Batu Mimpang and Gili Biaha inaccessible. Average visibility is 15 meters, but after rainfall or when there is big swell it can be reduced to 5 meters at the sandy sites around Amuk Bay. During the dry season, visibility can be 30 meters plus. Water temperature is warmest during the wet season and reaches 29 degrees, whilst from July to October thermoclines as cool as 21 degrees are present around the Gili rock pinnacles. Most operators offer both short and long suits depending on the season. If you are diving the pinnacles, a long suit is recommended year round.

Nitrox is readily available from Sanur operators and some Padang Bai dive centers. Operators generally limit dives to 25 to 30 meters and dive times tend to be 60 minutes. If you are diving Mimpang, Biaha or Tepekong, a DSMB (Delayed Surface Marker Buoy) is strongly recommended. For other sites and providing you know how to operate one, then it is a nice addition.

Padang Bai has a local clinic for minor injuries and ailments. For DCS or major health issues, it is best to head to Sanur for the recompression chamber at Sanglah Hospital and a range of international hospitals.

Recommended Operators

Diving

Bali Scuba (Author's Choice) Organized and professional operator based in Sanur offering 2–3 dive trips with hotel pick-ups and drop-offs, transfers to Padang Bai, lunch and diving. (See 'Bali Travel Planner', page 46). Tel: +62 (0) 361288610. www.baliscuba.com.
Geko Dive Based in Padang Bai. Tel: +62 (0) 36341516. www.gekodivebali.com.

Accommodation

Bloo Lagoon Village Eco Resort Padang Bai upmarket resort offering 25 eco villas situated to the north end of Padang Bai. Tel: +62 (0) 36341211. www.bloolagoon.com.
Puri Rai Padang Bai Jl Silayukti, No. 7X. Comfortable mid-range rooms and budget options. Tel: +62 (0) 3618528521. www.puriraihotel.com. Email: info@puriraihotels.com.
Pondok Ayu Upper mid-range resort in Sanur. www.pondok.com.au. Email: information@pondokayu.com.au.

This small species of frogfish is known as the clown frogfish and was pictured in Padang Bai.

NORTH SULAWESI

The lands of North Sulawesi are rich with nature: rolling green hills, volcanic peaks and a host of endemic species, from the crested black macaque and tiny tarsius to the anoa and babirusa. North Sulawesi's natural delights are not all terrestrial, though, and underwater there is a wealth of marine diversity to be expected from an area nestled in the heart of the Coral Triangle. The shores of Manado provide a mix of reef and critter diving and a small wreck and the city itself is an ideal stopover point for those with early or late flights and

Bunaken–Manado Tua
National Marine Park
75,265 hectares

Nain Besar I. Tampi

Helga Point

Bajo

Batu Kapal

Divex Point

Jalan Masuk

to Lirung, Tahuna

Tarabitan Pt.
Tarabitan Strait

Tarabitan

Tarabitan   Ser

Tangkasi

Tangkasi

Paputungan   Mobune

Barracuda Point

Sansilo

Montehage
Island

Kora Kora

Montehage

Tinangko

Tinabunan

Bango

Munte

Buhias

Kulu   Mal

Gorango

Lantung   Palaos   Werot

Totongapen

Darunu   Lansa   Kokoleh

Manado Tua

Alung
Banua

Siladen

Budo   Patokaan

Manado Tua

Bunaken

Talawan Bajo

Mt. Takaro
+556m

Bunaken

Wori

Tumbohon

Tiwoho

Tongkeina
Pisok Pt.

Mt. Tumpa
637m

Pandu

Waterfalls

Wasian

Barracuda Diving

Molas

Paniki
Bawah

Talawaan

Paleleh

Celebes
Sea

Baliang

Buha

Sam Ratulangi
Int'l Airport

Tetey   Talelu

Bitung
Karang Ria

Dimembe

Manado Bay

Manado

Kairogi

Blue Banter
Marina Beach

Maumbi   Laikit

Batu Nona Beach

Murex

Sario

Wenang

Kolongan

Mandolang Pt.

Malalayang

Kemangko

Waruga
Batu Megalit

Murex Dive Center

Tateli

Manado Beach

Tateli   Sea

Koha

Kaleosan   Air Madidi

Tanawangko
Bay

Mokupa

Pineleng

Tomb of Tuanku
Imam Bonjol

Koka

Sampiri   Lembean

Tasik Ria

Tasik Ria
Beach

Kali

Popo

Tanawangko

Kembes   Liang   Sawangan

Lemoh

Mt. Tawiran
1579m

Tinoor   Kali Waterfalls

Senduk

Rano Tongkor

Mt. Lokon
1595m

Tembona   Mt. Mahawu
1311m

Waterfalls   Waruga

Rano Tongi

Kakaskasan

Rurukan   Suluan   Tanggari

SEE BUNAKEN, SILADEN AND MANADO MAP

Tara Tara   Loloan

Temboan   Mt. Amemelar
+1081m

Munte

to Gorontalo, Palu
Tangkunel

Loloan Traditional
Village

Woloan

Tomohon

Kasuang   Tondano   Japanese Cave   Kinaleosan

to Palu   Uluindano

Merawas

for those who feel the need for some Western treats before heading on to their next destination. The towering coral-clad walls of Bunaken are vibrant and colorful and provide homes to an abundance of marine fish species and turtles, whilst the Lembeh Strait offers black sandflats and slopes that reveal a plethora of critters and weird and wonderful marine creatures rarely encountered in other parts of the Indonesian archipelago. Despite the close proximity of these two areas, the contrast between them could not be more extreme. If you are planning a trip to North Sulawesi, try to fit in both places as it will be well worth it!

Bangka Island

10 km
5 miles

N

Murex Bangka Resort

Sahaong Pt.

Bangka Strait

Sumoini Pt.   Pulisan Pt.

Likupang
Paradise   Tamba   Pulisan

Wineru

Kerbau Pt.

Maririsow

Rondor

Mogogimbun Island

Pante Pasar

Rincodoran

Pinenek

Batu Putih

SEE LEMBEH STRAIT MAP

Batu Kapal

Lirang

Tinerungan

Tangkoko-Batu Angus-
Dua Sudara Reserve

Lembeh Strait

Nusu

Mt. Batu Angus
1109m

Motto Pt.

Dua Sudara

Pinangunian

Kawasari

Motto

Mt. Dua Sudara
1351m

Makawidei

Posokan

Apela

Tanduk Rusa

Kungkungan
Bay Resort

Pintukota

Danowudu

Bitung

Kungkungan Beach

Girian   Japanese
Cave

Madidir   Aer Tembaga

Buriang

Papasungan

Lembeh Island

Sarimbala

Watu Dambo

Panchran

Pasir Panjang

Tanah Merah Beach

Dua I.

Kuning Pt.

to Kwandang, Lirung, Tahuna, Toli Toli

Maluku Sea

to Banggai, Gorontalo

to Ternate

North Sulawesi at a Glance
From Towering Peaks to Tropical Beaches

From wild volcanoes towering over lush, fertile, green plateaus to tropical white beaches and palm-fringed islands, North Sulawesi is vibrant, colorful and rich with breathtaking natural beauty. In just under 14,000 square kilometers, the area offers a diverse range of landscapes, from volcanic peaks above the clouds to stunning coral reefs underneath its seas.

North Sulawesi is the northern arm of the strange spidery-looking island of Sulawesi. To the north, south and east, the island is surrounded by water and to the west it borders Gorontalo. North Sulawesi is divided into four districts: Manado, Bolaang Mongondow, Talaud and Bitung. There are three main ethnic groups: the Bolaang Mongondow, the Sangihe Talaud and the Minihasa, the latter being the most culturally prevalent. There are also a number of minority immigrant populations.

The lands of North Sulawesi are amongst the most fertile in the archipelago. Nourished by volcanic ash and with near perfect growing conditions, the green plateaus of the highlands and lowlands yield abundant supplies of rice, coconut, clove, nutmeg, vanilla, vegetables and coffee. Annual temperatures range from 25 to 28 degrees although these decrease with altitude (approximately 1 degree for every 200 meters above sea level). The dry season runs from April until October and the rainy season from November to March. It is not only crops that flourish here. North Sulawesi also boasts numerous indigenous species, such as the anoa, a dog-sized dwarf water buffalo, the tail-less black macaque and the tiny tarsier which, despite having huge eyes, only grows to 10 centimeters.

Tangkoko Nature Reserve and Bogani Nani Wartabone National Park also provide refuge for many endemic bird species and giant fruit bats.

Manado is North Sulawesi's capital city and it embodies diversity, not only within its people but also its surrounding landscape. Just 25 kilometers from the heart of the busy, congested city you can escape to picturesque towns such as Tomohon, nestled on a plateau between two active volcanoes where the air is cool and fresh, flowers and exotic plants grow in abundance and life goes on at a much more leisurely pace.

Historically, abundant crop and rice supplies made Manado a strategic port for European traders traveling to and

Downtown Manado city offers Western eateries, shopping and traffic!

from the spice islands of Maluku. The Spanish built a fort in Manado much to the dislike of Manado's rulers who sought help from the Dutch in Ternate to overcome them. The Dutch obliged and took control of Manado in 1655, built a fort of their own in 1658 and expelled the last of the Spaniards shortly after. Dutch influence flourished in North Sulawesi and the people embraced the imported goods, culture and religion. In 1881, missionary schools were created in Manado and these were the first attempts at mass education in Indonesia. While anti-Dutch rebellions grew in Java, the relations between the Dutch and the Minahasans remained solid and earned the people of North Sulawesi the name *anjing Belanda* or 'Dutch Dogs'.

The main entry point to North Sulawesi is Manado's Dr Sam Ratulangi International Airport. International flights arrive from Singapore and domestic flights come daily from Jakarta and Makassar. Thirty-day tourist visas are available upon arrival at the airport (if you are not coming from an exempt county) and currently cost US$35. Manado has a range of accommodation available, from backpacker homestays to international hotels. In the city, most locals travel by motorbike or *mikrolet*, which are small blue buses that cruise the city and pick up passengers as they go along. Most dive operations will include airport transfers in their package prices or provide them for a small surcharge.

The Lembeh Strait is banked by lush green hills rich with foliage.

Manado's population is just under 410,000, 64 percent of whom are protestant, 31 percent Muslim, 4 percent Roman Catholic and 1 percent Hindu or Buddhist. Churches appear all around the city because religion is important here. Almost all Christian families belong to a church and many small businesses still close on Sunday mornings.

Music is important in North Sulawesi's culture. The people not only embrace modern music, from pop and rock to country classics, but also have a rich history of traditional music and even have their own instruments such as the *kolintang*, a type of wooden xylophone. As in most parts of the archipelago, music is nothing without dancing and the Minahasan traditional dances do not disappoint. The Kabasaran is a traditional war dance which expresses patriotism, heroism and courage and is one of the most impressive to watch as the men leap and cry out to frighten their enemies.

Rice is the staple food in North Sulawesi and, given its abundance, coconut is also found in many dishes. Local cuisine is spicy with chili peppers at the heart of most dishes. *Rica-rica*, a local favorite, can be made with fish or meat and is cooked with spicy red chili, shallots, garlic and tomato. Amongst the more daring of dishes is *paniki*, fruit bat cooked over burning coconut husks.

Diving North Sulawesi
Extreme Diversity and Full of Surprises

With warm, clear waters and extreme and diverse underwater topographies, from colossal vertical walls in Bunaken with schooling fish, turtles and pelagics to some of the world's best critter and muck diving in Lembeh, North Sulawesi's underwater reefscapes are as diverse and vibrant as the land itself.

Diving conditions around North Sulawesi are generally calm, so it is an ideal place for those learning to dive, less experienced divers and those who enjoy taking their dives at a relaxing pace. It also provides for great photography opportunities. For those seeking stunning corals, walls or deep diving, head over to Bunaken. Critter hunters will love the Lembeh Strait for the diversity of its weird and wonderful marine life. In short, you will not be disappointed whatever your diving preference. North Sulawesi rarely fails to impress.

Despite being far less developed for tourists than areas such as Bali, diving and getting around in North Sulawesi is surprisingly straightforward and stress-free with the majority of operators providing airport pick-ups and transfers included in their package prices or for small surcharges. Dive and stay full board packages are the norm. Less is definitely more for divers here. Whilst Bunaken and Lembeh host numerous resorts, boat traffic is less than in Bali.

In the last 10 years, dive tourism has developed across the region and, as such, more facilities for divers have emerged. Manado is not Indonesia's most picturesque city but it has a dive store, a recompression chamber and numerous ATMs. There is also a decent number of Western food eateries and most restaurants have wi-fi, and there is a range of hotels and places to stay.

With development across the region, competition between operators has grown and there are numerous resorts offering differing levels of service, from backpacker to luxury. Most operators offer courses in a variety of European languages and Indonesian. Two Fish Divers in Bunaken also offers instructor level training.

Many resorts have small shops for buying dive accessories such as masks,

Above Found in the Lembeh Strait, the coconut octopus exhibits unique behavior.

Opposite The Banggai cardinalfish is a highly localized species and can be seen amongst anemones in the Lembeh Strait.

clips and slates. If you are hoping to buy larger items such as BCDs or regulators, it is best to stop off in Bali or Jakarta on the way through.

Numerous resorts have nitrox available but not all, so check with your operator when booking. Some operators supply nitrox for free whilst others add a surcharge.

There have also been numerous positive environmental outcomes from development in the region. Marine parks have been established which ensure fishermen are not taking directly from the reefs. Clean-up dives are carried out regularly and coral monitoring and shark and turtle conservation initiatives are in place.

It used to be the case that to explore the reefs of North Sulawesi divers had to be based in Manado but now there are numerous resorts on Bunaken Island itself and Lembeh also hosts a decent variety of well spread out resorts. Neither destination has really developed outside of the resorts, which are unassumingly nestled into the landscape. If you are looking for comfortable accommodation and astounding marine life combined with a feeling of remoteness amongst breathtaking natural beauty, then North Sulawesi is a must!

USEFUL CONTACTS

Medical Centers

Manado Siloam Hospital Manado (SHMN), Boulevard Center, Jalan Sam Ratulangi No. 22, Manado. Tel: +62 (0) 431888 3131.

Hospital (Rumah Sakit) Prof. Dr R. D. Kandou Manado, Jalan Raya Tanawangko No. 56, Manado. Tel: +62 (0) 431838203 or 838305.

Bitung RSAL Bitung Jalan Vos Sudarso No. 26, Bitung. Tel: +62 (0) 43821264.

RSUD Bitung Jalan Manembo-nembo , Bitung. Tel: +62 (0) 43831881.

Recompression Chamber

There is a recompression chamber at Rumah Sakit Prof Dr Kandou Hospital. Tel: +62 (0) 431853191.

Dive Stores

Lautan Berkat Dive Shop Kawasan Mega Mas Blok Smart 3, No. 20, Jalan Piere Tendean Boulevard Manado. Cressi and Mares dealership with a range of dive equipment, spares. Servicing is also available. Tel: +62 (0) 4318881185 or + 62 (0) 8123819919. www.lautanberkat-diveshop.com.

Master Selam Aqualung stockiest with retail outlets in both Bali and Jakarta. www.masterselam.com.

Others

Garuda Indonesia 24-Hour Call Center. Tel: +62 (0) 8041807807 or +62 (0) 21 23519999. www.garuda-indonesia.com.

Sriwijaya Air Call Center. Tel: +62 (0) 21 29279777 or +62 (0) 8041777777. www.sriwijayaair.co.id.

Lion Air Assistance Line Tel: +62 (0) 21 63798000. www.lionair.co.id.

North Sulawesi
TRAVEL PLANNER

North Sulawesi offers two distinct dive areas: Bunaken Marine Park (including Siladen and Manado) and the Lembeh Strait. Transit from one to the other is remarkably simple with relatively short travel times. Manado Airport to Lembeh is around a 90 minute car journey to Bitung followed by a 10 to 20 minute boat ride to your chosen operator. Manado Airport to Bunaken or Siladen is around a 45 minute car journey to Manado harbor from where you transfer to boat which takes around another 45 minutes to reach Bunaken, depending on your operator.

As operators in both regions are full board dive resorts, all offer pick-ups and drop-offs either included in their pricing or for a small surcharge. If you are transiting from Bunaken to Lembeh, have your Bunaken operator transfer you back to Manado and your Lembeh operator pick you up from there, and vice versa if traveling from Lembeh to Bunaken. The trip from one to the other can comfortably be made in a morning or afternoon, but if you prefer to take things at a more leisurely pace, would like a dive-free day or want to explore Manado, then an overnight stay in the city with a pick-up

the next morning is entirely possible. Just be sure to let your operator know your plans in advance.

There are a number of operators based around Manado who offer diving in the Bunaken Marine Park and along the Manado coastline, but staying on either Siladen or Bunaken Islands puts you closer to the wall dive sites, for which the area is best known, and gives a truly remote island getaway feeling to your trip.

It is worth noting that the following operators have resorts on both Bunaken and Lembeh: Murex Dive Resorts (also with a third resort on Bangka Island) www.murex-dive.com; Two Fish Divers www.twofishdivers.com; Bastiano's www.bastianos.com; Froggies Divers www.divefroggies.com.

Unless you have a specific preference for either walls or critters, both areas offer equal amounts to explore and see. Thus, dividing your time evenly between the two makes good sense. There is easily enough to entertain most divers for at least a week in both destinations and for many divers two weeks would not be enough as these are both unique, diverse and intriguing areas.

Murex Dive Resort Manado offers comfortable accommodation in an oceanfront tropical garden setting.

Diving Bunaken, Siladen and Manado
Breathtaking Walls and Vibrant Corals

The walls around Bunaken Island have not become world renowned without good reason. Hosting vibrant corals, abundant fish and a healthy population of green and hawksbill turtles, Bunaken's topographically impressive sites reveal more and more with every glance. Manado offers a mix of reef and muck diving sites with a range of critters that reflects its proximity to the Lembeh Strait. For those who favor wreck diving, the *Molas* wreck off Manado offers some interesting swim-throughs and marine inhabitants. Siladen provides a mix of critters and reef and a successful sanctuary for assisting and releasing sea turtles.

Whilst Manado is a fast-developing city, the islands around it have remained quaint and traditional. Tourism is limited to full board dive resorts and there are very few other facilities for tourists outside of these. Nightlife is limited to your dive resort bar, which means evenings are usually quiet and early. Both islands have small local populations who mainly fish and farm for subsistence, with the exception of a few who have sought work in Manado and those who are employed in the diving industry in one way or another. Dive guides, boat captains, dive crew and hotel staff all tend to be from the islands.

Agriculture on the islands is a mixture of coconut plantations, cassava, banana,

Above Two Fish Divers, Bunaken, offers a range of bungalows, swimming pool and full service dive center.

Left Two Fish Divers also operate traditional wooden boats that make for comfortable sailing around the dive sites.

mango and lontar palm and the local diet is largely based around rice and fish and is famed for being amongst the hottest and spiciest in Indonesia. Bunaken and Siladen Islands are fringed with white sand beaches, mangrove forests and stunning coral reefs which now fall under the protection of the Bunaken National Park that was formally established in 1991 and also encompasses the islands of Manado Tua, Mantehage and Nain.

HIGHLIGHTS Tropical islands with postcard scenery, colossal, vibrant and colorful walls, turtles, sharks, eagle rays, critters and reported dugong sightings.

Left Honeycomb moray eels are one of North Sulawesi's most secretive species of moray.

Below Drifting along the walls of Bunaken Island is an experience not to be missed.

DIFFICULTY LEVEL Bunaken and Siladen have mild to medium level currents, warm water and good year round visibility which makes the diving suitable for all levels.
LOGISTICS Bunaken and Siladen are small neighboring islands just off the coast of mainland Manado. Bunaken has several full board dive resorts. Siladen has just two resorts. For those in the area wanting just a day dive trip, Manado has a selection of dive centers, dive resorts and hotels. Staying on Bunaken or Siladen Island puts you closer to the best sites and provides for a truly relaxed tropical island getaway where you literally have the ocean sleeping at your feet. Manado offers a range of accommodation and restaurants but the city itself is not a picturesque destination. The main airport is Dr Sam Ratulangi International in Manado and most operators offer airport pick-ups: a car journey to the harbor followed by a 40 minute boat ride to either island. If you are arriving in the evening, you may need to overnight in Manado before taking the boat the next morning.

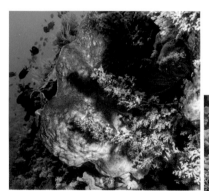

Above Bunaken National Marine Park is home to huge sponge corals and numerous soft coral species.

Right Due to successful conservation programs, green and hawksbill turtles abound in the Bunaken Park.

unaken, iladen and anado Dive Sites

Montehage Island

Barracuda Point
Tangkasi
Montehage
Tangkasi
Bango
Tinangko
Buhias
Gorango

to Lirung, Tahuna

Tanjung Kopi
Pengalingan
Totongapen
Manadotua 1
Manado Tua Island
Mike's Pt
Terigi Pt.
Sachiko's Pt.
Silanden Utara
Siladen Island
Benny's Pt
Cha Cha
Siladen Timur
Alung Banua
Tanjung Parigi
Manadotua 2
Bualo
Bualo
Raymond's Pt
Bunaken Island
Bunaken Manado Tua Marine National Park Headquarters
Siladen
DJ Pt
Tengah
Talawan Bajo
Mandolin
Fukui
Bunaken Timur 1
Negeri
Ron's Pt
Celah Celah
Bunaken Timur 2
Sal's Pt
Liang Beach
Bunaken
Pangalisang Beach
Kima Bajo
Johnson's Wall
Lekuan 3
Pangalisang
Tihowo
Wori
Alung Banua
Lekuan 2
Ghuntur's
Lekuan 1
Muka Kampung
Buhown
Tiwoho
Abang Pt
Talasa Beach
Mt. Tumpa 637m
Kalumpung
Gabet
longkaina
Pisok Pt
Engine Pt
Pandu
Tg Pisok
Barracuda Diving
Napo
Molas
Mera's
Batu Hitam
Baliang
Molas Shipwreck
Barracuda
Buha

Celebes Sea

Bitung
Karang Ria

Manado Bay

Marina

N

Reclamation Pt
MANADO
Sario
Batu Nona Beach
Murex
Blue Banter Marina Beach
Wenang
km
New Mandarin Pt
Malalayang
miles
Mandolang Pt.
45 Bananas
Murex Dive Center
Tateu
Tateli
Pygmy Pt
Sea
Pineleng
Tasik Ria House Reef
Mokupa
Koha
Critter Circus
Tasik Ria
ngko ay
Kali
Tasik Ria Beach
Kembes
Tanawangko
Lemoh
Tinoor

BUNAKEN, SILADEN AND MANADO'S BEST DIVE SITES

SILADEN JETTY

A phenomenal wall dive off the southwest corner of Siladen Island offering stunning clear water shallows, abundant healthy coral and a multitude of caverns, overhangs and recesses that make excellent habitats for the abundant critter life that this site houses.

The entry point is next to the jetty of Siladen Island where the reef crest is at approximately 5 to 10 meters. The top of the reef boasts abundant soft corals that form a patchwork of colors in the sunlight. The reef then drops away dramatically and comprises a mix of hard and soft coral characterized by fans and sponges with branching corals and plates adding other textures.

The site can be dived in either direction depending on the current, usually minimal. Head down to your maximum depth and then make your way steadily back up the wall to a safety stop either in the shallows or at the crest of the reef.

On the wall, scorpionfish lie camouflaged against the corals, ostentatious nudibranchs perch on ledges, spider crabs blend into fans, orangutan crabs burrow into bubble corals, thorny oysters can be found in the many recesses and green turtles and sharks are also frequent visitors. Amongst the critter life, reef fish also flourish here. Parrotfish, sweetlips, triggerfish and snappers all add to the blend. The variety of species that can be viewed in one dive is quite exceptional and almost everything deserves a second glance!

KAMPUNG BARU AND TIWOHO

Gradually sloping dark sand sites which provide for excellent muck diving. Whilst at first glance these sites appear sparse,

Numerous species of nudibranch are commonly seen around Siladen, such as the one shown here.

they play host to an abundance of critters and some of the areas most flamboyant marine life.

Both of these sites are situated on the coast of the mainland, to the north of Manado city, approximately 30 minutes by boat from either Bunaken or Siladen. The entry points are just offshore in the shallows at approximately 5 to 10 meters where there is a band of coral reef. Below 10 meters the reef peters out to sand, which eventually slopes to a maximum depth of 30 meters. Whilst there is a shallow reef here, the dive is mainly over the sand and the majority of critter life is in the 15 to 20 meter range.

When exploring the sand, look out for anything that could provide a habitat for critters as sporadic hard corals, anemones and natural debris can all be the base of some mini ecosystems. Common seahorses, pygmy lionfish, a variety of frogfish, ornate ghost pipefish, stonefish, octopus, ribbon eels, cuttlefish and blue spotted stingrays are all here with regularity.

As you begin to shallow up, the reef also reveals an abundance of interesting occupants. Mantis shrimps, nudibranchs, crocodilefish, pipefish, moray eels and cleaner shrimps are all present in abundance amongst the plates, tables, sponges and soft corals.

For critter fanatics, these two sites provide a plethora of species, easy conditions and some amazing photography opportunities. Whilst being a far cry from Bunaken's stunning coral walls, the variety of marine life here makes them no less impressive.

BUNAKEN TIMOR AND PANGALISANG

Wall dives on the east coast of Bunaken Island with dense coral coverage, enchanting shallow water coral gardens, turtles, critters and kaleidoscopic colors.

Entry to each of these sites is by boat just over the drop-off which is at between 5 and 10 meters. On the top of the reef crest there are soft coral gardens and an abundance of small fish. The walls are dived in either direction depending on the current and they can be dived shallow or deep. The walls here bottom out at well over 40 meters and coral coverage is excellent to at least this depth with huge gorgonians present at 35 meters plus.

Coral coverage is a mix of hard and soft with soft corals taking precedence as the depth increases. The colors at these sites are truly spectacular—reds, purples and pinks mingled in with green, blues and turquoises—contributing to a colorful patchwork effect.

These east coast walls provide a wealth of fish life, with sweetlips, snappers, parrotfish and puffers being amongst the most abundant of medium-sized fish whilst the reef is alive with smaller species: damsels glimmering in the sun, cardinalfish sheltering in branching corals, schools of fusiliers streaming by. The blue is densely populated with clouds of pyramid butterfly and red toothed triggerfish. These sites also provide ideal conditions for numerous large green turtles which are often seen feeding on the reef or surfacing in the blue. Banded sea snakes are also seen here.

Left Bunaken is home to numerous species of land crab. This one is carrying a large clutch of eggs.

Below Divers can enjoy the gentle drifts around Bunaken and take in the stunning sights of the reefs.

On the reef itself there is a good range of critter life. A variety of crabs, shrimps, scorpionfish and nudibranchs lie camouflaged on the wall's many ledges.

SACHIKO AND CHA CHA

These two drift dive sites, situated on the northeast corner of Bunaken Island, feature steep slopes and walls of healthy vibrant coral, diverse fish life, interesting critters and occasional passing eagle rays.

The reef crest is around 5 meters and offers beautiful shallow water corals which drop away dramatically into the blue. The sites are both dived as drift dives, with mild to medium currents, which makes for easy diving conditions. The sites can be dived shallow or at depth making them suitable for all levels.

Corals here are mixed but some of the more notable species include large sponges, barrels, plate corals and boulder corals with soft corals such as hydroids, tubers and sea whips interspersed between them. There is also a collection of gorgonian sea fans which are known to occasionally harbor pygmy seahorses.

The reef is characterized by a number of recesses which are worth exploring for spiny lobsters, shrimps and other shade dwellers.

The two sites have abundant fish life, with schools of butterfly fish and blue triggers in the blue. A wide array of moray eels are often found hiding in the reef and turtles commonly cruise through. Numerous species of reef fish are seen at both sites. Unicornfish, surgeons, parrots and triggers all inhabit the reef and numerous small fish such as damsels and basslets add splashes of color to the reef scene.

These are two great sites for experiencing comfortable drifts, almost guaranteed turtle encounters, diverse coral and reef life. With the possibility of eagle rays and other pelagics in the blue, these sites are well worth exploring.

Left Porcupinefish are covered in spines which they use when attacked. They are found across North Sulawesi.

Below Colorful soft and hard coral clusters like this one are found on the walls around Bunaken.

Siladen Island Turtle Sanctuary

Siladen Island Turtle Sanctuary was started in 2006 by Siladen Resort in conjunction with the North Sulawesi Water Sports Association. Green sea turtles (*Chelonia mydas*) and hawksbill turtles (*Eretmochelys imbricata*) had long been attracted to the long white sandy beaches of Siladen Island. However, due to the consumption of turtle meat and eggs by the islanders, the turtle population had come under pressure and this, coupled with the low survival rate of infant turtles and the relatively late age of maturity, led to a decrease in turtle numbers within the marine park.

A marine biologist was engaged at the start of the program to educate resort staff about turtle reproduction and provide practical training concerning operating the hatchery and the correct methods for digging up eggs, transporting them and repositioning and resetting them. Once the hatchery was ready, the program was explained to the local villagers and a turtle egg purchasing scheme was put in place. The ongoing work of the sanctuary includes educating the villagers and schoolchildren about the importance of turtles to the park and the economy and how and why they should be safeguarded.

The program has been a great success. Now, when local villagers find a nest they report it to the sanctuary and the eggs are carefully collected, repositioned, buried on the beach in front of Siladen Resort and the area is marked out with bamboo and monitored.

Once the eggs hatch, the infant turtles are placed in a maturing tank where they stay for three to four months. The maturing turtles are fed on a diet of fresh fish until the time of their release. Releasing a more mature turtle gives it a substantially better chance of survival compared to a new hatchling.

Each nest holds between 60 and 100 eggs. The sanctuary's first hatch of 82 eggs was in 2006 and since then it has gone on to assist and release over 1,000 turtles into the Bunaken Marine Park. Numbers appear to be on the increase with more turtles being sighted on each dive. In 2013 alone, the sanctuary assisted over 500 hatchlings. For the local people of Siladen, egg reporting provides additional income and more eggs are being reported and incubated each year.

On a day-to-day basis, the sanctuary is funded and managed by Siladen Resort. Funding is mainly through souvenir sales but donations are also welcomed.

Below Green turtle numbers in Bunaken are increasing every year.

Bottom A hatchling in the maturing tank at Siladen Island Turtle Sanctuary.

BUNAKEN, SILADEN AND MANADO TRAVEL PLANNER

The majority of dive sites concentrated around Bunaken Island offer everything from stunning shallow water coral gardens to towering walls that seem to extend down indefinitely into the blue. Off the coast of Manado there are some excellent sandy muck diving sites inhabited by a diverse mix of critters, perfect for those who do not have the time to visit Lembeh in the same trip.

Despite the deep waters (up to 1,500 meters), the annual water temperature range is from 27 to 29 degrees and most operators hire short 3 mm wetsuits as standard. Annual visibility ranges from 15 meters from December to February and it can stretch as far as 30 meters from June to August. After heavy rainfall and wind, it can drop as low as 5 meters at some sites.

Dive sites are accessed by boat, and as the sites are relatively close together travel times are usually less than 30 minutes.

Bunaken offers phenomenally deep sites but the most abundant marine life tends to be in the 25 meter upward range with a diversity of both coral and fish species which you would expect from an area in the heart of the Coral Triangle. Turtles abound on the reef, critter life is varied and colorful, fish numbers on the reef are healthy and you never know what to expect out in the blue!

Whilst diving in the Bunaken Marine Park is suitable for all levels, an advanced level certification will allow you to explore deeper areas of the walls. The area is also ideal for technical diving (currently offered by Two Fish Divers). Whilst there is abundant marine life in the shallows, larger pelagics are more frequently seen below 20 meters.

Divers are required to obtain an entry permit to the Bunaken National Park, usually purchased from your operator. At the time of writing, a one day ticket is IDR50,000 or a tag valid for one calendar year is IDR150,000. The proceeds of the tag system are used to assist waste disposal projects, attempts to abolish destructive fishing practices, to maintain mooring buoys and to fund marine conservation education programs and reef and mangrove rehabilitation initiatives.

Recommended Operators

Siladen Resort and Spa (Authors Choice) Upmarket eco resort on Siladen island with private bungalows and swimming pool, dive and stay packages, courses, nitrox, equipment hire available. Up to 3 dives per day plus night dive. Home of Siladen Island Turtle Sanctuary. $$–$$$. Tel: +62 (0) 431856820. www.siladen.com. Email: info@siladen.com.

Murex Dive Resorts Dive resorts in Manado, Lembeh and Bangka Island, multiple destination trips available with diving on boat transfers between resorts. Full service dive centers with a range of facilities and accommodation. Professional service and excellent boats. $$–$$$. Tel: +62 (0) 431838774. www. murexdive.com. Email: reservations@ murexdive.com.

Two Fish Divers PADI 5 Star IDC resort based on Bunaken Island with dive training pool and full service dive center, dive and stay packages with a range of bungalows available. Resorts also in Lembeh, Nusa Lembongan, Bali and Lombok. Multi-location packages available. Tel: +62 (0) 8135687 0384. www.twofishdivers.com. Email: info@ twofishdivers.com.

Living Colours Diving Resort Upmarket Bunaken dive resort. $$. Tel: +62 (0) 812430 6063. www.livingcoloursdiving.com. Email: info@livingcoloursdiving.com.

Accommodation in Manado

Swiss-Bell Hotel International hotel in the center of Manado offering a range of facilities. $$$. Tel +62 (0) 431861000. www.swiss-belhotel.com.

Diving the Lembeh Strait
World Class Muck Diving

Famed for being the 'Critter Diving Capital of the World', the Lembeh Strait is awash with some of Indonesia's weirdest and wildest creatures. The black sandy slopes are a macro photographer's dream and boast some unique and 'must see' species, including flamboyant cuttlefish, rhinopias, mimic octopus, hairy frogfish, Ambon scorpionfish, spiny devilfish, blue ring octopus, various seahorses, pipefish and a plethora of nudi-branchs, crabs and shrimps, to name but a few. The Lembeh Strait is muck diving at its best: black sand flats and slopes which yield a candy shop pick-a-mix of critters and creatures of a diversity hard to beat elsewhere.

The island of Lembeh is to the east of North Sulawesi. The major port town is Bitung, the main source of employment in the area. Bitung Port not only services numerous industrial cargo ships but is also a passenger ferry terminal and home to coconut oil refineries and cement and canned fish factories.

Bitung has several mini-marts for buy-ing basic supplies, but if you are looking for shopping then Manado has much more choice. There are a number of hospi-tals in Bitung which are able to deal with minor ailments and injuries, and there are also several pharmacies. For more serious health issues, Manado has a wider range of hospitals and an internationally recognized recompression chamber.

If you are arriving on a late flight or leaving on an early flight, it may be nec-essary to stay overnight in Manado where there are more hotels, restaurants, malls and other facilities as opposed to Bitung, which is basic by comparison.

Dive operations are based to the north and south of Bitung harbor on both Lembeh Island and on the mainland side of the Lembeh Strait. Most operators, including all of those on Lembeh Island, are accessed by boat.

Lembeh Resort offers upmarket accommodation and diving with critters@Lembeh Resort Dive Center.

The calm waters of the Lembeh Strait are bordered by green hills and rocky outcroppings.

DIFFICULTY LEVEL Warm waters, mild currents and relatively shallow sites make Lembeh suitable for beginners, but muck and critter diving is often a taste acquired by more experienced divers. Photography opportunities here are spectacular and suit all levels from amateur photographers to world-renowned and published professionals.

HIGHLIGHTS Lembeh is all about muck diving and is known as the 'Critter Diving Capital of the World' for good reason. Rhinopias, mimic octopus, wunderpus, numerous species of frogfish, shrimps, scorpionfish, nudibranchs, crabs, cuttlefish (including flamboyant) and almost every weird and wonderful marine species imaginable are here.

LOGISTICS Access to Lembeh is through Manado's Dr Sam Ratulangi Airport. From here it is a 90 minute car journey to the port of Bitung and then a short boat ride to your chosen operator. In general, operators organize airport pickups and transfers to resorts as part of the package price or for a small surcharge.

Above The hilltop lounge at Divers Lodge Lembeh offers both comfort and stunning views.

Left Indonesia is home to numerous species of scorpionfish, all of which are masters of disguise.

mbeh Dive Sites

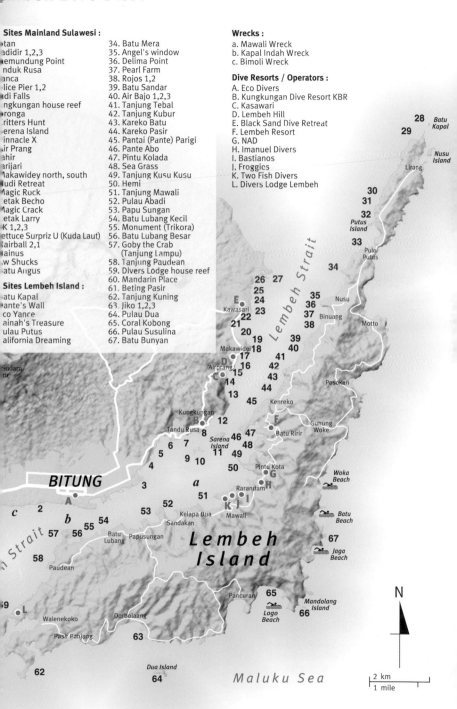

Sites Mainland Sulawesi :

- tan
- adidir 1,2,3
- emundung Point
- nduk Rusa
- anca
- lice Pier 1,2
- di Falls
- ngkungan house reef
- ronga
- ritters Hunt
- erena Island
- innacle X
- ir Prang
- ahir
- arijari
- lakawidey north, south
- ludi Retreat
- Magic Rock
- etak Becho
- Magic Crack
- etak Larry
- K 1,2,3
- ettuce Surpriz U (Kuda Laut)
- airball 2,1
- ainus
- w Shucks
- atu Angus

34. Batu Mera
35. Angel's window
36. Delima Point
37. Pearl Farm
38. Rojos 1,2
39. Batu Sandar
40. Air Bajo 1,2,3
41. Tanjung Tebal
42. Tanjung Kubur
43. Kareko Batu
44. Kareko Pasir
45. Pantai (Pante) Parigi
46. Pante Abo
47. Pintu Kolada
48. Sea Grass
49. Tanjung Kusu Kusu
50. Hemi
51. Tanjung Mawali
52. Pulau Abadi
53. Papu Sungan
54. Batu Lubang Kecil
55. Monument (Trikora)
56. Batu Lubang Besar
57. Goby the Crab
    (Tanjung Lampu)
58. Tanjung Paudean
59. Divers Lodge house reef
60. Mandarin Place
61. Beting Pasir
62. Tanjung Kuning
63. Jiko 1,2,3
64. Pulau Dua
65. Coral Kobong
66. Pulau Susulina
67. Batu Bunyan

Sites Lembeh Island :

- atu Kapal
- ante's Wall
- co Yance
- ainah's Treasure
- ulau Putus
- alifornia Dreaming

Wrecks :

a. Mawali Wreck
b. Kapal Indah Wreck
c. Bimoli Wreck

Dive Resorts / Operators :

A. Eco Divers
B. Kungkungan Dive Resort KBR
C. Kasawari
D. Lembeh Hill
E. Black Sand Dive Retreat
F. Lembeh Resort
G. NAD
H. Imanuel Divers
I. Bastianos
J. Froggies
K. Two Fish Divers
L. Divers Lodge Lembeh

BITUNG

Lembeh Island

Maluku Sea

N

2 km
1 mile

LEMBEH STRAIT'S BEST DIVE SITES

NUDI FALLS
☆ AUTHOR'S CHOICE

This site is on the west bank of the Lembeh Strait to the north of Bitung Harbor (No. 7, map). It has a range of topographies and bottom compositions making it home to a wide variety of Lembeh's critters, including numerous species of nudibranch. Entry is made in front of the small wall that forms the bank of the strait. The descent is down to the sand and rubble reef top at around 5 meters, which then gradually slopes away. Upwards of 15 meters the slope is dotted with small sporadic coral bommies. Below 15 meters the hard coral formations peter out and the bottom composition becomes a mix of sand, algae and occasional short soft corals. There are some pretty whips and tubers here in a range of colors but overall the impression is one of a layer of plant-like weeds blanketing the sand. Rhinopias have previously been spotted nestled amongst the vegetation and mantis shrimps favor the rubble for making their holes. Heading south at 18 meters, the bottom of the wall comes into view and has surprisingly good corals considering this is an area famed for muck, with

The squat shrimp, also referred to as the sexy shrimp, is found around and under the edges of anemones in the Lembeh Strait.

dense coverage and an impressive range of sponges. Along the base of the wall are some fans which are worth checking for pygmy sea horses whilst on the wall itself numerous lionfish lie flattened, a variety of nudibranch species dot the corals, frogfish take camouflage, crocodilefish lie on the bottom and reef fish, including Moorish idols, triggerfish, butterfly fish and wrasses, are all drawn to the reef. This is also a good site for spotting the endemic Banggai cardinalfish (*Pterapogon kauderni*), which is often found hiding amongst anemones. Nudi Falls definitely lives up to its name, with the species seen here changing from season to season but always with good variety. The ascent is usually up the wall or the adjacent slope. There are several shady areas along the bottom of the wall that are worth investigating. Nudi Falls offers a change from black sand diving with a more varied reef scene and plenty of critter action!

HAIRBALL II, TK III AND AIR BAJO III

These three sites are real muck diving black sand slopes which at first glance may appear barren and lacking in life

Ornate ghost pipefish are frequently found in pairs around soft corals and feather stars.

Left The blue ring octopus flashes its electric blue rings at predators when it is under threat.

Below Many of Indonesia's nudibranch species have unique and detailed markings.

save for the smattering of green or red algae that coats the sandy bottom in places. Both Hairball II (No. 24, map) and TK III (No. 22) are on the west bank of the strait whereas Air Bajo (No. 40) is to the east, off Lembeh Island. There are very sporadic small croppings of halimeda algae, natural debris, some unnatural debris and random small sponges. Check them all for inhabitants hiding beneath, behind or simply in plain view but relying on their own camouflage mechanisms for disguise. Entry to these sites is just off the shore and the top of the reef flats are at approximately 6 meters, with the drop away at around 45

degree angles. All three sites provide ideal environments for garden eels, cockatoo waspfish, short fin lionfish, flounders and gobies and their hard-working shrimp partners. Hairball II is characterized by occasional flying gurnards, dwarf cuttlefish, pipefish, coconut octopus and, on good days, flamboyant cuttlefish. TK III slopes to around 20 meters and then levels out and has similar critter life to that found at Hairball II but it also hosts some random anemones in which porcelain crabs, squat shrimps and commensal shrimps are common guests. It is worth noting that nudibranchs are also known to be quite common here.

TIP BOX Lembeh has a large number of black sand muck diving sites, all of which offer a wide range of critters which move around from time to time. It is best to let guides know in advance what you are hoping to see and they will know which sites will give you the best spotting opportunities.

The Coconut Octopus *Amphioctopus marginatus*

The coconut octopus, also referred to as the veined octopus, has a sturdy looking brown body detailed with fine darker lines. It is one of the smaller octopus species, with arms growing up to 30 cm, and it can change color dramatically from bluish hues to bright white. It usually buries underneath the sand to escape predators but also lodges itself inside empty bivalve shells. When shells are in short supply, the octopus substitutes them with more readily available coconut husks, hence its name. If no husks or shells are present, the octopus will use natural debris or trash, including beer bottles! When moving around, it carries its host underneath its mantle while it walks on extended arms as if on stilts. This use of tools and the apparent forward planning makes the octopus an interesting species to observe. Once inside the shell, or chosen host, the octopus uses its suckered arms to hold itself inside and pull the other half of the shell or piece of debris over the top, thus creating a tightly sealed trapdoor!

This coconut octopus has inserted itself into the neck of a broken beer bottle in Lembeh.

The octopus uses a shell, which it carried to the bottle itself, as a door that it can close from inside!

The individual shown here was photographed in the Lembeh Strait. When we first saw the octopus, it was hiding inside an old broken beer bottle (top photo) and half of a bivalve shell was around a meter away. We settled on the sand and calmly waited while the octopus observed us and the distance to the shell. After a few minutes it began to unfurl its arms from the bottle and attempt to stretch them to the shell. It soon realized the distance was too great and steadily it came out of the bottle and swam swiftly over to the shell, positioned itself over it and carrying it back to the bottle under its mantel. Once it was back at the bottle, it quickly deposited the shell within reaching distance, inserted itself back into the bottle and began to draw the shell, using its suckered tentacles, up in a drawbridge-like manner to seal itself inside (bottom photo).

Coconut octopus are seen in many parts of Indonesia but the Lembeh Strait is one of the easiest places to find them. They are worth watching for some time as their intelligent behavior is quite intriguing!

Air Bajo III has also had sightings of orangutan crabs, mimic octopus, blue ringed octopus, painted frogfish and Ambon scorpionfish. Whichever of these sites you dive, you can be assured of a range of hidden gems, and whilst the topography is simple the marine life is anything but!

AIR PRANG AND JAHIR

These two sites (No's 13 and 14, map), situated on the west bank of the strait, are black sand flats which start at around 6 meters. Whilst called flats, they are actually very gentle sloping topographies as opposed to the slopes above which drop at almost 45 degree angles. Entries are made just off the banks of the mainland over the shallow sand. The sites tend to be dived in a zigzag search-like pattern, taking you down the gentle slopes, which are around 15 degrees, and then repeating the pattern back up. This allows for maximum bottom coverage and spotting opportunities. Common to both dive sites are numerous diadema

Orangutan crabs can be found in several anemone species and bubble corals.

sea urchins in the shallows, mimic octopus and flamboyant cuttlefish, snake eels, blue spotted stingrays, scorpionfish and lionfish. Jahir has had frequent sightings of hairy frogfish, wunderpus, Ambon scorpionfish and blue ringed octopus whereas Air Prang is better known for clown frogfish, occasional harlequin shrimp, a range of nudibranchs and coconut octopus. For macro photographers, these sites are must do's, and as they tend to be dived shallow you have extended bottom times and can focus on getting the shot that you want without being hurried.

The Ambon scorpionfish is one of the smaller and more unusual looking scorpionfish species.

meters and stretches down to 40 meters. The wall also attracts a healthy selection of fish life. Small schools of fusiliers dart by in the blue, damselfish, angelfish, Moorish idols, a range of triggerfish and occasional schools of shrimpfish suspended out from the wall all make this site a nice contrast to Lembeh's black sand sites.

Above The ability of the mimic octopus (*Thaumoctopus mimicus*) to imitate other marine life is astonishing.

Right Juvenile yellow boxfish are extremely shy and will back into the reef when approached.

MAGIC ROCK

This site (No. 18, map) is similar to Nudi Falls in that it boasts a range of topographies and bottom compositions which make for varied critter sightings in one dive. If you are diving the site from north to south, you should start out on the sandy rubble bottom which gradually becomes a sloping coral reef and then a wall. There is also a nice hard coral garden in the shallows which is ideal for snorkeling. Starting out over the sand and rubble there is a mixture of small anemones, soft coral and hard coral formations until the slope begins at around 8 meters. The site is named after a rock at 15 meters which forms a cleaning station staffed by a multitude of shrimp species. A wealth of other critters are often seen here too. Heading along the slope, there is a mixture of sponges bubble corals, whips, hydroids and leather corals interspersed by sandy spots and other hard corals. Continuing south, the wall starts at around 21

There are a number of fans on the wall which are also worth checking out for pygmy seahorses and skeleton shrimps. Look carefully also at every anemone for commensal shrimps hiding amongst the tendrils. The corals here are also home to numerous reef critters. Lionfish, pipefish, a host of different nudibranch species, rounded porcupinefish, juvenile harlequin sweetlips, frogfish, octopus and cuttlefish can all be found at this site. Magic Rock offers such a variety of critter life that dives here really can be 'magic', and on days when the critters are hard to find the shallow water hard corals are really quite impressive photography subjects too.

If this type of site ticks all the boxes for you, then Nudi Falls and Critters Hunt (No. 10, map) should also be on your list.

LEMBEH STRAIT
TRAVEL PLANNER

At first glance, which is usually from Bitung Port, the Lembeh Strait does not seem like an area where diving could be possible, never mind incredible. Dive boats look like toys compared to the huge container ships and cranes towering above them. Fortunately, once you are clear of the harbor area, which is also home to some phenomenal sites, the banks of the Lembeh Strait are green with forest-clad hills bordered by black sand beaches and a range of bays that look more like stereotypical dive sites. To the inexperienced eye, Lembeh's black sand flats may appear sparse and deserted, but to a muck diving enthusiast every dive is like flipping through the pages of the best critter diving reference book imaginable.

Water temperature is relatively constant throughout the year at 27 to 28 degrees. In July to August it can drop to around 26 degrees. Average visibility is from 10 to 15 meters but can drop substantially after rainfall and with big waves. On the best of days, it doesn't stretch much beyond 20 meters.

The busiest time for diving in Lembeh is late May to early November as this coincides with the dry season, which gives slightly better visibility, little rain and warm sunny spells. It does, however, mean more divers. Diving in December means fewer dive boats and still relatively good weather. The critters here do not appear to be seasonal but different individual species appear to come and go and move from site to site from time to time. Dive times are relatively long in Lembeh, with many operators offering unlimited dive times and just a 50 bar surfacing requirement. Dives are rarely below 25 meters. Nitrox is widely available as are dive courses and equipment hire.

Recommended Operators

Diver's Lodge Lembeh Eight eco bungalows catering for up to 14 people with fan cooling and hot water. The resort is set amid the hills and trees bordering the Lembeh Strait. All resort areas and guest rooms have great views over the strait or the lagoon. The resort also uses solar panels and aims to reduce their impact upon the environment. Good value dive and stay packages include three meals per day, 2 to 3 boat dives per day plus night dive options, unlimited dive times, tailored schedules also possible, nitrox available, services in English, German and Indonesian. Two destination trips available with Weda Reef and Rainforest Resort, Halmahera. $$. www.diverslodgelembeh.com. Email: info@diverslodgelembeh.com.

Lembeh Resort Upmarket resort and spa overlooking the Lembeh Strait. An excellent choice for photographers with small groups and good guides. A range of rooms are available, swimming pool, bar and restaurant. Also offers a number of land tours, including the Tangkoko National Park, North Sulawesi Highlands and village trips. The critters@ Lembeh Resort dive center is part of the reputable Murex Dive Resort Group which also has resorts in Manado and Bangka Island. Multi-destination packages available. $$$. Tel: +62 (0) 4385503139. www.lembeh-resort.com. Email: reservations@lembeh-resort.com.

Two Fish Divers Small resort on Lembeh Island offering full board dive and stay packages and PADI courses. Has resorts also in Bunaken, Nusa Lembongan, Bali and Lombok. $$. Tel : +62 (0) 82194806676.www.twofishdivers.com.

Kungkungan Bay Resort (KBR) Upmarket resort with all-inclusive bungalows situated in a private bay. Nitrox, equipment hire, courses and swimming pool. $$$. www.divekbr.com.

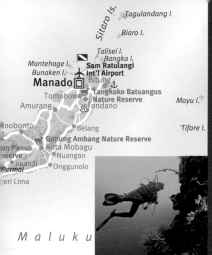

Sitaro Is.
Tagulandang I
Biaro I.
Talisei I.
Bangka I.
Mantehage I.
Sam Ratulangi
Bunaken I.
Int'l Airport
Manado
Bitung
Tomohon
Tangkoko Batuangus
Amurang
Nature Reserve
Mayu I.
Tondano
Inobonto
Belang
Tifore I.
Gunung Ambang Nature Reserve
Kota Mobagu
an Panua
Nuangan
serve
Imandi
Ong, gunolo
Permai
eri Lima

Maluku

I.
Todeli
a
Penu
Dofa
Mangole I.
Taliubu I.
Wayhaya
Mangole
Fagudu
Waykilo
Loseng
Sanana
Sula Islands
Manaf
Kabau
Sulabesi I.
Waygay

NORTH MALUKU
NORTH MALUKU
MALUKU

North Banda
Basin

CENTRAL, SOUTH AND SOUTHEAST SULAWESI

This region may not suit those looking for lively night life and tourist attractions but the central, south and southeast parts of Sulawesi are arguably amongst the best regions for diving in Indonesia. Reefs vary from fringing and barrier reefs to atolls, and with such a central position in the world's Coral Triangle the diversity of corals and marine life does not disappoint. It would be hard to find someone unimpressed by this region. With beaches that rate amongst the most beautiful in Indonesia, quiet dive sites, top class critter life, pristine reefs and an array of pelagics and large predators, there is something for everyone.

Central and Southern Sulawesi at a Glance
Natural Beauty and Friendly Faces

Surrounded by some of Indonesia's deepest waters, Central and Southern Sulawesi's fertile lands, rich with a diversity of flora and fauna, make this area amongst the most naturally beautiful and bountiful in the whole archipelago.

Sulawesi is the fourth largest land mass in Indonesia and the third most highly populated. It is divided into six provinces: North Sulawesi (see previous chapter), Central Sulawesi, which includes the Togean Islands; Gorontalo; South Sulawesi, which encompasses Selayar Island; West Sulawesi and Southeast Sulawesi, which includes the Wakatobi Islands. Historically, Sulawesi was used as a stopover port for ships traveling east to the Spice Islands. Today, it is still a seafaring hub with coastal areas relying on trade from ships. Fishing, both for subsistence and export, is a major industry. Inland Sulawesi provides excellent growing conditions for numerous crops, ranging from coffee to corn, which has led to deforestation in many areas. On low-lying lands, rice is grown commercially. Paddy fields stretch as far as the eye can see and the rice produced is exported both domestically and internationally. Sulawesi not only boasts natural beauty, but is also rich in natural resources, including gold, silver and nickel. Sadly, mining for such resources has also resulted in further deforestation.

The people of Sulawesi are predominantly Muslim though Christians form a large minority, almost 20 percent of the population. The largest city in South Sulawesi is Makassar, which is the

Sunsets over the Togean Islands in Central Sulawesi offer a spectrum of colors.

Traditional boats carrying people, goods and fish are a common sight across Indonesia's islands.

administrative capital and is situated on the west side of the southern part of the region. Palu is the capital of Central Sulawesi and Kendari the capital of Southwest Sulawesi. Makassar is the main entry point to the region and has its own airport, the Sultan Hasanuddin International Airport, 12 kilometers from the capital. There are also smaller domestic airports in Gorontalo, Luwuk, Wangi Wangi, Selayar and Kendari.

Transport around the region is primarily by road or domestic air travel and by ferry to the coastal island chains.

Sulawesi is famed throughout Indonesia for its spicy seafood. Most traditional dishes feature fish and rice or, for sweet treats, bananas and coconuts which flourish in the local climate. The rainy season runs from November to February and the dry season from April to September. The further south you travel, the drier the wet season, with Bira and Selayar having markedly less rain than Makassar. At sea level, Sulawesi is hot and humid, but venturing into the moun-

tainous highlands can be remarkably fresh and even chilly.

Traveling south in Sulawesi takes you off the beaten track, and whilst tourism is evident in small localized pockets, tourists are still fairly new and cause for curiosity to the friendly local people. It is not an area that boasts a large choice of operators and places to stay but there are a handful of beautifully located resorts. Sulawesi's underdevelopment leaves it with an atmosphere which is slightly bohemian yet exclusive, charming and relaxed.

Selayar Dive Resort in South Sulawesi boasts a beautiful and well-maintained 1 kilometer beach.

Diving Central, South and Southeast Sulawesi
Tropical Islands and Bountiful Reefs

This region may not suit those looking for lively night life and tourist attractions but the south, southeast and central parts of Sulawesi are arguably amongst the best for diving in Indonesia. Reefs vary from fringing and barrier reefs to atolls, and with such a central position in the world's Coral Triangle the diversity of corals and marine life does not disappoint. It would be hard to find someone unimpressed by this region. With beaches that rate amongst the most beautiful in Indonesia, quiet dive sites, top class critter life, pristine reefs and an array of pelagics and large predators there is something for everyone.

Central and southern Sulawesi are arguably home to some of the most pristine beaches that Indonesia has to offer and within only meters of these beaches are some of Indonesia's most phenomenal dive sites. Walls abound around Selayar, Bira, Wakatobi and the Togean Islands where coral diversity and health is nothing short of what you would expect from areas centralized in the Coral Triangle.

Sinking beneath the surface of the aquamarine waters reveals colorful reefscapes, staggering walls and a vibrancy of life which matches that found on the land of Sulawesi. With hundreds of species of fish and corals, it is hard not to be impressed.

The diving is not the most accessible in Indonesia and if you are looking for happening night life, shopping and plenty of tourist facilities then this may not be the right destination for you. However, if you are seeking a truly tropical and secluded island diving destination with natural beauty that is hard to match, then the island archipelagos of this region have everything to offer.

The majority of the diving is relatively easy but there are some sites which can have slightly stronger currents and drifts.

The reefs around Tukangbesi are teeming with life, such as these colorful schooling antheas.

Una Una in the Togean Islands is home to a healthy turtle population.

The entire Sulawesi land mass is surrounded by some of the deepest waters found in Indonesia and some of the wall dive sites can be up to hundreds of meters deep. However, most can be dived at a range of depths and offer abundant and dense coral coverage and plentiful fish life at all levels. Water temperatures do not range as much as in other parts of Indonesia as the temperature holds steady at around 28 to 30 degrees year round. There are occasional seasonal lows of 26 degrees in some areas. Visibility is generally good, and despite it lowering after rainfall and big waves, the usual range is from 15 to 40 meters.

Most diving areas in the region are fairly remote, and whilst there are recompression chambers in Makassar and Manado it is important to remember that Makassar is the best part of 8 hours from the south of Selayar, 5 hours from Bira and over a day from Wakatobi and the Togeans. Divers are recommended to take this into consideration. Many operators limit dive times and depths, the exception being in Selayar where some excellent deep diving is available for divers with experience of the deep.

The majority of operators are Western-owned dive resorts offering full board accommodation and diving packages. Resorts are few and far between, which means the chance of seeing another dive boat at a dive site is virtually non-existent but it does mean that booking needs to be in advance and if you require equipment hire or courses make sure that you specify this at the time of booking. The exception to this is Bira where there are several standalone dive centers which accommodate guests in local homestays.

Equipment purchasing in the region is very difficult. Most operators purchase supplies from Bali which takes time to be delivered. While it is possible to pick up small items such as clips and mask straps from some operators, it is best to carry your own or buy gear in Bali or Jakarta beforehand.

Central and southern Sulawesi offer year round diving with above average visibility, relatively calm conditions and substantially less rainfall than in other parts of Indonesia. Selayar operates seasonally from October to May due to swells from May to September which limit accessibility. Check with your operator before booking for availability.

Sea fans and feather stars decorate the reefs around Wakatobi.

CENTRAL AND SOUTHERN SULAWESI TRAVEL PLANNER

Sulawesi covers a large area and the best diving regions are spread out, which makes exploring more than one region best suited to those who are planning longer trips. Divers should keep in mind that each individual area offers tremendous diving and spending two weeks in one location would still not be long enough to get bored of the dive sites! Due to the remoteness of many areas, operators provide transfers and pickups and whenever possible it is recommended to make use of these even when there is a surcharge. It will save a lot of hassle and time compared to trying to make arrangements yourself!

10 days Bira and Selayar Island: Walls, Drifts and Stunning Beaches

This itinerary suits those who want to experience two destinations but without having the hassle of taking domestic flights. The schedule allows for two full days of diving in Bira and five to five and a half days of diving in Selayar. The majority of the time should be spent in Selayar where the natural beauty of the island itself is just as impressive as the diving but time can be apportioned to suit.

Day 1 Arrive at Makassar Airport and transfer to Bira by car, approximately 5 hours. Overnight in Bira.

Days 2 and 3 Diving in Bira, 2 to 3 dives per day.

Day 4 Transfer to Selayar Dive Resort by speed boat, about 2.5 hours. Possible afternoon dive.

Day 5–9 Diving in Selayar, 2 dives per day plus possible night dives/fluoro dives/ unlimited House Reef dives.

Day 10 Morning transfer back to Bira by speedboat and then car to Makassar for departing flight.

15 Days Selayar and Wakatobi: Walls, Caverns and Pristine Reefs

A 15 day itinerary amidst the breathtaking natural beauty of both Selayar and Wakatobi. The diving in either of these destination can easily be altered to longer durations. When traveling to or from Selayar, it is also possible to add in extra days to dive around Bira. Once in Wakatobi, additional days can be added to cover diving around both Tomia and Wangi Wangi. This schedule allows for 5 days of diving in both Selayar and Wakatobi and involves one return domestic flight.

In the Bajo villages around Wakatobi, the most common local transport is still paddle boat.

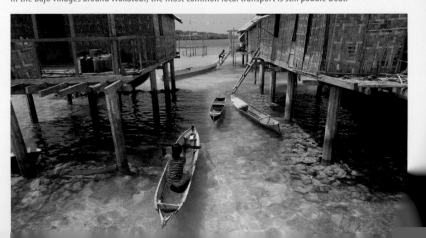

Day 1 Arrive at Makassar Airport and transfer to Bira by car, approximately 5 hours. Speedboat to Selayar Dive Resort, 2.5 hours and overnight. (If you arrive on a late flight, then an overnight in Bira may be necessary.)

Day 2 Either a morning speedboat to Selayar followed by afternoon dives or a full day of diving in Selayar depending on arrival time on Day 1.

Days 3–7 Diving in Selayar, 2 boat dives per day plus unlimited House Reef dives and night or fluoro dives as applicable.

Day 8 Early morning speedboat transfer to Bira followed by car to Makassar. Overnight in Makassar.

Day 9 Morning flight from Makassar to Wangi Wangi (Lion Air) for diving in Wakatobi. Most operators have pick-ups from Wangi Wangi but check with your chosen operator when booking. Possible afternoon dive.

Days 10–13 Diving in Wakatobi, 2 to 4 dives per day plus night dives.

Day 14 Early morning dives only, depending on flight times the next day.

Day 15 Transfer from your resort back to Wangi Wangi and fly to Makassar for your onward flight to your next destination.

23 Days South, Southeast and Central Sulawesi: Full Circle Tour

A 23 day itinerary which includes five days of diving in Selayar, Togean and Wakatobi with comfortable transit times between them. The schedule involves two return domestic flights and one return overnight ferry crossing. Whilst this itinerary involves more travel time, you have reasonable length stays in each destination in order to get an overview of the best of the best! *Note:* Day 16 should be a Friday as the Tuna Tomini Ferry to Wakai only leaves Gorontalo on Tuesdays and Fridays and returns on Thursdays and Saturdays.

Days 1–15 The same as for Day 15 itinerary above, but overnight on Day 15 in Makassar.

Day 16 Flight from Makassar to Gorontalo.

From Gorontalo Airport take a taxi to the main ferry terminal for the overnight ferry (Tuna Tomini) to Wakai, departing at 5 pm.

Day 17 Disembark from overnight ferry in Wakai at 5 am. Togean operators pick up guests in Wakai for a 20 minute boat ride to Kadidiri Island which is where dive operations are based. Late morning and afternoon diving in Togean.

Days 18–21 Diving Togean, 2 to 3 dives per day plus night dives are available.

Day 22 Optional morning dives. Operator transfer boat back to Wakai for the return ferry (Tuna Tomini) to Gorontalo which leaves at 5 pm.

Day 23 Disembark ferry in Gorontalo at 6 am, car/taxi journey to Gorontalo Airport for a flight to Makassar for your onward flight to your next destination.

USEFUL CONTACTS

Makassar Recompression Chamber RSU Wahidin Sudirohusodo, Jalan Perintis Kemerdekaan Km 11, Tamalanrea Kampus UNHAS, Makassar. Tel: +62 (0) 411584677.

Manado Recompression Chamber Malalayang Hospital (Rumah Sakit Malalayang), Manado. Tel: +62 (0) 811430913.

Sultan Hasanuddin International Airport (Makassar), Jalan Raya Airport No. 1, Makassar. Tel: +62 (0) 411553183.

Gorontalo Jalaluddin Airport (GTO) Tel: +62 (0) 435890494.

Luwuk Syukuran Aminuddin Amir Airport (LUW) Tel: +62 (0) 46121524.

Garuda Indonesia 24 Hour Call Centre Tel: +62 (0) 8041807807 or +62 (0) 2123519999. www.garuda-indonesia.com.

Lion Air Assistance Line Tel: +62 (0) 2163798000. www.lionair.co.id.

Sriwijaya Air Call Centre Tel: +62 (0) 2122 79777 or 0804 1 777 777. www.sriwijayaair.co.id.

Diving the Togean Islands
Easy Diving Along Breathtaking Walls

Diving in the Togean Islands makes the extra effort it takes to travel there worthwhile. From the first sunrise over the islands to the final safety stop, the Togeans offer immense coral walls with kaleidoscopic colors and a diversity of hard and soft corals that are hard to match. Togean is relaxed and laid back and the diving is easy with little current. Sites around Una Una offer more abundant fish life and generally more challenging conditions for experienced divers. The Togeans are casual and peaceful, making them the perfect island retreat.

Kadidiri, off the northwest tip of Togean island, is just 5 kilometers long. The island is skirted by white sand beaches and the interior is rainforest. There is no town or local community on Kadidiri. The only occupants are the few dive resorts based around the bay. The nearest town is Wakai, just off Togean Island, which is a small harbor town with local shops, *warung* food stalls and a bustling market. As Wakai is the entry point to diving in Togean, the people are used to foreign travelers and basic English is under-stood. The main language spoken in Togean is Bahasa Indonesia and the people are predominantly Muslim.

Agriculture is the main industry in the Togean islands where the equatorial climate provides ideal conditions for growing cocoa, cloves and coconuts. The driest months are from May to October and the wettest months from December to February. Resorts all open all year round.

At the time of writing, the Togeans are in the preliminary stages of becoming a Marine Protected Area (MPA).

Clear water around Selayar Island means excellent visibility, coral growth and light, even at depth.

DIFFICULTY LEVEL Warm water, good visibility and little current make the dive sites of the Togeans suitable for divers of all levels. For experienced divers looking for more challenging conditions, there are a couple of deep sites with stronger currents.

HIGHLIGHTS Stunning walls with world class corals off Kadidiri, abundant fish life at Una Una and some interesting muck diving with a variety of critters. The small number of operators in the area makes diving in the Togeans an exclusive experience.

LOGISTICS The Togean Islands are an archipelago in the Gulf of Tomini, Central Sulawesi. Most operators are based on Kadidiri Island which is accessed either by taking the overnight ferry from Gorontalo to Wakai or a 3 hour ferry from Ampana to Wakai. Ferries from Gorontalo and Ampana to Wakai run twice a week only and dive operators will pick up guests from Wakai, which is a 20 minute boat ride from Kadidiri.

Top left Hard corals, soft corals and anemones compete for space on the reefs in Sulawesi.

Top The Togean Islands are home to a jellyfish lake where you can swim without fear of being stung.

Above These razorfish were pictured in their usual nose down position.

Gorontalo Airport is serviced by domestic airlines only so transit is usually via Makassar. Private boat charters to Wakai are possible. Check with your operator in advance if you do not want to take the public ferry. If you are staying at Walea Dive Resort, fly into Luwuk.

These schooling barracuda were photographed as they cruised towards the reef top.

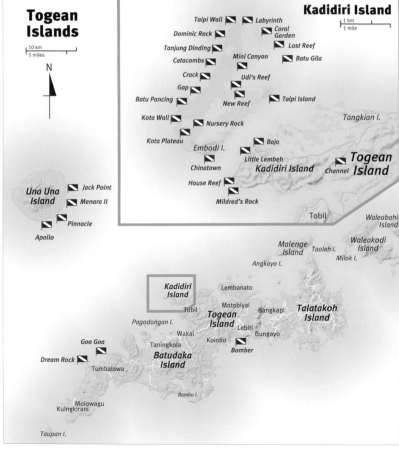

Togean Islands

10 km
5 miles

N

Una Una Island

Jack Point

Menara II

Apollo

Pinnacle

Kadidiri Island

1 km
1 mile

Taipi Wall   Labyrinth
Dominic Rock   Coral Garden
Tanjung Dinding   Lost Reef
Catacombs   Mini Canyon   Batu Gila
Crack   Udi's Reef
Gap
Batu Pancing
Kota Wall   New Reef   Taipi Island

Tangkian I.

Kota Wall
Kota Plateau   Nursery Rock

Embodi I.   Bajo
Chinatown   Little Lembeh
Kadidiri Island   Channel   *Togean Island*

House Reef

Mildred's Rock

Tobil   *Waleabahi Island*

Malenge Island   Taoleh I.   *Waleakodi Island*
Angkayo I.   Milok I.

Kadidiri Island

Lembanato

Tobil   Motobiyai   Bangkapi   *Talatakoh Island*
Togean Island
Pagodongan I.   Lebiti
Wakal   Bungayo
Goa Goa   Taningkola   Kololio
Dream Rock   *Batudaka Island*   Bomber
Tumbalawa

Bambu I.

Molowagu
Kulngkirani

Taupan I.

TOGEAN ISLANDS' BEST DIVE SITES

KADIDIRI ISLAND: THE LABYRINTH, CATACOMBS AND MINI CANYON

These three sites are all open water seamounts off Kadidiri's northern outer barrier reef which offer stunning, dense coral garden plateaus with a range of bordering walls and steep sloping reefs. The tops of the seamounts are between 5 and 10 meters with mooring lines to the surface. The descent is down the mooring line onto the shallow water plateaus which drop off steeply down to white sand bottoms at between 30 and 40 meters. Despite being open water seamounts, currents at these sites are minimal and they can be dived either shallow or deep.

Coral coverage extends from the plateau to the base of the mount and the variety of species is phenomenal. Huge barrels and fans stand out against the densely packed branching corals, sponges, plates and boulders, while tubers, sea squirts, anemones and other soft species cover any spaces left between.

Fish life on the mounts is not as prolific as at Una Una but small schools of yellow back fusiliers and neons pass through the blue and damsels congregate over the corals catching glimpses of the sunlight. Critter life on the walls and slopes, though, is both abundant and varied. Hunting lionfish, moray eels, nudibranchs, porcelain crabs, a range of shrimps and Christmas tree worms inhabit the seamounts' rugged and craggy walls. Overhangs create huge caverns that are worth exploring for shade dwelling shrimps and macro life as well as resting batfish.

These three sites, whilst being similar, also have some distinguishing features. At the base of the Labyrinth seamount is a haphazard collection of various sized rocks and boulders creating a coral-encrusted maze. Eagle rays, bumphead parrotfish, stingrays and Napoleon wrasse are often seen here. Catacombs is bordered by staggering walls with bulbous overhangs, huge gorgonians, rifts, faults and craggy caverns which makes for some phenomenal scenery, while Mini Canyon features a wall with a protruding arm offering ledges, critter-filled recesses and undulating corals.

All three mounts have a range of tropical reef fish: puffers, triggerfish, angelfish, gobies, antheas, butterfly fish and wrasses all weave in and out of the reef. But the highlight is definitely the species variation and density of the coral, which is nothing short of breathtaking.

Hard corals in Sulawesi make excellent stations for a variety of floral looking worms.

UNA UNA ISLAND: THE PINNACLE AND MENARA DUA

Whilst Kadidiri diving is all about the coral, the diving around Una Una is definitely more about the fish. Schooling fish in the blue, a multitude of both small and medium sized reef fish and turtles, eagle rays and passing predators are frequently seen here.

The Pinnacle is a small steep-sided pinnacle to the south of Una Una while Menara Dua is a small seamount slightly further north. Both sites offer divers deep walls and steeply sloping reefs of abundant coral hosting numerous critters. The dive profiles are similar at each site with the top of the Pinnacle and Menara Dua being at between 5 and 10 meters. Make the descent to your maximum depth and then traverse the mounts in the direction of the current as you make your way back up.

Menara Dua's walls offer a rich mix of corals ranging from tables, staghorn and boulders to huge gorgonian fans, leather corals and sponges. The coral coverage is dense, healthy and colorful and the multitude of species creates a dazzling patchwork effect in the sunlight. The corals host an abundance of marine life, from hoards of damsels to tiny squat lobsters. Turtles often feed and take a break on the reef. Keep an eye out to the blue for eagle rays passing through.

The Pinnacle also boasts rich and varied corals, but with abundant fish life in the blue it is easy to be distracted as schools of fusiliers stream by, barracuda hover menacingly and snappers and surgeonfish cruise past. The north and west sides of the pinnacle bottom out at 25 meters and the east and southern sides are deeper, stretching down to around 40 meters.

Hairy squat lobsters are commonly found in the crevices between the ridges of barrel sponges.

Looking into the reef, lionfish, moray eels, cuttlefish and nudibranchs are hidden in the corals and sailors' eyeballs ('bubble algae') are nestled down on the substrate. Turtles are often spotted in the area, particularly in the shallows.

There can be a little more current at these sites than in Kadidiri so check the direction of the current at the beginning of the dive and drift along with it. An SMB is recommended so that you are visible to the boat crew after you have surfaced.

The Great Barracuda *Sphyraena barracuda*

Great barracudas, often called giant barracudas, are a common predator in Indonesian waters where they are seen as both solitary individuals and in small groups, usually around coral reefs where they prefer relatively shallow water, often upwards of 15 meters. Solitary individuals are also spotted in the open ocean and sightings have been recorded at depths of up to 100 meters.

Their long cylindrical bodies range from a brownish to bluish silver. They can grow up to 1.8 meters in length and may display between 18 and 23 dark bars on the upper side which are most noticeable when resting.

The great barracuda's powerful jaw profile is one of its most distinguishable features, with a lower jaw that protrudes below the upper one, allowing glimpses of their complex dentistry. Great barracudas have two sets of teeth: a small set of razor-sharp teeth on the outside of the jaw and a larger set of dagger-like triangular 'fangs' set within these. The teeth are closely set and the longer fangs have their own holes on the opposing jaw which enables the barracuda to be able to close its mouth tightly shut, trapping any prey inside with little possibility of escape. The great barracuda feeds on smaller species of fish, the

The great barracuda can be an imposing sight, especially when one notices its fang-like dental arrangement.

smallest ones being swallowed whole whilst larger species are cut into smaller pieces and then swallowed one piece at a time.

Great barracudas are opportunistic hunters and hunt mainly out in the water column where they are a menacing predator. Their body shape is well suited to fast attacks and it is estimated that they can reach speeds of up to 58 kilometers per hour. Because of their size and speed, they have very few predators. As adults, however, prior to reaching full maturity, they are known to have been attacked by sharks, tuna and goliath groupers. Juveniles fall prey to numerous reef predators.

The great barracuda is estimated to have a life expectancy of around 14 years. Male individuals reach sexual maturity at approximately two years and females at four.

These impressively large, powerful and occasionally threatening looking fish are seen in various locations around Indonesia and generally pose little threat to divers although it is wise not to approach too close or with little warning as on a few occasions they have been reported to react defensively.

LITTLE LEMBEH

Little Lembeh is situated just a few minutes north of Kadidiri and, as the name suggests, is a muck diving and critter site where some of Togean's most unusual species can be found. The site is a long, shallow shore reef dive which slopes down to a vast sand bottom consisting of numerous small sandy peaks. The reef is a mix of medium density undulating hard and soft corals with sandy areas in between. In the shallows, small fish life is abundant. Electric blue

Little Lembeh in the Togean Islands is home to numerous critters, including common seahorses like this one.

and yellow damsels dart back and forth over branching corals and basslets bask in the sunlight. The rolling coral reef is home to numerous anemones which host a range of anemonefish, porcelain crabs and cleaner shrimp. Amongst the hard corals, moray eels, reef cuttlefish and octopus hide out. The branching corals are also home to brittle sea stars and small aggregations of cardinalfish.

The coral reef begins at around 6 meters and extends down to 15 meters where it peters out to the sand which slopes very gradually down to around 22 meters. Entry is made over the reef. Then descend down to the sand where most of the dive time is spent. This site can be dived in either direction depending on the (usually minimal) current. Allow enough time to make your way steadily up the reef as the corals also have a lot of marine life to offer.

The sandy area below the reef may look sparse and barren at first glance but this is where some of the most interesting critters can be found. Muck diving on the sand reveals an abundance of sea cucumbers with outstretched feeding tentacles and dwarf cuttlefish hiding behind sand dunes. The beak-like heads of snake eels can be found staring up at you, and gobies and their hard working shrimps busily burrow. The common seahorse is also found here.

Little Lembeh is home to a host of critters and certainly lives up to its name.

TOGEAN ISLANDS
TRAVEL PLANNER

Water temperature in the Togean Islands ranges from 28 degrees in January and February through to 32 degrees in October and November. Togean's protected location means very little rainfall. The wettest months are January and February but rainfall is not torrential and mainly during the night. The driest months are July and August. Visibility is weather-dependent and can range from as low as 5 meters immediately following rainfall but stretch as far as 40 meters from March to May. Average visibility is 20 meters.

Togean diving is based around both Kadidiri and Una Una. Kadidiri boasts a selection of topographies from muck diving sandy slopes to coral reefs and vertical walls of stunning corals. Una Una offers more abundant fish life, the opportunity of passing pelagics, a spectacular pinnacle and beautiful walls. For wreck diving enthusiasts, there is a B 24 bomber wreck located on the south side of Togean Island, and if you have a day off from diving there is also a jellyfish lake which makes for some interesting snorkeling.

There is no denying that the Togean Islands are not the easiest dive destination in Indonesia to access, but waking up on the ferry as it nears Wakai at sunrise makes it all worthwhile, and this is only a taste of what is to come. White sand beaches, rock pinnacles, turquoise water, lagoons and sunsets that take your breath away make the Togean Islands as awe-inspiring on land as they are underwater.

Sinking beneath the surface reveals a density and variety of coral that is hard to match: walls with overhangs, ledges, caverns, branching fans and

attention-grabbing side profiles that will astound even the most seasoned divers.

The Togeans are one of Indonesia's hidden gems. They are relatively untouched with pristine reefs, secluded paradisiacal islands and a true display of the natural beauty of the underwater realm.

Recommended Operators

Black Marlin Dive Resort Beautifully located on Kadidiri Bay, dive and stay packages, range of accommodation, restaurant and bar, massage center, dive center, equipment hire, daily dive trips, PADI and SSI courses, pick-up and drop-off service by boat from Wakai, experienced guides and small groups. Tel: +62 (0) 85657202004. www.blackmarlindiving.com.

Walea Diving Resort and Spa Upmarket resort on Waleabahi Island. Offer pick-ups and transfers from Luwuk Airport. Tel: +62 (0) 411402101. www.waleadiveresort.com.

Black Marlin Dive Resort in the Togeans offers diving for all, including children.

BLACK MARLIN
DIVE RESORT

Take Only Photos and Leave Only Bubbles

Indonesia boasts incredible areas of stunning natural beauty and is home to what are undeniably some or the world's most spectacular marine ecosystems. Whilst the reefs have come under a number of pressures, there are now many marine parks and conservation projects across the archipelago working to protect them and their aquatic inhabitants. In recent years, it is not only foreign-owned dive shops that are behind these efforts. There has also been an increase in the number of Indonesian-owned operations working tirelessly to educate others and protect and conserve their reefs. Government involvement has also increased significantly. Whilst marine protection in Indonesia still has a long way to go, all conservation efforts need as much support as possible from those visiting the area.

The following is a set of guidelines which visitors should follow to help conserve both Indonesian marine and terrestrial environments:

Recommendations for Becoming a Responsible Marine Tourist

1. Bring a refillable water bottle with you. It is important to stay hydrated, but buying several disposable plastic bottles of water a day adds up to a lot of plastic. Refills are advertised in many areas and in others just ask. Refills are often free.
2. Try to avoid leaving showers and taps running for longer than necessary. In many parts of Indonesia, fresh water is a scarce commodity.
3. If you are not in your room, turn off your AC and lights. Electricity is a problem in many areas, so try not to waste it.
4. In many areas, bins are now being provided for different types of waste, such as plastic, glass, etc. Try to make use of these as it generally means the waste will be recycled.
5. If you bring batteries with you, please take them home for disposal. There are very limited facilities for dead batteries in Indonesia. Bringing rechargeable batteries is the best solution.
6. Do not touch, tease, chase or harass marine life. Most reputable operators already have strict policies concerning this. If you are diving in an area to see a specific creature, listen to the briefings about interactions. (See also the manta and mola diving guidelines on page 59 of this book.)
7. Do not collect shells from the beaches or during dives as they are part of the ecosystem.
8. Avoid contact with the reef at all times. If you have to hold on in strong currents, find a non-living part of the reef such as a rock rather than a coral which may be damaged by coming into contact with your skin (and may sting you).
9. Do not buy souvenirs which have been made from products of the ocean, such as shell or coral ornaments and jewelry.
10. When diving in a marine park in Indonesia, check the park regulations and abide by them.
11. When you see plastic waste during a dive it is very sad but don't just complain about it. Pick it up and take it

with you back to the dive center for proper disposal. They will thank you!

12. Try to limit the amount of waste plastic that you generate in Indonesia. Often stores will automatically put your purchase into a plastic bag, even an item as small as a box of matches. If you do not need a plastic bag, let them know and do not take one.

13. Do not eat fish. Whilst many people want to enjoy seafood on their holiday, overfishing is an issue in Indonesia, so much so, in fact, that restaurants in some areas import their fish. Divers are urged not to eat fish or seafood, but if you cannot resist at least make sure that it is fish that has been caught away from the reef.

14. Join in with marine conservation projects that are happening in the area you are visiting, such as beach and reef clean ups.

15. Choose a reputable operator who follows responsible marine tourism dive practices, such as:
    i) Not dropping anchors on the reef. Mooring buoys are now in many areas, and where there are not mooring buoys dive boats will usually follow divers along at the surface.
    ii) Organizes clean ups, reef monitoring programs, educational marine life talks or other conservation initiatives. These will vary from area to area.
    iii) Does not feed fish or other marine life.
    iv) Operates out of an environmentally aware or eco resort that tries to limit its impact on the local environment. In some areas it is easier for operators to limit their carbon emissions than in others, for example, in areas with no mains power they often have no other option but to use generators.
    v) Provides dive guides and instructors who model marine conservation dive practices such as those listed above.

Above Colorful soft corals will grow on any solid substrate in the right conditions.

Host anemones and their resident clownfishes flourish on reefs across Indonesia.

Diving Wakatobi (Tukangbesi Islands)
Picture Perfect Beaches, Pristine Reefs

This remote archipelago off the south of Southeast Sulawesi is home to pristine reefs, some of the world's most diverse coral life and a plethora of marine species ranging from tiny macro organisms to large pelagics. It is easy to believe the claims that Jacques Cousteau described Wakatobi as 'probably the finest diving site in the world'. Resorts are few and far between, meaning that dive sites are usually an exclusive experience, and whether you are diving on the fringing, barrier or atoll reefs there is always something to see and marvel at.

Wakatobi is an acronym for the islands of the Tukangbesi archipelago, the four main islands being **Wa**ngi Wangi, **Ka**ledupa, **To**mia and **Bi**nongko. The islands form a north to south chain to the southeast of the main island of Sulawesi. To the northeast they are bordered by the Banda Sea and to the southwest by the Flores Sea. The Wakatobi islands have been a marine conservation area since 1996, and in 2002 they were declared a National Park which encompasses the reefs around the islands as well as mangrove forest, lowland and coastal forest and rainforest. The islands are stereotypical picture perfect, with white sand, palm-fringed beaches, azure blue clear water and beautifully diverse flora and fauna.

Wanci is the administrative capital for the Wakatobi region and is situated on Wangi Wangi Island. Kendari on the east coast of the Southeast Sulawesi peninsula is the provincial capital for Southeast Sulawesi.

Anemonefish are one of only a few species that have the ability to change from male to female.

As this image of divers in the distance shows, the visibility around Wakatobi can be staggering.

The predominant religion in Southeast Sulawesi is Muslim and the local people of the Wakatobi region largely belong to the Bajau ethnic group, a group with a long seafaring history. Industry and work have traditionally been based around the ocean, with many people relying on fishing for both subsistence and trade. In some areas there are still traditional Bajo villages where the houses are built on stilts over the water.

DIFFICULTY LEVEL Wakatobi has sites suitable for all levels. Currents generally range from nothing to medium but some pinnacle sites have stronger currents and there are numerous deep diving opportunities as well.

HIGHLIGHTS Diving in the Wakatobi National Park, world-class pristine reefs, stunning wall dives and abundant marine life, particularly in the Tomia area. Turtles, rays, sharks and a whole host of critters, quiet dive sites and good visibility.

LOGISTICS There are two main diving destinations in Wakatobi. The first (and most pristine) is around Tomia Island, including the islands of Tolondono (also known as Onemobaa Island), Sawa and Lintea. The second is around Wangi Wangi Island, including the islands of Kaledupa and Hoga. For both destina-

tions, check transport and transfer information with your chosen operator. There is an airport on Wangi Wangi Island (Matahora Airport), which is serviced by flights from Makassar that can be reached from either Bali or Jakarta and internationally from Singapore. If you are diving the Wangi Wangi region, it is just a short boat or car ride to your destination. If you are diving around Tomia, there are public boats leaving Wangi Wangi every morning to Tomia Island. Alternatively, it is possible to charter a private boat. Wakatobi Resort provides air transfers from Bali (see recommended operators).

Hawksbill turtles such as this one commonly have algae growing on their carapaces.

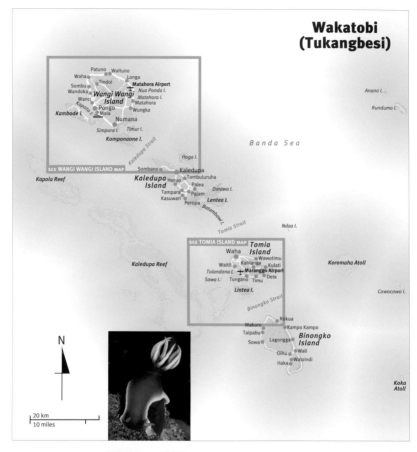

Wakatobi (Tukangbesi)

Patuno   Waituno   Longa
Waha   Tindoi
Sombu   *Wangi Wangi*   **Matahora Airport**
Wandoka   *Island*   Nua Ponda I.
Wanci   Pongo   Matahora I.
Kambode I.   Mola   Matahora
Numana   Wungka
Simpora I.   *Timur I.*
Komponaone I.

SEE WANGI WANGI ISLAND MAP

Hoga I.

Sombano   Kaledupa
Kapola Reef   *Kaledupa*   Horuo   Tambuluruha
Island   Palea
Tampara   Pajam   *Darawa I.*
Kasuwari   Peropa   *Lentea I.*

Anano I.

Runduma I.

Banda Sea

Ndaa I.

SEE TOMIA ISLAND MAP   *Tomia Island*
Waha   Wawotimu
Kaledupa Reef   Waiti   Kahianga   Kulati
Tolandona I.   **Maranggo Airport**
Sawa I.   Tongano   Timu   Dete
Lintea I.

Koromaha Atoll

Cowocowo I.

Rokua
Makoro   Kampo Kampo
Taipabu   *Binongko*
Sowa   Lagongga   *Island*
Oihu   Wali
Haka   Waloindi

Koka Atoll

N

20 km
10 miles

Top Nudibranch species range vastly across Indonesia and from season to season. **Above left** Cuttlefish, also known as sepia, are from the molluscan class Cephalopoda. **Above** Reef lionfish are incredible hunters found across many of Indonesia's reefs.

WAKATOBI'S (TUKANGBESI ISLANDS) BEST DIVE SITES

TOMIA ISLAND: ROMA

Roma Reef is a large submerged sea-mount situated at the northern end of the east coast of Tomia Island that takes its name from a large formation of potato corals which loosely resemble the Coliseum in Rome, Italy!

The mount sits on a roughly east to west axis and bottoms out to sand at around 30 meters to the north and 40 meters to the south. Entry is made over the top of the mount which is only a few meters deep and which is covered in a mix of coral rubble, anemones, rocks, pinnacles, bommies and potato corals. Fish life here is abundant, and immediately after entry it is possible to see schools of red toothed triggerfish and fusiliers out in the blue. The site is usually dived by heading down the south slope first and then traversing around the reef to the north side and working your way back up to the entry point. The reef is a mix of undulating mounds, slopes, rocks and bommies, all of which display healthy fish life. Every bommie and formation is worth investigating as there is a wealth of macro life and critters: leaf scorpionfish, ribbon eels, lionfish, scorpionfish, winged pipefish, blue spotted rays hiding out under ledges and numerous species of nudibranch. Out in the blue, occasional barracuda cruise through along with jacks and the odd eagle ray. Coming up the north side reveals a variety of reef fishes. Parrotfish, Moorish idols and anemonefish add dashes of color. As you near the shallows, schools of antheas and damselfish glimmer in the sunlight. Look out for banded sea snakes here, too, as this site

Despite having narrow bodies, ribbon eels are deceptively long when viewed in the open.

is renowned for them. This is an easy dive with little current, suitable for all, and with wide-ranging, stunning and abundant marine life it has something for everyone.

TOLANDONO ISLAND: TURKEY BEACH

Turkey Beach is an extension of the House Reef dive site of Wakatobi Resort and it is situated on the south side of Tolandono Island. The site is a gentle drift dive along a stunning sloping reef that has excellent coral coverage and soft

Ornate ghost pipefish are one of Wakatobi's most sought after critters by photographers.

and sponges, all adding color and texture. Diving this site under bright sunlight reveals mind-blowing colors which are equally as impressive as the marine creatures seen here. Turtles (both green and hawksbill) are frequent visitors as are blue spotted stingrays, lobsters, cuttlefish and crocodilefish. Schooling fusiliers are another common sight, along with hoards of antheas and damselfish over the corals in the shallows. This is another site that is suitable for all divers and which has a diversity and abundance of marine life to keep all levels entertained.

TOLANDONO ISLAND: ZOO

Zoo is another site on the south side of Tolandono Island, towards the eastern point, and it is well worth a visit for divers whose preference is critter diving. The site takes its name from the sheer number of different species that can be seen in one dive here and there are some superb candidates to choose from. Ghost pipefish, leaf scorpionfish, frogfish, mantis shrimps and pygmy seahorses have all been seen here.

The shallow reef at 5 meters is a mix of sandy patches, lettuce coral and coral rubble and the drop down to the slope begins at between 5 and 8 meters. The slope bottoms out to sand from between 22 and 30 meters but diving between 18 and 20 meters gives the best spotting opportunities. Whilst this is a dive mainly for macro sightings, do not be surprised to encounter turtles here along with black tip reef sharks close to the bottom of the slope and passing sea snakes. The reef is a mix of hard and soft corals, all of which provide shelter for the reef's inhabitants. Stonefish lie camouflaged underneath small table corals, robust ghost pipefish masquerade as sea grass over the sandy patches and spiny

corals with intense colors and variety. In the shallows there is an overhang which continues along the reef from around 5 to 10 meters and it is worth checking under here for critters and other shade dwellers. The reef runs on a roughly north to south axis and can be dived in either direction according to the current. The reef bottoms out to sand at around 30 meters but usually this site is dived shallower where the best coral coverage is at around 20 to 25 meters. There are two canyons here which often play host to schools of batfish and yellow snappers. Along the reef there is a healthy mix of gorgonians, whips, tubers lobsters take cover in crevices with only their antennae exposed.

Zoo is also an ideal site for both night dives and mandarinfish dives. At sunset, the mandarinfish can be seen emerging from the corals to find a partner. The mating 'routine' involves the male and female rising up around a meter from the reef in a belly to belly position before the sperm and eggs are released in a cloud and the two fish part and dive back into the reef. Night dives at Zoo reward divers with cuttlefish and octopus sightings, sleeping parrotfish inside their protective cocoons, numerous shrimps and crabs and, on occasions, the twin spot lionfish can be seen.

Fans growing on the walls around Wakatobi can reach well over 2 meters in diameter.

LINTEA ISLAND: FAN 38 (EAST AND WEST)

These are two sites which border each other on the north side of the outer barrier reef of Lintea Island. Both sites are predominantly wall dives with some steep sloping areas and, as the name suggests, they are alive with gorgonians of all different colors and sizes from small to unbelievably huge and over 2 meters in diameter. These sites offer opportunities for deep diving, but for those who would prefer to stay shallow they can be enjoyed at any depth. The walls are a mixture of ledges and overhangs and crevices and canyons. The huge outstretched fans combined with wispy and wild-looking black coral formations just adds to the pristine and untouched look of these sites. These are

Wangi Wangi has good coral variety, such as the tubular sponges pictured here.

the nooks and crevices of the walls. Remember to keep an eye out to the blue for passing barracuda, trevally and other pelagics.

With two stunning areas suitable for all levels and with healthy coral growth stretching down as far as one can see, these sites provide for some excellent deep diving for those with suitable experience.

WANGI WANGI ISLAND: WAHA WALL

Waha Wall is situated on the northeastern point of Wangi Wangi Island and provides divers with good coral variety from the reef crest down to the deep. The drop starts at between 5 and 10 meters and the wall continues down in excess of 40 meters, providing for some deep diving opportunities for more experienced divers. The site is a favorite of divers who are hoping to encounter larger pelagics such as eagle rays, barracuda and passing tuna. The wall is a myriad of colors with fans, tubers and whips making colorful side profiles against the blue. Barrels, sponges and plate corals add to the mix and fish numbers are reasonable. Schools of basslets and damsels hover over branching and table corals in the shallows and a wide range of reef fish dart in and out since parrotfish, triggerfish, sweetlips and a wide range of wrasses have all made their homes here. Looking out to the blue, streams of fusiliers glide by and turtles are often seen resting in the shallows or swimming up to the surface.

definitely sites for wide-angle photographers! The sites are relatively easy but there can be some drift. Aim to time the dives to just before high tide if you are looking for less current but be aware that the current does bring fish with it too!

The walls not only have stunning fans but also a good range of hard and soft coral diversity and a variety of reef fish. Red toothed triggerfish and pyramid butterfly fish cloud in the blue, neon and yellow back fusiliers stream by and devil rays, eagle rays and turtles are not unusual. On the reef itself, pygmy seahorses have an overwhelming choice of fans to inhabit, ghost pipefish hide out amongst feather stars and soft corals and a wealth of macro life exists in amongst

The Hawksbill Turtle *Eretmochelys imbricata*

The (IUCN) critically endangered hawksbill turtle is frequently spotted around Wakatobi and several other areas in Indonesia. Its sharp and curved 'beak' makes it easily distinguishable from other turtle species at a glance but there are other features peculiar to the hawksbill. It has a flattened body shape and flipper-like 'arms' which it uses for swimming. Like other species, its shell is made up of thick scutes and, like them, it has five central and four lateral scutes. However, the rear scutes of a hawksbill's shell overlap, resulting in a serrated saw-like appearance from behind. It is also unique in that it has two pairs of prefrontal scales on the top of its head and each flipper usually has two claws.

Hawksbills are one of the smaller turtle species, measuring up to around 90 cm in length and weighing up to 70 kg. They are highly migratory and spend time in both the open ocean and in lagoons and on shallow reefs where they are often seen resting in caves or on ledges.

Hawksbills are omnivores, with sea sponges making up a high percentage of their diet, but they are also known to regularly feed on jellyfish and algae. Their life expectancy is estimated at 30 to 50 years. Females nest only every two years when they return to the beach where they were born. Following a successful mating, the females come ashore to lay their eggs and bury them in sand. Clutches can comprise up to 140 eggs, but with low infant and juvenile survival rates their numbers have declined. Unhatched eggs are hunted and eaten by numerous land-dwelling species and newly hatched hawksbills fall victim to several sea predators. Once a hawksbill reaches maturity, however, it has few predators due to its size and hard shell.

Hawksbills face a number of issues aside from predators. Their shell was traditionally traded for decorative tortoiseshell materials, their habitats and nesting beaches are being degraded, they are susceptible to long-line fishing and, in certain areas, both the hawksbills and their eggs are hunted for human consumption. These factors, coupled with their slow growth rate and low juvenile survival rate, have led them to be listed as critically endangered. The capture and trade of hawksbill turtles and hawksbill products is now prohibited by CITES (the Convention for International Trade in Endangered Species) and it is hoped that this, combined with other conservation efforts, will protect their numbers from further decline.

Hawksbill turtles have a distinct curved and overhanging beak-like tomium.

Numerous species of anemone and anemonefish can be seen in a single dive around Wakatobi.

If this was not enough, there is a wealth of critter life hiding on the wall's many ledges and in crevices. Commonly seen critters include porcelain crabs hiding amongst anemones, nudibranchs, scorpionfish, lionfish and moray eels. Waha Wall offers good all round variety, and with little current it can be enjoyed by divers of all levels.

HOGA ISLAND: OUTER PINNACLE

Outer Pinnacle is to the north and slightly east of Hoga Island and, as the name suggests, it is a submerged pinnacle which peaks at around 5 meters under the surface and stretches away with ridges to the north and south. Current here varies and the site can be dived in either direction, but the preferred route is to enter in the shallows on the top of the pinnacle, make your way down the south side's slope to around 25 to 30 meters and then follow the sloping side of the pinnacle around to the north side as you make your way back up to the peak for the safety stop.

The coral here is decent, with huge sponges and a variety of soft and hard formations although there are some rubble and broken areas. Fish numbers here are impressive, though, and schools of fusiliers speed past in the blue and up and down the reef bringing with them some of the larger predatory pelagics such as tuna, great barracuda, giant trevallies and Naploean wrasses. Both black and white tip reef sharks are also occasionally seen here along with schooling chevron barracuda.

Looking into the reef, there is a good mix of macro life and critters, ranging from scorpionfish, crocodilefish and leaf scorpionfish to different species of pygmy seahorses, blue spotted rays and moray eels. The safety stop on the pinnacle peak is also a good place for critter hunting. It is a nice pinnacle with a good diversity of both corals and marine life.

KAPOTA ISLAND (ALSO CALLED KAMBODE ISLAND): KAPOTA POINT

Kapota Point is on the northernmost tip of Kapota Island and offers stunning wall diving with huge gorgonians and a tapestry of colors for which the Wakatobi region is so well renowned. The wall has varied topographical features, including a number of overhangs, ledges and crevices which provide ideal conditions for shade dwellers, critters and occasional larger pelagics, including resting reef sharks. As this site is situated on the tip of the island, currents can be stronger here than at other sites in the region and the depth is also in excess of 50 meters in places, making this a dive for advanced divers with experience in both currents and deeper diving.

Schooling fish are drawn to the currents, and fusiliers and snapper gather in the blue with occasional tuna and trevally keeping them in check, whilst on the reef a multitude of brightly colored reef fish shimmer under the sunlight.

The reef, as with most others in the area, supports a range of critter life also, ranging from blennies, dragonets and crocodilefish through to an assortment of moray eels, lionfish and nudibranchs.

The site can be dived in either direction, so check the current first and go with the flow, keeping close to the wall, and enjoy the ride!

Crocodilefish are found camouflaged on several reefs around the Wakatobi Islands.

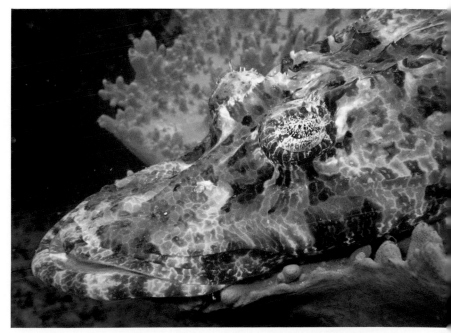

WAKATOBI (TUKANGBESI) TRAVEL PLANNER

Wakatobi has generally mild currents, good visibility and most sites can be dived at any depth. Reefs are a mixture of fringing reefs, barrier reefs and atolls with some excellent shore diving opportunities in addition to boat dives going further afield.

Annual water temperatures average 28 to 30 degrees with a cooler period from July to September when temperatures can drop to 26 degrees, ensuring coral health and no bleaching effects. The wet season runs from December to February with annual rainfall being less than in other parts of Indonesia. As there are no rivers washing out, visibility remains consistently good, averaging around 30 meters all year round.

Equipment hire is available from most operators as are courses, which should be booked in advance. Nitrox is available through some operators. Check at the time of booking. Dive times are around one hour but operators vary. As the islands are remote, decompression diving is not recommended. Currents are mild but an SMB is advisable for boat pick-ups. With few operators in the region, dive boats are few and far between and divers often have sites to themselves.

Destructive fishing practices are prohibited within the park. Whilst most sites are incredibly stunning, around some islands there is evidence of previous reef damage.

Recommended Operators
Tomia

Wakatobi Dive Resort (Author's Choice) Luxury eco dive resort based on Tolandono Island (also known as Onemobaa Island) offering a range of individual bungalows, full board dive and stay packages, up to 3 boat dives per day plus night dives, fluoro dives and unlimited House Reef dives. Nitrox, equipment hire, courses and private guide options are available. Air transfers from Bali using the resorts privately chartered plane and airstrip on neighboring Tomia Island. Also operates the *Pelagian* liveaboard. $$$. Tel: +62 (0) 361759669. www.wakatobi. com. Email: office@wakatobi.com.

Tomia Scuba Dive Dive center on Tomia Island offering diving only or full board dive and stay packages using local guest houses with choice of fan or AC rooms. Daily dive trips, night dives and equipment hire available. $. www.tomiascubadive.com.

Wangi Wangi

Wakatobi Patuno Resort Dive resort on Wangi Wangi with a range of bungalows. Full board dive and stay packages with 2 to 3 dive day options, free airport transfers from Wangi Wangi. Equipment hire and courses available. $$. Tel: +62 (0) 811400 2221. www. wakatobipatunoresort.com. Email: info@wakatobipatuno-resort.com.

Wakatobi Dive Resort is a divers' paradise with stunning reefs and luxury accommodation.

Diving Selayar Island (including Bira)
World Class Walls, Pelagics and Critters

Selayar Island is an idyllic tropical island destination with pristine beaches set against a backdrop of tropical rainforest. Underwater is just as awe inspiring, with deep walls with caverns and overhangs, diverse corals, good visibility and truly world-class marine life. The marine reserve surrounding Selayar Dive Resort boasts an array of stunning walls that are inhabited by a range of critters and fish, from tiny macro species to huge schools of jacks, turtles, rays, sharks and numerous passing pelagics. Easy diving is available for beginners and there are numerous deep opportunities for those with more experience.

Bira (or Tanjung Bira) is located on the southernmost tip of the southwesterly 'arm' of Sulawesi and boasts a beautiful white sand beach. Bira is a harbor town with a large passenger and cargo port. It is also a major shipbuilding area. There are numerous small guest houses and *warung* but there are no major international hotels yet. Mid-range accommodation is available and is charmingly rustic but by no means top of the range. If heading to Selayar Island, you may need to overnight in either Makassar or Bira unless your flight arrival is very early in Makassar. Selayar Dive Resort, located in the south of Selayar, is a 2.5 hour speedboat journey. A domestic flight to Selayar is also available from Makassar. Check with your operator when booking if you would prefer this option as flight schedules are flexible.

Selayar Island is approximately 90 kilometers from north to south and only a few of kilometers from east to west. It sits directly below Bira, with the small islands of Pulau Kambing and Pulau Pasitanete in between. The west coast of Selayar has most development. Situated in the center of the west is Benteng, the island's main town, which is spread along the coastal road. Benteng has a local clinic-cum-hospital, but for more serious

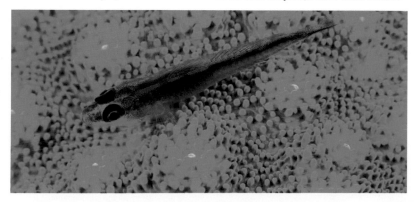

Fluoro diving at Selayar Dive Resort is a colorful highlight not to be missed.

The walls around Selayar Dive Resort are adorned with sponges and a range of coral species.

issues there are larger hospitals in both Bira and Makassar. The eastern side and southern tip of Selayar, which are home to Selayar Dive Resort and its marine park, are as yet undeveloped. Thus, when traveling the east coast by boat, the scenery is spectacular. Green peaks, waterfalls and sandy bays with turquoise shimmering water and interesting rocky outcroppings form picture perfect views.

Selayar Dive Resort is based on a kilometer-long stretch of white sand beach, also favored by nesting green turtles, with a long wooden jetty that stretches out over the aquamarine lagoon, and traditional yet comfortable beach bungalows set along the sandy bay in front of a backdrop of lush green rainforest.

Divers should note that the west coast and northern section of the east coast of Selayar Island have been damaged by destructive fishing practices. It is only the area protected by the Selayar Dive Resort marine park that offers world-class

diving. If you are diving outside of the Selayar Dive Resort area or with another operator, you may well be disappointed as diving within the park is an experience not to be missed!

For those who do not have the time to dive from south Selayer, Bira offers a range of dive centers with dive sites around Bira, Pulau Kambing and Pula Pasitanete. Be wary of cheap operators as safety and equipment standards can vary widely and currents can be incredibly strong.

DIFFICULTY LEVEL From easy to advanced. Sites are deep but are mainly walls that can be dived at any depth. Currents range from non-existent to reasonable drifts with only occasional up and down drifts. Operators time dives according to tides to ensure conditions suit guests' experience levels.

HIGHLIGHTS Stunning walls with exceptional coral diversity, a wealth of macro life, pygmy seahorses, turtles, passing pelagics, including sharks and a range of rays. Fluoro diving around Selayar Dive Resort Jetty and House Reef is an experience not to be missed.

LOGISTICS Accessing Bira, which is the boat departure point for Selayar Island, takes around five hours from Makassar by car. The picturesque journey takes you through endless rice paddies, local villages with traditional and colorful Minahasan houses and a regular stream of roadside markets rich with local produce. The main operator on the island is Selayar Dive Resort and it is within its marine park that the world-class diving is to be found. The resort offers transfer from Makassar as part of its packages.

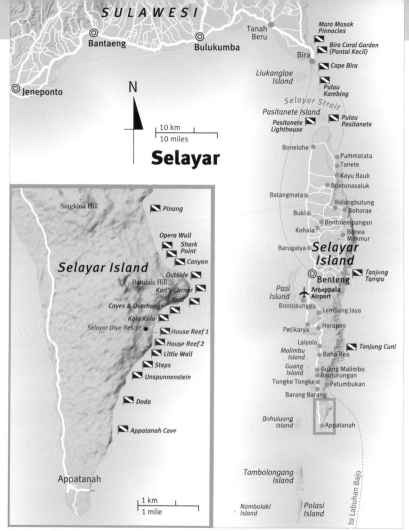

SULAWESI

Bantaeng

Bulukumba

Tanah
Beru

Jeneponto

Mara Masak
Pinnacles

Bira Coral Garden
(Pantai Kecil)

Bira

Cape Bira

Liukangloe
Island

Pulau
Kambing

Selayar Strait

Pasitanete Island

Pulau
Pasitanete

Pasitanete
Lighthouse

Bonelohe

Pammatata

Tanete

Kayu Bauk

Bontonasaluk

Batangmata

Balangbutung

Buki

Bohorae

Bontolempangan

Kohala

Bonea
Makmur

Barugaiya

Selayar
Island

N

10 km
10 miles

Selayar

Benteng

Tanjung
Tampu

Pasi
Island

Aroeppala
Airport

Bontosunggu

Lembang Jaya

Patikarya

Harapan

Laiyolo

Tanjung Cuni

Malimbu
Island

Baho Rea

Guang
Island

Guang Malimbo

Bauturungan

Tongke Tongke

Patumbukan

Barang Barang

Bahuluang
Island

Appatanah

Tambolongang
Island

to Labuhan Bajo

Nambolaki
Island

Polasi
Island

Singkina Hill

Pinang

Opera Wall

Shark
Point

Selayar Island

Canyon

Outside

Batulaia Hill

Karl's Corner

Caves & Overhangs

Nel2

Kolo Kolo

Selayar Dive Resort

House Reef 1

House Reef 2

Little Wall

Steps

Unspunnenstein

Doda

Appalanah Cave

Appatanah

1 km
1 mile

The Selayar Dive Resort jetty provides easy access to the House Reef and magnificent views.

SELAYAR ISLAND'S BEST DIVE SITES

SHARK POINT
☆ AUTHOR'S CHOICE

This is a wall dive that offers phenomenal deep diving opportunities for experienced divers. The drop in point is on the north side of the headland to the north of Selayar Dive Resort where the top of the wall sits at around 5 meters. The wall features many clefts and rifts which provide sheltered areas for schooling bannerfish, snappers and jacks. If diving when the current is running, it is not unusual to find yourself swimming through layer upon layer of schooling fish hovering off the reef. Close to the wall, schools of juvenile fusiliers obscure the view, whilst looking out to the blue reveals exceptional activity and life. Great barracuda are often seen hanging out from the wall, schools of unicornfish occupy the reef top and giant trevallies patrol menacingly.

The initial wall drops to around 30 meters from where it becomes a steep sand slope featuring sea whips, large gorgonian fans, occasional barrel sponges and scattered formations. At 50 meters it drops again to a 60 meter ledge which drops into the blue. This dive is all about looking out to the open ocean. Large, densely packed schools of shimmering silver jacks can be found swimming into the current whilst huge tuna, a range of barracuda species and sharks circle out in the blue. Common shark species here include black and white tips and grey reef sharks. Overhead, passing mobula and eagle rays 'fly' over and large stingrays often cruise down the reef. If the current is running fast, it may be necessary to hold on, sit tight and watch the action!

Heading back up the reef, numerous turtles can be seen in one dive, the coral becomes a little patchy, and as it begins to level out from 8 meters upwards there is a mix of healthy corals and coral rubble which makes for some wonderful critter spotting opportunities. Leaf scorpionfish, ribbon eels, various small stingrays and other bottom dwellers all favor the shallow reef.

For those diving shallower, the wall offers stunning corals, the chance to see pelagics and turtles and abundant and varied marine life.

For experienced divers, this is an adrenaline-pumping ride, with deep, decent currents, patrolling pelagics and teeming schools of fish.

APPATANAH CAVE

A diverse wall dive situated on the southernmost tip of Selayar Island which boasts a large cathedral-style cavern 45 meters long with a swim-through and a large recessed shelf, an excellent site with some interesting topographical features, deep water pelagics and shallow water critters. This site can be dived shallow, and on the reef top from 10 meters upward there is some excellent white sand muck-style diving.

If diving the cavern, which is actually a swim-through, the entry point for the dive is almost immediately above it with a drop straight down the rock and sandy based wall to 45 meters. If you are diving the site from south to north, the cavern has a large opening framed by huge sponge corals, and as you swim out through the north side, a distance of only a few meters, fans and black corals adorn the bordering edges. When passing through the swim-through, look for the schools of small fish that inhabit the shadows parting to make way for you. On the north side of the cavern there is

a huge recessed ledge where the bottom of the wall inverts and this is a good place for looking out to the blue and below for passing sharks and rays. On the reef there are numerous nudibranchs and shrimps hiding out amongst the densely packed mixed corals and fans. Fish numbers are healthy with schools of juvenile fusiliers swaying in the current, damselfish and antheas darting in and out of the reef and parrotfish, Moorish idols, sweetlips and all other manner of reef fish cruising through. The wall then continues to the north with a range of hard and soft corals and the ascent takes you up the wall to where it levels out at between 10 and 15 meters onto a white sandy area which often hosts large numbers of garden eels. As you make your way up the sandy slope, there are sporadic small and medium sized coral bommies, rubble patches and rock formations which make for excellent critter and muck diving. The sand here is very fine, so watch your fins! Looking around the base of the bommies, blue spotted stingrays are often tucked away, stonefish,

Shark Point at Selayar Dive Resort is a hunting ground for grey reef sharks.

Bio-Fluorescence Night Dives

For divers and photographers, some of the best dives are the ones with the most color, whether it's the colors on the reef, the corals or the fish and other creatures around us. If colors are your thing, then bio-fluorescence diving, also known as fluoro diving or blue light diving, is not an experience to miss. Imagine the neon lights of any major city or a 1970s disco or a carnival and picture that vividness, brightness and outright boldness underwater. That is fluoro diving. It's not just about the colors, though, it's also about seeing things and details which you just can't see with the human eye without assistance. Moreover, fish that would usually swim away under ordinary torchlight stay still and quiet and you can get exceptionally close as the blue lights do not affect them in the same way.

Fluoro diving involves using either a UV light or an LED light with a blue lens and amber tinted eye shields. If you have ever experienced a night dive with luminescence you may understand some of the science behind it. Certain marine organisms produce proteins that are capable of generating fluorescence when they absorb blue light. The proteins absorb the photon of the blue light, which results in an increased energy level. This increased energy is used to emit a photon of light in return with a longer wave length. This is fluorescence and it is usually visible as fluorescent reds, oranges, blues, and greens depending on the individual protein affected.

Not all marine organisms react in this way but corals are amongst the best reactors and unveil a myriad of details which are usually unseen. Most crustaceans hiding within them will stand out equally as brightly, like gaudy baubles on an already overdressed Christmas tree. Nudibranchs, cephalopods, worms, clams and jellyfish all react well, too. Some fish will react and others won't, but for nocturnal species which usually shrink away from torchlight, they won't be startled by a blue light, allowing for some phenomenally close encounters and photography opportunities.

Fluoro diving is like seeing the reef for the first time. Hidden gems are produced where you would least expect them and the creatures you have always wanted to closely inspect but have never been able to, allow you to study them closely and for longer periods. Try it and you will be surprised!

Corals that would normally retract under torchlight are unaffected by blue lights, Selayar Dive Resort.

It is possible to see huge marbled stingrays at all of the sites within the Selayar Dive Resort marine park.

ragged scorpionfish and moray eels hide out in the shade, whilst leaf scorpionfish and a range of shrimps decorate the corals.

After experiencing the cavern and larger pelagics, the switch to muck and critter diving is quite remarkable. With little current in the shallows, this is a site that offers something for everyone.

OPERA WALL

This is a remarkable wall dive starting to the north of Shark Point and drifting south. Entry is over the sandy and gravel reef top at 7 meters which then drops away vertically into the blue. The wall is curved, which forms vertical rifts and clefts characterized by horizontal ledges and overhangs. This is a wall to rival those found in the Togeans and Halmahera: stunning and rugged topography with an abundance of soft coral which grows out from the wall giving the effect of a chaotically overgrown vertical garden. Fish life is impressive. Red toothed triggerfish and pyramid butter-

flies school in the blue whilst juvenile fusiliers dart up and down the reef streaking it with purples and blues. Fans punctuate the face of the wall (look out for pygmy seahorses) and at 35 meters there are some impressive black coral formations reaching up to 3 meters across. Schools of cardinalfish shelter behind the overhanging soft corals and abundant critter life can be found on the wall's many facets. As you near Shark Point, shallow up to around 15 meters, which is where schools of snapper hover off the reef, great barracuda are often spotted, as are hunting trevallies and numerous turtles. As you continue drifting south, the wall begins to turn into a slope at 15 meters and the number of sandy patches increases. This is a great place for looking for bottom dwellers but keep an eye on the blue, too. Schooling barracuda, tuna and Napoleon wrasse often speed through. The slope levels out at around 5 meters and this is where turtles are often seen nestled down on the reef. Blue spotted stingrays are also

often seen here as well as sea snakes, and look out for huge giant trevallies cruising back and forth just under the surface. Opera is a magnificent wall. Home to abundant and varied marine life, there is a lot of action out in the blue and it is definitely a favorite of Selayar's green turtle population!

Green turtles are common in Selayar. This one was pictured on the reef top of the Steps dive site.

STEPS

Steps is a deep wall site to the south of Little Wall, which starts at around 7 meters and then, as the name suggests, drops down in a series of steps and shelves. The side profile of the wall is a topographical overload with the sheer size of the wall being the primary wow factor. Once accustomed to the towering reef, the steps and numerous recesses and clefts add to the effect and the coral growth, which forms a patchwork covering of colors and textures, will leave even the most well-traveled of divers in awe. Fish life here equals the reef in terms of diversity and abundance. Eagle rays cruise through the blue, huge groupers rest on the reef's ledges, jeweled fairy basslets and bright juvenile fusiliers add another layer of color to the scene. The walls are a healthy mix of hard and soft corals. Most notable are some impressive fans, wild looking sponges and large black corals which harbor schools of glassfish. At 55 meters there is an abundant display of black corals, an impressive sight for those who are making deeper dives.

Looking out to the blue, solitary titan triggerfish and schools of red toothed triggerfish, pyramid butterfly fish and schooling bannerfish mingle off the reef whilst neon fusiliers, blue fin trevally, large tunas and jackfish stream past.

The ledges of the reef make ideal resting places for some of the largest of green turtles which are often accompanied by their remoras whilst resting. The many ledges and recesses are worth peering into. Reef sharks and a variety of rays also choose to rest here. Continuing up the wall, the crest onto a stunning platform of soft corals is at around 7 meters. Turtles feature highly here as well as blue spotted fantail, porcupine and other stingray species on the sandy patches.

Currents can pick up a little here and if they are running fast it is also possible to cover part of Little Wall in the same dive. Little Wall is another vertical wall with the healthy coral diversity and fish life that you come to expect from Selayar Island's dive sites.

Other notable wall dives around Selayar include Karls's Corner, Netz and Caves and Overhangs. For those interested in critter diving, try Opera Sands for excellent macro life.

SELAYAR TRAVEL PLANNER

Selayar Dive Resort's southeast dive sites comprise a range of walls which plummet dramatically from 5 meters to a few hundred and form a mix of topographical features, including overhangs, ledges, caverns and swim-throughs. The diversity of coral species is exceptional and the walls easily rival those in Togean, Halmahera and Bunaken, but fish life is more abundant here and pelagics are more frequently spotted. Shark numbers are healthy and may be on the rise due to the MPA created by Selayar Dive Resort. Annual water temperature ranges from around 27 to 30 degrees, visibility is on average 20 meters but ranges from 15 meters after rainfall to 30 meters plus on calm days.

Selayar Dive Resort is a natural beauty hot spot both on land and underwater. Huge butterflies pass through the resort, turtles nest on the beach, and lizards, squirrels and numerous other local fauna live amongst the beach bungalows.

Diving is usually scheduled for two boat dives per day, timed according to the tides, with unlimited House Reef diving available. Night dives and 'blue light' or fluoro diving is available and highly recommended. The marine park boasts a wealth of critter life along its stunning walls and beautiful reef-scapes and the opportunity to spot larger pelagics.

Diving

Selayar Dive Resort (Author's choice) Diving and full board accommodation packages, stunning eco beach resort with 9 bungalows all with hot water and ocean views, AC available, restaurant and dive center, maximum of 15 minutes to reach dive sites. The area around the resort is a protected marine park and no-take zone which the resort diligently patrols day and night. Conservation is a key focus here and due to the marine park and the resorts commitment to environmental preservation, the dive sites are full of life with both macro and large pelagics and have stunning coral coverage. Closed May to the beginning of October due to the monsoon season. Advance booking required. $$. www.selayar-dive-resort.com or selayar-dive-resort.de. Email: info@selayar-dive-resort.com.

Bira Divers On Bira Beach, this operator offers fun diving and PADI and SSI courses.

Accommodation

Bara Beach Bungalows (Bira) Basic to mid-range bungalows looking out over Bira beach, stunning views, AC and hot water. Tel: +62 (0) 82291816872. www.bara-beach.com.

Selayar Dive Resort offers comfortable bungalows, all with ocean views and their own private beach area.

NUSA TENGGARA

The Nusa Tenggara region is vast, stretching from Lombok in the west to Timor in the east. It encompasses hundreds of tiny islands, ranging from mere pinnacles to substantial land masses, and boasts thousands of kilometers of coastline and reef. It also offers divers everything from submerged seamounts, walls and drop-offs to freshwater caves, gentle slopes and sandy muck diving bays. For the most part, currents can be strong across the Nusa Tenggara region, making the greater part of the diving suitable for those with a reasonable amount of experience. But for those who dive here, the challenging conditions make the rewards all the more worthwhile: numerous species of sharks and rays, including hammerheads and mantas, big schools of fish, dolphins, whale sightings, colorful reefs and exhilarating conditions. As you head east across Nusa Tenggara, the diving areas become more remote and more exclusive, with dive boats being few and far between, if any at all. This is an area rich in natural beauty and diversity. If you are looking for an adventure both underwater and on land, Nusa Tenggara has everything to offer.

Nusa Tenggara

Nusa Tenggara at a Glance
A Vast Area That Invites Exploration

Nusa Tenggara is a chain of islands running from Lombok in the west to Timor in eastern Indonesia. Also known as the Lesser Sunda Islands, the chain is divided into two distinct geographical arcs, with the northern arc encompassing Lombok and the islands of Flores through to Alor, and the southern arc including the islands of Sumba through Roti to Timor. The contrast between the two arcs couldn't be greater. The northern islands are characterized by lush, green, tropical jungle and fertile soil in complete contrast to the dry, dusty and barren islands in the south.

The formation of the Nusa Tenggara island chain began approximately 15 million years ago when the Asian and Australian tectonic plates collided, resulting in the birth of one of the most active and geologically complex regions on earth. Whereas the northern arc, which is volcanic in origin, has a number of active volcanoes, the islands of the southern arc are non-volcanic. The Nusa Tenggara region is characterized by numerous small islands which are often divided by deep ocean trenches. Such trenches limit the ability of species to cross from one island to the next, resulting in numerous endemic species, the most famous being the Komodo dragon, which is the worlds's largest living species of lizard, reaching up to 3 meters in length. Other notable endemic species of Nusa Tenggara include the Lombok flying fox, the Flores shrew and numerous species of bird.

MICRO CLIMATIC CONDITIONS

Nusa Tenggara has the driest of all climates found in Indonesia. In particular, the southern islands closest to Australia have the longest of dry seasons and the least annual rainfall. The wettest months are December through March and the driest are from May to October. It is because of these climatic conditions that the original and predominant vegetation in the south of the region is dry forest as opposed to rainforest. On many of the southern islands, the dry forests have now been substantially cleared to make way for settlements and crops.

THE SOUTHEASTERN ISLANDS

Nusa Tenggara literally translates from Indonesian as 'Southeastern Islands'. It was in 1958, after gaining independence from the Dutch, that ndonesia established three provinces in the Lesser

Komodo has numerous quiet bays that are perfect for liveaboards.

Sunda Islands: Bali, West Nusa Tenggara and East Nusa Tenggara. West Nusa Tenggara covers Lombok, the Gili Islands and Sumbawa, whereas East Nusa Tenggara encompasses Flores and Komodo, the Solar archipelago between Flores and Alor, the Alor archipelago, West Timor, the Sawu Islands and Sumba. In total, 566 islands fall under the umbrella of East Nusa Tenggara.

Blue Marlin in Gili Trawangan operate a number of traditional style dive boats.

Collectively, East and West Nusa Tenggara cover a land area of approximately 70,000 square kilometers and are home to just under 10 million people. The people here are as diverse as the landscape itself, with Lombok and Sumba being predominantly Muslim areas, whilst moving east towards Timor the majority religion is Christian, most of whom are Roman Catholic, together with a large percentage of Protestants.

The Gili island, which lie just off the north of Lombok, are a major tourist attraction and take the bulk of foreign travelers. Whilst some tourists travel on to Lombok to climb the mighty volcano Rinjani, it is only a relatively small percentage of travelers who make it any further east than this. The people of the more eastern islands survive mainly by subsistence farming and fishing as there is little industry in the area. The climate here can be harsh, particularly on the islands of the southern arc where the long dry seasons mean that drought is not unusual. In the northern arc, the climate is kinder and there is a healthy period of rainfall during the wet season. The northern islands are able to grow rice but in the south corn or lontar palm, which can survive with little water, are more common.

LOCAL PRACTICALITIES

The two main cities in Nusa Tenggara are Mataram in Lombok, the administrative capital of the west, and Kupang in Timor, the administrative capital of the east. A wide variety of local languages as well as Bahasa Indonesian are spoken throughout the region and basic English is understood in the major towns, cities and tourist areas.

When moving from island to island in Nusa Tenggara, travel is by either plane or boat. The major airports are on Lombok, Maumere, Kupang and Labuan Bajo. Boat travel is seasonally reliable, with many boat crossings being delayed or cancelled in the wet season when sea conditions can be difficult.

Traditional food from Nusa Tenggara features less rice than other cuisines and more sago, corn and cassava, largely due to the difficult growing conditions. Fish is a staple protein throughout and the local people rely heavily on the surrounding waters for food. *Sepat* is a widely available dish of shredded fish in coconut and young mango sauce. *Jus poket* (avocado juice) is also a regional favorite.

Diving Nusa Tenggara
Undeniably Impressive

Nusa Tenggara is a vast area with thousands of kilometers of coastline that offer divers a variety of difficulty levels, topographies, marine life and reef formations. From the gentle, warm waters of the Gili islands, which are suitable for learners and novices, to the choppy, challenging waters of southern Lombok and the fast drifts over pristine reefs of Alor, there is something for every level and type of diver in Nusa Tenggara.

Access to emergency services is often limited in Nusa Tenggara because of the remoteness of some areas. Thus, it is recommended to always choose a reputable operator that has oxygen, first aid kits and communication devices on hand. Decompression diving should be avoided at all costs as recompression chambers are almost always a long trip away, in some cases many days by boat. Most operators set maximum depth limits of 25 to 30 meters and dive times of up to 60 minutes.

With the exception of the Gili Islands and Labuan Bajo where diving is a major tourist industry, many operators are based in remote areas and have limited equipment for hire. Bringing your own is therefore strongly recommended. Most airlines allow 20 kg baggage allowance but some smaller aircraft operators only allow 15 kg. Excess baggage fees range from RPI10,000 to 40,000 per kg. If you

Above Colorful coral reefs are a consistent feature across Nusa Tenggara.

do not own your own equipment, then make sure you let operators know in advance that you will require rental gear and provide them with the sizes.

East of Flores, tourism is on a very small scale with few places to stay and limited international facilities. Aside from liveaboards, the majority of diving is done through the few Western dive resorts that have cropped up that offer diving and accommodation packages. These tend to be small-scale but generally very well run and organized operations. Due to the remoteness of many resorts, they do not anticipate walk-in bookings, and if you try just turning up there is no guarantee of a place. Booked in advance, however, you will be met at the airport and transported to the resort of your choice.

Diving resorts in Nusa Tenggara tend to be above average and range from comfortable rustic bungalows with onsite dive shops, boats and compressors to markedly high-end accommodation with AC, wifi, swimming pools, nitrox compressors and luxury boats. Because the resorts are invariably in remote locations, most operate on a full board basis with the daily rate including diving, accommodation and three to five meals a day.

Check with your operator to see what is included in your package.

There are numerous liveaboards around Nusa Tenggara. Some cover the entire area as well as parts of Raja Ampat and Maluku whilst others are very localized, such as the Komodo-based liveaboards which offer 3 to14 day trips around the Komodo National Park. Liveaboards vary from backpacker style with open sleeping areas to luxury vessels offering high-end service.

Visibility and water temperatures vary across the region and according to the season. Check with your chosen operator for temperatures at the time you are visiting and for recommended exposure protection. If in doubt, take additional exposure protection as many areas have cool thermoclines.

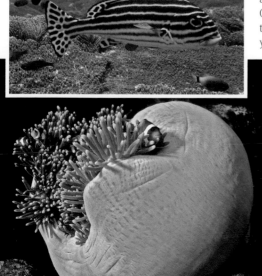

Top This reef octopus takes shelter and changes color to match its surroundings.

Above left The oriental sweetlips is just one of many sweetlips species found in Nusa Tenggara.

Left This magnificent anemone has begun to close around its anemonefish residents.

Liveaboard Options for Nusa Tenggara

Despite the vast area that Nusa Tenggara covers, which makes it ideal for exploring by liveaboard, there are surprisingly few liveaboard trips crossing the entire region. Komodo has by far the most liveaboards, with around 50 percent of them being stationed there all year round and only undertaking trips within and around the Komodo National Park. The other 50 percent tend to split the year between Komodo and Raja Ampat, usually operating in Raja Ampat from October to April/May and then in Komodo from May to September. However, as the boats move between the two areas in the offseason, from April through May and again in September through to October, they operate a couple of cruises across the region, so during these limited periods it is possible to take liveaboard trips that start in Komodo and head towards Raja Ampat, or vice versa. These trips are limited and places are often booked up to a year in advance, but if you are lucky enough to secure a spot the trips go via a number of possible locations, including Alor, Maumere, Ambon and Banda.

The plus side of these trips is that many of the spots that the liveaboards visit en route are in areas where there are no shore-based operators as yet and so diving in these areas is simply not possible by any other means, at least not without a significant amount of organizing, expense and risk.

For liveaboard trips solely around Komodo, there are a number of options. Some liveaboards operate on a hop-on, hop-off basis, such as the *Ikan Biru* (see opposite), where guests are taken by speedboat to the liveaboard in the park where they stay for their chosen number of days, and then return to Labuan Bajo by speedboat whilst the liveaboard vessel stays out in the park. Alternatively, there are traditional liveaboard trips that embark and disembark in Labuan Bajo. Trip durations vary from 3, 5, 7, 10 to 14 days depending on the operator.

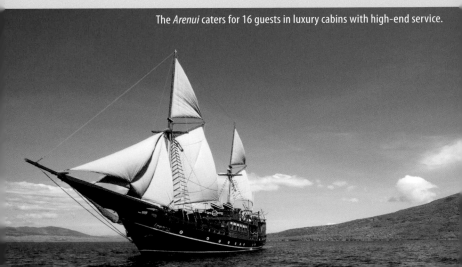

The *Arenui* caters for 16 guests in luxury cabins with high-end service.

Seven Seas has smaller tender boats for quick access and pick-ups at dive sites.

Below Large guest cabins on board the *Seven Seas* are specifically designed for comfort, storage space and light.

Below The Gili Islands offer easy and pretty dive sites, perfect for beginners.

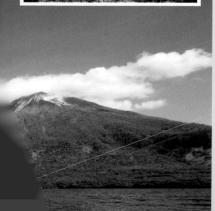

Recommended Operators

Seven Seas 45 meter Indonesian sailing schooner with 8 state cabins for 16 guests. www.thesevenseas.net. Email: info@thesevenseas.net.

Amira 52 meter Indonesian-style *phinisi* with 8 double cabins, 2 single cabins. www.amira-indinesia.com.

Arenui 43 meter luxury liveaboard with 8 cabins catering for 16 guests. www.thearenui.com. Email: info@thearenui.com.

Aurora 40 meter *phinisi*-style liveaboard covering a number of destinations, including Komodo and Raja Ampat. www.auroraliveaboard.com. Email: info@auroraliveaboard.com.

Best Value Recommendation
Ikan Biru Excellent budget liveaboard option great for those with limited schedules. Stationed in Komodo National Park, operating on a hop-on, hop-off basis. Up to 8 recreational divers or 6 technical divers, sleeping arrangements on the upper deck. www.ikanbiru.com. Email: info@bluemarlinkomodo.com.

NUSA TENGGARA TRAVEL PLANNER

If you are planning to visit a few different dive areas in Nusa Tenggara, consider carefully if the diving is within your capabilities. Komodo, southwest Lombok and Alor have sites suitable for beginners but the bulk of the diving can be challenging, with strong currents, and experienced divers will get a lot more out of these areas than beginners. The Gili Islands offer perfect conditions for those who want easy diving. Kupang also offers easy diving but, as a commercial harbor and provincial capital city, it is not an ideal holiday destination.

If you are hoping to see hammerheads in Lombok, then you should aim to stay 3 to 5 days as sites are not always accessible and are dependent on sea conditions. Komodo and Alor have a vast number of sites and spending 2 weeks in either of these alone would still not get you to every site on the map. The best of the diving in the Gili Islands can be covered in 2 to 3 days, but with the islands' relaxed, tropical atmosphere it's easy to see why people like to stay longer.

It is also worth considering how remote you want to go. The Gili islands are fully geared towards tourism, with restaurants, bars and numerous facilities. Labuan Bajo is also pretty well developed, although nowhere near to the same extent. Alor is by far the most remote, with little tourist infrastructure, so if you cannot cope without Western food and home comforts this may not be the place for you. South Lombok is similarly undeveloped, with only one place to stay in Belongas Bay.

8 Day Gili and Lombok Itinerary: Sharks, Turtles and Reefs

This itinerary is suitable for all levels of divers and allows two days of diving in Gili and four days in Belongas Bay. Transfers are all by car and boat.

Day 1 Arrive in the Gili Islands, either at Trawangan, Air or Meno. If starting from Bali, the easiest way to Gili is by fast boat from Sanur. If you are flying into Lombok, most Gili operators will provide pick-up services for a surcharge. Check with your operator when booking. Overnight on the Gili Island of your choice.

Day 2 Full day of diving around the Gili Islands. Overnight in the Gilis.

Day 3 Morning dives in the Gilis followed by afternoon boat transfer to Lombok and taxi to Senggigi for an overnight stay in Senggigi ready for an early morning pick-up the next day.

Day 4 Early pick-up from south Lombok operator and transfer to Belongas Bay Lodge. Possible afternoon dives in Belongas Bay sites according to experience level.

Days 5–7 Diving in Belongas Bay. Up to 4 dives per day, possible night dives.

Day 8 Check out of the Lodge and transfer to the airport or Senggigi for fast boat transfer back to Bali.

14 Day Lombok and Komodo Itinerary: Mantas and Sharks

This itinerary offers five days of diving in both Komodo and Belongas Bay. It begins in Labuan Bajo and ends in Lombok and requires one domestic flight. The Komodo portion of the trip can be by liveaboard or through an operator based in Labuan Bajo. (See Recommended Operators, page 175.)

Day 1 Arrival in Komodo Airport, pick-up by chosen operator and transfer to Labuan Bajo to board liveaboard, or check in to accommodation. Depending on arrival time/liveaboard schedule, possible afternoon dives or night dive.

Days 2–6 Diving in Komodo by liveaboard or day trips from Labuan Bajo. If you are diving by liveaboard, you should aim to be disembarking in Labuan Bajo either on the evening of Day 6 or early morning on Day 7.

Day 7 This is a non-diving day spent in Labuan Bajo to allow 24 hours for off-gassing prior to flying.

Day 8 Morning flight to Lombok and pick-up by Belongas Bay operator for car transfer to Belongas Bay. Check in to Belongas Bay Lodge. Possible afternoon dives in Belongas Bay.

Days 9–13 Diving in Belongas Bay. Aim to finish diving by lunchtime on Day 13 if you are flying out of Lombok the next day. If you are traveling back to Bali by boat, Day 13 can be a full day of diving.

Day 14 Transfer by car to either the airport or harbor.

21 Day Lombok, Komodo and Alor Itinerary: Island Explorer

This is a longer itinerary that takes you around some of Indonesia's most pristine reefs and is best suited to experienced divers. The itinerary allows for five days of diving in each of the three destinations and starts in Kupang and ends in Lombok. Four domestic flights are required and additional days can be added for cavern diving in Kupang.

Day 1 Arrive in Kupang and overnight there close to the airport ready for an early morning flight to Alor the next day. If you want to dive the freshwater caves in Kupang, this can be done on Day 1 if you arrive early. If you have an afternoon arrival, add an extra day and dive the caves the next day and then pick up the schedule again from Day 2.

Day 2 Morning flight to Alor (45 minutes) and meet operator for transfer to resort. 2 to 3 dives around Alor, possible night dive.

Days 3–7 Diving around Alor, 3 to 4 dives per day plus night dives are possible. On Day 7, make early morning dives only to ensure ample time between diving and flying the next day.

Day 8 Morning flight back to Kupang followed by an afternoon flight to Komodo. Pick-up in Komodo by chosen operator and transfer to Labuan Bajo to board liveaboard or check in to accommodation.

Days 9–21 Follow the same itinerary as Days 2–14 of the 14 day Lombok and Komodo Itinerary on page 160.

USEFUL CONTACTS

Recompression Chamber Rumah Sakit Sanglah, Jalan Diponegoro, Denpasar. Tel: +62 (0) 361227911.

Lombok International Airport (LOP) Jalan Raya Tanak Awu, Lombok Tengah. Tel: +62 (0) 370 6157000. www.lombok-airport.co.id.

Komodo Airport (LBJ) Situated in Labuan Bajo, Flores. Domestic services only but expansion plans are under way. Tel: +62 (0) 38541132.

Timor Airport (KOE) El Tari Airport, Jalan Adi Sucipto, Kupang. Tel: +62 (0) 380881668. www.eltari-airport.co.id.

Alor Airport (ARD) Mali Airport. Flights from Kupang only. Tel: +62 (0) 38621710.

Maumere Airport (MOF) Domestic flights **Garuda Indonesia** 24 Hour Call Center Tel: +62 (0) 8041807807 or +62 (0) 2123519999. www.garuda-indonesia.com.

Sriwijaya Air Call Center Tel: +62 (0) 21 29279777 or +62 (0) 8041777777. www.sriwijayaair.co.id.

Lion Air Assistance Line Tel: +62 (0) 216379 8000. www.lionair.co.id.

Merpati Assistance Line Tel: +62 (0) 8041621 621. www.merpati.co.id.

Transnusa Assistance Line Tel: +62 (0) 380 822555. www.transnusa.co.id.

Diving the Gili Islands
A Great Place for Beginners

The Gili Islands are easily accessible and cover just about every option, from sun-drenched beaches, tropical waters and the choice of partying until the early hours on Gili Trawangan, or a Robinson Crusoe-style getaway on Gili Meno. Underwater, parts of the Islands have suffered from destructive fishing practices in the past but there are still some pretty reefs, and even those that have sustained damage host a range of critter life. Turtle numbers are high and diving conditions are relatively easy.

With white sand beaches and turquoise tropical water surrounding these small, idyllic islands, it is no wonder that they are such a popular spot. Gili Trawangan, the liveliest and most developed of the islands, is the furthest west and has numerous dive centers and accommodation options. Meno, the centrally positioned island, is the quietest. Air is the eastern island with the largest local population. It also has a range of accommodation and dive centers.

Up until the end of the 1960s, the Gili Islands were pristine mangrove habitats with no permanent settlers. As water supplies and transport improved, small settlements began in the 1970s. In the 1980s, the Gili Islands were discovered by backpackers and tourism began to grow. Most resorts are Western-owned

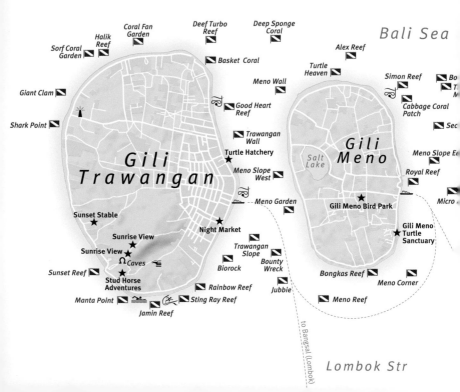

and there are few local establishments on Trawangan. As boat services from Bali have increased, tourism has boomed, and now that Lombok has an international airport the boom looks set to continue. Trawangan is a popular spot for young beach lovers who are looking for sun, sea and lively night life. Gili Meno is a much more rustic affair, better suited to those seeking a more remote island experience, while Gili Air falls between the two.

Gili has the same monsoon cycle as Bali and Lombok with most rain falling from November to April, but given their low lying landscape the islands have a much drier micro-climate.

The local religion in the Gili Islands is Muslim as most local workers originate from Lombok. However, particularly on Trawangan, there is a much more Westernized culture and beach clothing is

Clownfish never fail to excite beginner level divers.

acceptable. Since the 1980s, recreational drugs (Magic Mushrooms) have been widely available on Trawangan and they are still advertised for sale. Whilst policing appears slack, drug offences in Indonesia have very serious consequences.

DIFFICULTY LEVEL Year round warm water, little current and shallow reefs make the Gili Islands a popular choice for those learning to dive.

HIGHLIGHTS Reasonably reliable shark sightings. Numerous turtles can be seen on almost all sites and manta rays occasionally pass through.

LOGISTICS The three Gili Islands are situated off the north of Lombok and access is by boat either from Lombok, Bali or Nusa Lembongan. If traveling to Gili from overseas, transit must be through Denpasar Airport in Bali or Lombok International Airport. There is a plethora of dive centers and a wide range of accommodation in the Gilis, the majority being on Gili Trawangan, but there are also operators on Gili Air and Gili Meno, albeit on a smaller scale. Gili Trawangan is the largest island, measuring approximately 3 by 2 kilometers. There is no motorized transport on the Gili Islands, so getting around is by foot, bicycle or traditional horse and cart 'taxi'.

Gili Islands

1 km
0.5 miles

N

Takat Sirah

Segaluh Reef

Batfish Point   Gogos Reef

Frog Fish Point

ll

Hans Reef

Gili Air

Air Home Reef

Nemo City
Tanjung An Reef
rbor Reef   ★ Pearl Farm

to Bangsal (Lombok)

GILI ISLANDS' BEST DIVE SITES

GILI TRAWANGAN: MANTA POINT
☆ AUTHOR'S CHOICE

Manta Point is a gentle, sloping reef off the south coast of Gili Trawangan. The shallow waters are a mix of fire coral, hydroids and coral rubble. Whilst far from being Indonesia's most beautiful reefscape, it can be good for spotting swimming moray eels, cowfish and anemonefish nestled in their hosts. From 10 meters to 15 meters there is medium patchy coral coverage, predominantly soft species, coupled with sporadic hard coral, including branching corals and some healthy sized tables. From 18 meters and below, the coral peters out to sand with a maximum depth of 20 to 25 meters. Despite its name, manta rays are not regularly seen here although they are known to pass through on occasions. Shark sightings are much more reliable and schools of yellow snapper are often in the area, too. The dive is a straight-forward swim along the reef. The coral makes a 'band' from approximately 10 to 15 meters which you can follow either east or west depending on the current, usually only mild. Fish life is not abundant and the reef is mediocre, but if sharks are on your bucket list, it is worth donning your fins if you are in the area!

White tip reef sharks are frequent visitors to Manta Point, Gili Trawangan.

GILI TRAWANGAN: SHARK POINT

Situated off the west coast of Gili Trawangan, Shark Point is arguably one of the Gili Islands' best dive sites due to the variety of species that can be seen in one single dive. The reef itself is not world class when compared to other areas of Indonesia, but it plays host to a surprising amount of critter life, sharks, turtles and some schooling fish. The reef begins at the entry point at around 12 meters and largely consists of hydroid soft corals, fire corals and patches of coral rubble. Unfortunately, damage to the reef is obvious in some places. From 12 meters, the reef slopes down with a series of canyons to a maximum depth of around 40 meters. The ideal depth to dive is 20 to 25 meters for a good chance of shark sightings. The reef becomes more interspersed with sand the deeper you go below 25 meters.

Amongst the canyons is a good range of sponges, boulder corals adorned with feather stars and rocky formations that provide for interesting topographical features and form sheltered areas for hiding turtles, octopus, moray eels, ribbon eels and leaf scorpionfish. Blue spotted stingrays are often seen on the sandy areas and, of course, reef sharks are frequent visitors here. As you progress along the reef, work your way up over the soft, shallow corals, which are brightened by small schools of electric blue and yellow damselfish, and look out for the numerous turtles that hunker down in hollows on the reef. It is not unusual to see several in one di

Green Turtles *Chelonia Mydas*

The green sea turtle is very commonly seen around the Gili Islands where it flourishes on the surrounding shallow reefs. This larger species of sea turtle can weigh up to 300 kkilograms (average 150 kilograms) and its carapace can be as long as 1.5 meters. Green sea turtles are herbivores as mature adults and feed on a mix of sea grass and algae but juveniles are omnivores and will consume jellyfish, sponges and small molluscs.

The green sea turtle is distinguishable by the single pair of prefrontal scales on its small blunt head and its boney, ridgeless carapace which is composed of large, non-overlapping scutes. The green turtle's name derives from the fat underneath its shell. Shell coloration varies widely, from pale or dark green to brown and even black and grey in some areas. On paler colored individuals, it is easy to see radiating stripes on the carapace. Unlike hawksbill turtles, which are also commonly seen in Indonesia, the green sea turtle has only one visible claw per flipper rather than two.

Green sea turtles prefer coastline habitats and are most frequently seen around islands, bays and protected shores. They generally do not live in the open ocean

The radiating steaks are clearly visible on each scute of this green sea turtle's carapace.

but are capable of migrating over huge distances—up to 2,250 kilometers—from their feeding grounds to nesting areas.

Females will return to the beach on which they were hatched for breeding, which occurs only every two to four years. In a nesting year, a female may nest up to nine times with there being 75 to 150 eggs in each nest. As with most turtle species, the percentage of eggs that hatch can be very low due to land-dwelling predators. The percentage of juveniles reaching maturity is similarly low. Other factors that have led to the green sea turtle being listed by the IUCN as endangered are the degradation of feeding and nesting habitats, mature individuals falling victim to longline fishing and drowning in fishing nets, ocean pollution and trade in green sea turtle eggs, meat, leather and shells.

A green sea turtle's lifespan is estimated to be at least 80 years in the wild, and once they have reached maturity they have few known natural predators. Gili Trawangan is also home to a turtle sanctuary and thus turtle numbers in this area are healthy.

Turtles around the Gili Islands seem comfortable with divers and close encounters are not unusual.

GILI MENO WALL

Gili Meno Wall is off the west coast of Gili Meno and offers a steep sloping reef and wall which is excellent for turtle sightings. The reef itself starts at approximately 5 meters where there is a mix of coral rubble and branching corals. The reef then drops down to around 18 meters before it peters out to a white sand bottom. The wall is in two sections and in between the two parts both green and hawksbill turtles are frequently spotted. The reef has a rocky underlying base which has medium density coral coverage of both soft and hard corals. Plates,

small tables, branching corals, brain corals, sponges and hydroids feature highly. During daylight hours, the wall boasts lionfish and a range of moray eel species that make the most of the crevices and shady areas. When dived at night, the critter life includes a variety of crustaceans, shrimps and lobsters. Whilst life on the reef is not abundant, there is a good mix of reef fish. Damselfish aggregations are seen over table corals, and parrotfish, sweetlips, angelfish, small puffers, boxfish and occasional batfish flit in and out of the reef as they pass through. The site can be dived in either direction depending on the current, which is usually only mild, making this site suitable for all levels. Meno Wall is an overall easy dive with pretty colors and turtle sightings, which makes it a perfect spot for novices.

Gili Meno Wall is home to a variety of moray eel species that hide amongst the reef.

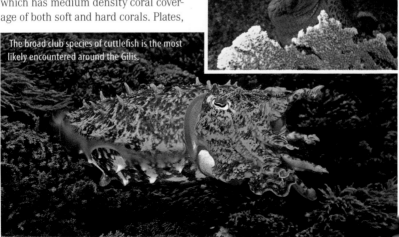

The broad club species of cuttlefish is the most likely encountered around the Gilis.

GILI ISLANDS
TRAVEL PLANNER

Whilst the diving in Gili is reasonable, it is not world class as the reefs have suffered from destructive fishing practices and in many areas have been reduced to rubble. The number of fish species is also not as varied as in other locales, nor is it as abundant. That being said, the Gili islands do provide excellent training conditions and ample marine life, including sharks and turtles, for those who want to learn to dive whilst enjoying a beach holiday in the sun.

Annual water temperature is approximately 29 degrees and most operators hire 3 mm short suits as standard. Average visibility ranges from 10 to 20 meters. Dive training is now a big industry in the Gilis, with all centers offering recreational courses and several also offering instructor level programs, technical diving and free diving. With many dive centers around the islands, the dive sites can be busy during high season (June to September). During the wet monsoon, sea conditions can be choppy.

Recommended Operators

Blue Marlin (Author's Choice) Established dive center on both Trawangan and Meno, courses, equipment hire, tech and fun diving available. Dive and stay packages with a range of accommodation. Tel: +62 (0) 3706132424. www.bluemarlindive.com. Email: info@bluemarlindive.com.

Other reputable operators include: **Trawangan Dive** Tel: +62 (0) 3706149220. www.trawangandive.com. Email: info@trawangandive.com. **Manta Dive** Tel: +62 (0) 3706143649. www.manta-dive.com. Email: info@manta-dive.com. **Oceans 5 Dive Resort** (Gili Air) Tel: +62 (0) 81338777144.

www.oceans5dive.com. Email: info@oceans5dive.com. **Big Bubble Dive** Tel: +62 (0) 370625 020. www.bigbubblediving.com. Email: info@bigbubblediving.com.

Accommodation

Pesona Resort Gili Trawangan Comfortable Indian-themed accommodation and restaurant to suit a range of budgets. $–$$. Tel: +62 (0) 3706123521. www.pesonaresort.com. Email: pesonaresort@hotmail.com.

Villa Ombak Trawangan Upmarket international hotel with full range of facilities. $$$. Tel: +62 (0) 3706142336. www.hotelombak.com. Email: info@hotelombak.com.

Below Blue Marlin in Gili Trawangan is a popular operator for those learning to dive.

Bottom Manta Dive Resort bungalows are built in a traditional style and offer comfort and space.

Diving Lombok
Rugged Seascapes, Exhilarating Dives

Lombok's southern coastline is untouched, remote and has a quality of beautiful wilderness that has to be experienced. Rugged rock pinnacles and crashing waves can have your adrenaline pumping before you even reach some of the sites, but with the promise of seasonal schooling hammerhead sharks, mobula and eagle rays, for those with more experience this could soon become the next diving mecca in Indonesia. Dive sites closer to the mouth of Belongas Bay, towards the western end of the coastline, offer easier all round conditions for all levels of divers, combined with beautiful corals, excellent macro opportunities and occasional passing rays and pelagics.

Belongas Bay is an exquisite location with a long beach and a bay that is millpond flat. The area is remote and there is little in the nearby village, but the local people are friendly and keen to exchange a few words with visitors. The lands of South Lombok are low lying with undulating hills which support ricefields and tobacco leaf plantations. For the people of Belongas, the local fishing industry is a main source of income as well as pearl and seaweed farming in some areas. The local dialect is Bahasa Sasak but the younger generations speak Bahasa Indonesia and some English. As this area is so remote, there is limited

Above Schooling mobula rays are one of the big draws of diving in South Lombok.

internet and phone reception and thus it is best to buy a local Sim card for your devices before traveling to Belongas. There is, however, a satellite phone at the lodge for emergencies. Electricity at the lodge is 24/7 provided by the mainland power grid. During the occasional power outage, power is supplied by generator. The majority of the locals are Muslim and as such alcohol is not widely available outside of tourist hotels and visitors should dress conservatively if venturing out.

DIFFICULTY LEVEL South Lombok has everything, from some of Indonesia's most challenging sites to easy submerged coral reefs suitable for all levels. **HIGHLIGHTS** Stunning, untouched, remote beaches and coastline. Schooling hammerheads at the Magnet site from late June to late October, as well as schooling eagle rays, reef sharks, mobula, marble rays, tuna and great barracuda. Exhilarating, challenging dives for experienced divers and more relaxed picturesque reefs for those who prefer a more laid-back diving experience. **LOGISTICS** Belongas Bay (meaning Bay of Tranquility) is located on the southwest of Lombok. There is currently one operator in the area, Dive Zone, in partnership with Two Fish Divers who also have resorts in Bunaken, Lembeh and Nusa Lembongan. If you are flying into Lombok Airport, they will provide pick-

Diving in South Lombok also offers some less challenging sites over picturesque reefs.

ups providing you arrive before 8 pm. If arriving later, an overnight stay near the airport is necessary. pick-ups are also available from Sekotong, Senggigi and Kuta Bay. Day trips to Belongas Bay from these areas are also available with pick-up times being between 6 and 7 am. Belongas Bay Lodge is the only accommodation in the area and is Dive Zone's diving base. Surcharge per car (maximum 8 people) applies for pick-ups.

SOUTH LOMBOK'S BEST DIVE SITES

THE MAGNET
☆AUTHOR'S CHOICE

The Magnet is South Lombok's most iconic site, the one that most people come to dive as it offers the chance of both scalloped and great hammerheads schooling from late June to late October.

But this is not a site for inexperienced divers or the faint-hearted. The Magnet is a rock pinnacle out in the open ocean which rises up from around 60 meters. The site is a 30 minute boat ride from

Above Allied cowries such as this one are less than 2 cm long but their detailed markings are exquisite.

Left Despite their feathery appearance, the spines of the common lionfish are venomous.

This scorpionfish nestled itself amongst the coral to add to its camouflage.

the shore and the sea conditions can be rough, especially during hammerhead season, and the surge around the pinnacle is visible from the surface with waves crashing into the rock. A negative entry, out from the pinnacle, in the center of the north side is required so that you drop through the surge zone as quickly as possible. In the 18 meter upward range, stay around 10 meters away from the pinnacle wall to avoid being sucked up and down with the water movement. Below 18 meters the surge is still felt but it eases off. The dive is generally back and forth across the north side. Be careful of getting too close to the east and west edges as the currents coming in from the south whip around the pinnacle. On the calmest of days, it is actually possible to circumnavigate the entire pinnacle, but even then this is not an easy dive. The wall is completely coral-encrusted with short, colorful close-cropped corals. But this is really a site for looking out to the blue. Huge tuna, mobula rays and eagle rays, barracudas, big schools of fusiliers, and black tip, white tip and grey reef sharks are seen here. The sheer volume of fish is astonishing. At 30 meters there is a small alcove which provides useful shelter on dives where the surge and currents are particularly strong. As you make your way back up the wall, move

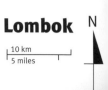

Lombok N

10 km
5 miles

SEE GILI ISLAN

Gili
Trawangan

**Small Ferry E
to Gili Isl**
Pandanan Bay
Blambanan Point
Nipah Bay
Rumbeh Point
Mt. Mal

Mangsit Point
Mt. E
Senggigi
Senggigi Bay
Senggigi Beach
Pura Batube
Batu

Men
Pura Se
Selaparang
Amped

Tanju

Lombok Strait

Gunung Pengsong

Ferry from Padang Bai, Bali (3.5 hr.)

Gili Anyaran
Gili Rengit
Gili Layar
Gili Asahan
Gili Lontar
Gili Poh
Gili Nangu
Gili Tangkong

Besar Bay

Pes
Len
Selegong
Gili Gede Gili Genting
Pelangan, Gili Amben
Bathing Beach
Gili Su
Le

Mt. Gua
149m
Sekotong Barat
Scenic Area ★
Sekotong
Tengal
Pelangan Barat
Mt. M
Mt. Marmadi
490m
Mt. Embit
418m
Peretan Bay
Gili Solet
Mt. Belongas
299m
Marmadi Point
Mekaki Bay
Belong
Mt. Panggang
329m
Gili Wa
Batujonggat Bay
Uah Point
Gili
Sarang Burung
Panga
Belenam

Amoramor Bay
Emapaskodek Bay
Segoar Bay

Akarakar
Anyar
Sukadana
Kayangan
Selengan
Traditional Village
Loloan
Bayan
Obel-obel

Wetu Telu Mosque

Gangga Waterfall
Rempek
Sesait
Mt. Semboya ±820m
Traditional Village
Sidanggala Waterfall
Sajang
Mt. Turunanjalan 1026m
Mt. Kubu 552m
Belanting
Gili Lawang

Gili Sulat

Spring
ket
Jenggala
Gondang
Tiu Pupas Waterfall
Tiuteja Waterfall
Mt. Murmas 676m
Mt. Samurarung 2037m
Mt. Hau 1366m
Mt. Keliun 797m

Tanjung
Sokong
Mt. Bangketaji 693m
Mt. Pusuksuhur 900m
Base Camp Hot Springs
Sembalunlawang
Guesthouse
Mt. Sengkor 1490m
Mt. Mundung 1440m
Sambelia
Gubuk

nang
dan
Mt. Buanmangge 1916m
Plawangan I
Mt. Plawangan 2612m
Shelter Campsite
Sembalunbumbung
Plawangan II Campsite
Mt. Ayasa 2029m
Mt. Anjeman 465m
Camping

Mt. Peluntak 705m
Mt. Tanakawin 2664m
Mt. Batujai (Mt. Baru) 2351m
Lake Segara Anak
Mt. Propok 2077m
Mt. Rinjani 3726m
Mt. Atas Timur 2235m
Mt. Nangi 2330m
Mt. Transat 103m
Gili Pentangan

Mt. Peluntak 705m
ion
Mt. Masjidborok 1272m
Mt. Ketimunan 1602m
Mt. Seribu 1910m
Mt. Bukitbau 1668m
Gili Pasaran
Gili Lampu

Mt. Muteran 1083m
Mt. Meninting 1418m
Mt. Rinjani Reserve
Scenic Area
Sapit
Perigi
Kayangan
Ferry to Labuhan Tano, Sumbawa 1.5 hr.

gar
n
Mt. Pelola 593m
Suwela
Suntalangu
Ketangga
Labuhan Lombok
Belang Island

oo Crafts
gsari
afts
Pura Lingsar
Sesaot
Freshwater Spring
Dance & Music
Jeruk Manis **Freshwater Waterfall** **Spring & Views**
Freshwater Spring & Views
Karangbaru
Makam Selaparang
Pringgabaya

aram
Pura Suranadi
Freshwater Spring
Aikbuka
Perian
Wajageseng
Scenery & Walking
Scenery & Walking
Aikmel
Utata
Kembangkerang Lauk
Poh Gading
Kerumut

Sweta
Market
Batukumbung
Rinjani Country Club
Golong Golf Course
Pemepek
Kotaraja
Tanakbeak
Selubung
Kataraja
Tetebatu
Pengadangan
Weaving
Pringgasela
Aikmel
Wanasaba
Dance & Music
Apitaik
Korleko
Belusun Point

Narmada
Water Palace
Pura Meru
Kekalik
Bebuak
Jengik
Crafts and Pottery
Ledangnangka
Suralaga
Hikmah
Sumbawa Island

egara
Narmada
Bagu
Pringgarata
Pagutan
Montongterep
Terara
Masbagik
Pottery
Paokmotong
Kerongkong
Savong Bay

ak
aragara
Bonjeruk
Perina
Montongterep
Dasanbaru
Rarang
Semaya
Crafts
Sikur
Suradadi
Pancor
Jantuk
Kabar
Monday Cattle Market
Teros
Selong

Bengkel
Kuripan
Jagaraga
Jago
Aikmual
Monggas
Darmaji
Sakra
Montongtangi
Penedagandor
Sesait Island

eri
Ubung
Jelantik
Puyung
Dunutbook
Jurangjalen
Suwangi
Gunungrajak
Surabaya
Labuhan Haji

sasangeres
Sukarara
Unggo
Leneng
Weaving
Beraim
Sukarara
Rensing
Sepit
Pengkelekmas
Labuhan Haji Beach

Darek
Praya
Batujai
Semayan
Batunyale
Lekor
Beleka
Selayar
Alas Strait

Pengga Reservoir
Pottery
Penujak
Bonder
Crafts
Mujur
Ganti
Tundak
Canoe Making
Fish Market
Tanjung Luar

Mt. Raruna 357m
Tanakawu
Kateng
Lombok Int'l Airport
Marong
Semoyang
Traditional Sasak Village
Keruak
Gili Kere
Sesait Island
Banja

gsapah
Mangkung
Pengembur
Sengkol
Sukaraja
Gili Belek
Gili Merengke
Galuh Point

wok
u
Truwai
Rembitan
Sagikmateng
Salt Pans
Gili Areng
Keceling Bay
Sunut Bay
Gili Petelu
Jelengnya Point

k Scenic Area
Mt. Pandaleman 244m
Caves & Viewpoint
Sade
Traditional Sasak Village
Fishing Village
Gili Inus
Ringgit Point
Aikundur Bay
Jelenga

wok u
Caves
Kuta
Kuta Beach
Avang Bay
Caves
Mangkurun Bay
Cina Point
Benete

Tampa Bay
Gili Nusa
Nyale Ritual
Tanjung A'an Beach
Mt. Tunak 105m
Nyale Ritual
Scenic Area
Numu Point
Malok Point
Maluk

Scenic Area
Tanjung Aan
Serenting Bay
Teduwak Bay
Gumbang Bay
Sangulap Point
Seriwe Bay
Sekongkang

Desert Point
Bumgkulan Point
Sumbawa Island

IAN OCEAN
Ferry to Padang Bai, Bali

The Scalloped Hammerhead Shark *Sphyma lewini*

The scalloped hammerhead, also known as the bronze hammerhead and the kidney headed shark, is relatively easy to distinguish from other hammerhead sharks by virtue of the central indentation on the front margin of its broad head. It ranges in color from brownish grey to bronze on top with pale white or yellow undersides. Juveniles have dark second dorsal and pectoral fins. Fully mature males reach up to 1.8 meters and females 2.5 meters.

The scalloped hammerhead is a semi-oceanic species of shark which is commonly found around insular shelves adjacent to deep waters. By day it tends to stay closer to shore whilst at night it heads further offshore in search of prey. They have been seen from the surface down to depths of up to 275 meters.

Adults are seen individually, in pairs and in small schools, but young scalloped hammerheads live in large schools and newborns and infants live in coastal nurseries.

The scalloped hammerhead's diet is extremely varied and includes reef fish such as parrotfish, surgeons, wrasses and damselfish, pelagics such as barracuda, Spanish mackerel, other sharks and rays such as black tip reef sharks and stingrays. They are also known to feed on invertebrates, including squid, octopus, shrimps, crabs and lobsters.

Above Schooling scalloped hammerheads at the Magnet —an exhilarating sight and an exhilarating dive.

Female scalloped hammerheads move inshore to shallow water to pup and they give birth to live young following a 9 to 10 month gestation period. Litters are large and can range from 12 to 38 pups, which are just 15 to 18 inches long at birth. After pupping, females leave the young and return to deeper water. Hammerhead pups living in coastal nurseries are extremely vulnerable to fishing, pollution and habitat destruction. They are also prey to other larger shark species. As mature adults, scalloped hammerheads have no major predators. Despite having large litters though, only a small proportion of the pups will reach sexual maturity, but for those that do, life expectancy is estimated at 30 years or more.

The IUCN has listed the scalloped hammerhead as 'near threatened' and globally its numbers are in decline. Both game fishing and commercial fishing have had an impact on the species. They are also vulnerable to longlines and trawls and they are often a by-catch in drift net fishing. As with all shark species today, they are sadly also caught for their fins for the black market shark fin industry.

out from it before you enter the strong surge zone at 18 meters. The safety stop is usually made at around 10 meters out from the pinnacle. This is an exhilarating dive for experienced divers. Whilst it can be challenging, the possibility of seeing schooling hammerheads makes it all worthwhile.

When diving the Magnet and the Cathedral sites, listen carefully to your guide's briefing, pay attention and stay close and behind the guide during the dive. A delayed SMB is strongly recommended. If you arrive at the site and the guide thinks the conditions are too rough to dive, listen to the advice and save it for another day.

THE CATHEDRAL

This is another site that can have challenging conditions. Whilst it is generally easier than the Magnet, it is also recommended for experienced divers only. The Cathedral takes its name from a large rock pinnacle with two main peaks, much like a cathedral ceiling. The pinnacle bottoms out at around 45 meters and only the small upper portion is visible from the surface. The dive is made according to the currents and surge. On more challenging days, the dive is just along one wall. On days with less surge, it is possible to swim around the pinnacle. Like the Magnet, there is a lot of surge here, especially in the first 5 meters where visibility is also reduced due to the waves hitting the rock. Once you descend through the surge zone, there is a beautiful wall covered with soft corals, short tubers and sponges which host numerous nudibranchs, scorpionfish and lionfish. Looking out to the blue, this is another site for spotting larger species such as dog tooth tuna, schooling eagle rays, great barracuda, schools of smaller barracuda and reef sharks. Sea snakes are also commonly seen here with numerous individuals seen in one dive. Coming back up the Cathedral, move away from the pinnacle as you shallow up. As with the Magnet, if you are too close you will be caught up in the surge and risk being thrown into the rock. Usually the safety stop is 10 meters out from the pinnacle. The Cathedral is a challenging site, but for divers with experience of diving in tricky conditions it is another iconic South Lombok site.

GILI SARANG

Gili Sarang is a 20 minute boat ride from Belongas Bay and features a large rock which rises up, towering out of the water. Gili Sarang offers substantially easier conditions than those found at the Magnet and Cathedral sites. The rock bottoms out to white sand at around 35 meters, and surrounding the main rock are numerous boulders and bommies

Dense schools of fish are frequently seen in the currents around South Lombok.

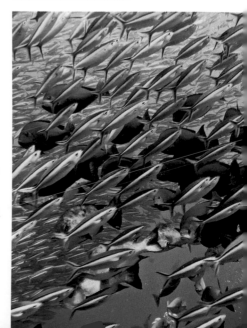

that appear to have been haphazardly scattered around its base. The numerous boulders are covered with soft corals, including leather corals, small fans, sponges and several black coral formations. After dropping in and heading down to your maximum depth, the dive is a swim-through and around these varied formations before gradually making your way back up. There is usually some level of surge at Gili Sarang but it is just a case of kicking when it goes in your favor and going with the flow! When making the initial descent, keep an eye out to the blue for schooling mobulas and eagle rays which frequently pass through, especially in August and September. In the boulder area at depth, reef sharks are often seen and this site is also good for smaller marine species. Pygmy seahorses, a range of shrimps, various nudibranchs, scorpionfish and lionfish are all spotted here. As you shallow up, the soft corals in the 15 meter and upward range really catch the light

Beautiful soft corals adorn some of Lombok's less ferocious dive sites.

from the sun and the colors are quite impressive. As with the other pinnacle sites in the area, if there is surge move away from the rock for the safety stop. Gili Sarang does not have the volume of fish that you see at the Magnet but it is a nice all round dive site with interesting topographical features, the chance of seeing some larger species and a good mix of macr olife as well.

CORAL GARDEN

Coral Garden is a site suitable for all levels of divers as it is situated in a more sheltered position, further in towards the mouth of Belongas Bay as opposed to being out in the open ocean. The site is a series of pinnacles of varying sizes which rise up to around 12 meters beneath the surface and bottom out at around 25 meters to sand. Entry is made over the pinnacles or slightly upcurrent.

The pinnacles boast abundant fish life and stunning corals. Whips, tubers, small gorgonians with bushy feather stars, leather corals and anemones adorn the rocky surfaces. Reef fish are varied with all of the usual suspects present. Lionfish, anemonefish, Moorish idols, parrotfish and numerous wrasses weave in and out of the reef and hoards of damselfish and basslets glimmer in the sunlight as they dart in and out of the corals. Coral Garden offers some great macro photography opportunities as there is a good range of shrimps, nudibranchs and crinoids. On good days, ghost pipefish and pygmy seahorses can be found here also. It's not just macro life and corals though. Schools of chevron barracuda are known to pass through along with sea turtles, marble rays and occasional eagle rays. All in all, Coral Garden offers relatively easy conditions and a good overview of the range of reef life in South Lombok.

For diving the more challenging sites in Belongas Bay—the Magnet and the Cathedral—divers require an advanced level certification as well as 50 logged dives between November and May and 100 logged dives between June and October. For other sites there are no such prerequisites but some experience is recommended. Whilst equipment hire is available, it is recommended that you bring your own. Surface marker buoys and dive computers are mandatory and are not for rent. Nautilus Lifeline Diver retrieval systems are available for rent at a small surcharge.

Belongas Bay Lodge offers a range of bungalows to suit divers' requirements.

Water temperatures range from 26 to 28 degrees on average, but during hammerhead season they drop as low as 21 to 24, so a good 5 mm wetsuit is recommended. Due to the extreme water movement at the pinnacle sites and the shallow depth at sites nearer the bay, visibility ranges from 10 to 15 meters.

There are no credit card facilities or ATMs at the Lodge or in the village, so payment must be in cash or paid in advance when booking.

Dive schedules vary according to sea conditions, but up to four dives per day are possible. Some sites are not diveable when there is a big swell.

Whilst the hammerhead season runs for several months, the best time to dive is from mid-July to early October. September is the best month for seeing schooling mobula and eagle rays.

Recommended Operators

Diving

Dive Zone Lombok (Author's Choice) Based at Belongas Bay Lodge, Dive Zone have ten years of experience in South Lombok and in the South Gili's where they also have operations. They offer fun diving trips to all Belongas Bay sites. Pick-ups (see Logistics, page 163), equipment hire and night dives are available. Equipment hire must be requested in advance. Tel: +62 (0) 81339544 998. www.divezone-lombok.com. Email: dive@divezone-lombok.com.

Dive Zone operate in partnership with Two Fish Divers who are a reputable operator with resorts in Bunaken, Lembeh and Nusa Lembongan, Bali. Multi-destination trips are possible as is dive training up to and including Instructor level. www.twofish-divers.com.

Accommodation

Belongas Bay Lodge Comfortable mid-range bungalows (two superior bungalows with AC and hot water and two standard rooms with fan and ensuite WC, shared hot water shower, set in a picturesque garden on the banks of Belongas Bay. Room rates include breakfasts whilst buffet-style lunches and dinners (IDR75,000 per meal) are not included. $$. Tel: +62 (0) 361710004. www.the lodge-lombok.com. Enquiry form on web page or can be booked through Dive Zone or Two Fish Divers.

Diving **Komodo and Flores**
Dramatic Scenery and Jurassic Dragons

From rugged uninhabited islands to rocky pinnacles and submerged seamounts, this area has a feel of being untouched by time. Underwater is no less impressive: sharks, manta rays, eagle rays, an astonishing volume of fish and vibrant reefs rich with color and diversity. Unpredictable and occasionally ferocious currents make the diving around Komodo an exhilarating experience from start to finish. Flores offers a number of easier sights, suitable for all levels, with a wealth of critter and macro life, passing rays, schooling fish and occasional predators. Diving in Komodo promises a lot and it certainly delivers!

Historically, diving in the Komodo Marine Park was almost exclusively by liveaboard but an increase in shore-based operators has resulted in numerous new facilities. Restaurants, cafes, bars and shops are cropping up along the main drag, Jalan Soekarno Hatta, which runs along the harbor coastline.

The local inhabitants of the Komodo islands are fishermen who came from South Flores, Sumbawa and South Sulawesi (from the Suku Bajau ethnic group, hence the 'Bajo' part of Labuan Bajo). The predominant religion is Islam and the locals are used to tourists who have been visiting the area to see the mighty Komodo dragons for decades.

Basic English is understood in the town, and with liveaboards stopping to pick up supplies, a surprising selection of Western products is available.

The Komodo National Park encompasses the three main islands of Komodo, Rinca and Padar, plus 26 smaller islands, and was founded in 1980 to protect the world's largest species of lizard, the Komodo dragon. In 1991, it was declared a World Heritage Site by UNESCO and conservation efforts have been extended to cover all aspects of marine and terrestrial life.

DIFFICULTY LEVEL Challenging topographies with wildly exhilarating and sometimes extreme currents suitable for

The Komodo dragon is the largest living species of monitor lizard in the world.

Above The dramatic scenery of the Komodo National Park is simply breathtaking.

Left Komodo's reefs offer exceptional coral biodiversity and marine biomass.

Below Manta rays, such as the manta alfredi pictured here, are resident in Komodo's Marine Park.

experienced divers. There is a range of calmer sites that are ideal for beginners and those who do not like diving in currents. Some sites can also be timed and dived so as to minimize currents.

HIGHLIGHTS Reef sharks, manta rays, eagle rays and a big variety of pelagics and predators, excellent biomass with schooling fish in abundance and a range of unique topographies and reefscapes.

LOGISTICS Most operators, including liveaboards, are based in the harbor town of Labuan Bajo in Flores. Komodo Airport in Labuan Bajo is serviced by domestic flights, and transit is through Bali or Jakarta. There are several passenger ferries traveling back and forth along the East Nusa Tenggara island chain.

KOMODO AND FLORES' BEST DIVE SITES

KARANG MAKASSAR (MANTA POINT OR THE AIRSTRIP)

This site is a drift along the northern section of the east coast of Komodo Island and is a favorite of Komodo's manta rays! The site is a long stretch of shallow, sloping rubble reef with very little living coral aside from small, sporadic patches. The maximum depth is around 12 meters as the mantas tend to be upwards of this and there is little to see any deeper. Current strength varies. If it is strong, drift with the flow and 'fly' along the reef. On dives with little current, the rubble is great for critter hunting.

This long shore site has interesting topography. The rubble undulates, forming 'banks' similar to golf bunkers where the rubble appears to have been deposited by tides or currents. The banks are each around 1 to 2 meters high. There is

nothing more rewarding than swimming up one to find a manta ray on top waiting to meet you! The mantas come here for cleaning and feeding when the water is plankton-rich. For cleaning, the mantas find a patch of coral to circle or hover over whilst the smaller reef fish go to work. If you stay low down to the bottom and remain calm and still, you can enjoy long and rewarding encounters. On good days, up to 20 mantas are seen here in one dive. For more manta ray information, see the Marine Life Feature and guidelines for diving with manta rays in the Bali chapter, page 59.

KOMODO: BATU BOLONG

This iconic Komodo site offers the chance to see hoards of fish, stunning, vibrant colors, huge schools of fish and large pelagics. But because there can be

Biomass in Komodo is phenomenal and huge schools of fusiliers are a common sight in the blue.

strong up and down currents, the dive site is for experienced divers only.

Current is visible from the surface hitting either the north or south side of the rock that marks the site. The south side is a craggy steep slope whilst the north side showcases a steep sheer wall with rifts, faults and interesting formations. Whichever side you dive, you can be guaranteed dense fish biomass, excellent coral coverage and an adrenaline-pumping dive.

Upon dropping in on the lee side of the pinnacle, the shallows are a myriad of dancing, weaving and darting colored antheas, fairy basslets and damsels that shimmer in the light. As you progress down the pinnacle, it is difficult to know how to allocate

Above Batfish such as the one pictured here are often seen in small groups over Komodo's reefs.

Left This tiny bobtail squid is one of Komodo's nocturnal critters often seen on night dives.

Below Every coral and space in Komodo appears to be harboring life, such as this big eye.

your time. The surrounding blue is packed with thousands of streaming neon fusiliers and clouds of red toothed triggerfish and surgeons. Larger predators, such as giant trevallies, tuna, Spanish mackerel, barracuda and occasionally sharks, pass through or hang out in the blue surveying the action.

Stay close to the reef which is littered with scorpionfish, nudibranchs and sheltering lionfish. In the 15 meter upward range, parrotfish, Moorish idols, large sweetlips, emperorfish, blue fin trevally and pyramid butterfly fish busily dart around the reef. The sheer volume of fish is phenomenal, and when coupled with the kaleidoscopic reef itself this is not a dive to miss. For those who love current diving, this is a site to really get your juices flowing.

KOMODO: TATAWA KECIL

This is an underwater playground off the northeast coast of Komodo comprising swim-throughs, ledges and overhangs formed by a multitude of large boulders haphazardly strewn around the base of the rock pinnacle of Tatawa Kecil. Currents can make this a challenging dive, but entering on the lee side of the pinnacle makes it manageable and a lot of fun, and with passing pelagics and dense schools of fish it is well worth it!

If the current is coming from the north, drop in on the south lee side close to the island and head down relatively quickly to the plateau area at 16 meters, which attracts schools of snappers, neon fusiliers and larger solitary fish. Look out for huge Napoleon wrasse, reef sharks, turtles, giant trevally, large groupers and jacks. At 20–25 meters there is a collection of crevices and clefts that can harbor anything from white tip reef sharks to cleaner shrimp. Heading east at 18 meters there are some swim-throughs, and at 15 meters is an almost entirely open-sided cavern housing schools of batfish and sweetlips.

Upwards of 15 meters, fish life is phenomenal. Schooling fairy basslets fight the current, lone titan triggerfish hover menacingly, and clown triggerfish, angelfish, Moorish idols and coral cods swim about the reef under curtains of yellow back fusiliers that sweep past overhead. This is a beautiful site packed with unique topographical features and stunning corals. Abundant fish life and passing pelagics are the icing on the cake!

KOMODO: CASTLE ROCK
☆ AUTHOR'S CHOICE

Another iconic northern Komodo site, this is a submerged seamount famed for sharks, pelagics and intense current. Castle Rock is dived according to the direction of the current. The lee side is most sheltered, but if you are here to see pelagics, your chances of doing so increase along with the current.

The seamount pinnacle is at 4 to 5 meters and the best entry is to drop in upcurrent from the pinnacle onto the side of the mount. A negative entry and quick descent are important to avoid being swept back and up over the top of the

Komodo

This magnificent anemone is host to several false clownfish, including juveniles.

These two manta ray alfredi are juveniles measuring only around 1.5 meters across.

The batfish is a shy fish species but is incredibly photogenic.

mount. Currents push both up and down, so stay within reaching distance of the reef. The east side extends to around 27 meters and the west side is in excess of 30 meters. Shallower dives are possible.

The dive profile is relatively simple. Head down to your maximum depth and watch the blue! White tip, black tip and grey reef sharks patrol the deeper sections. Giant trevally, tuna, Napoleons and Spanish mackerel are also visitors here,

Below The map puffer has very distinctive maze-like markings.

Bottom The ornate harlequin ghost pipefish is highly attractive to photographers.

together with schooling jacks and fusiliers in droves. The reef is a mix of hard corals: short-cropped branching corals, abundant plate corals, stubby fire corals, patches of rubble and colorful algae-covered boulders. Allow plenty of time for your ascent up to the pinnacle, particularly when the current is strong. From 15 meters up, the reef is a riot of color. Large angular boulders are encrusted with flat hard corals, sea squirts and small branching corals. The sheer volume of reef fish is impressive. Brightly colored antheas, damsels and basslets persistently battle the current. Keep glancing overhead as schools of fish stream through oblivious to the diving activities around them.

This is a popular site, so expect to see other divers if you are diving here from July to September.

KOMODO: THE CAULDRON

This site is not for the faint-hearted. With currents spiraling up through faults in the reef, streaming overhead and rushing by a sinkhole (from which the site takes its name), and with topographical features named the Shot Gun and Sling Shot, it is an adrenaline-pumping ride from start to finish.

The site lies in the passage between the two islands of Gili Lawa Laut and Gili Lawa Darat, and bottoms out to a large sinkhole (cauldron) reaching 22 meters. On a high tide, the entry point is on the southeast point of Gili Lawa Laut over a pretty white sand sloping reef. The sinkhole sits slightly to the west. The walled edges on the north side are uneven, with ledges, overhangs, faults and crevices covered with every type of soft and hard coral. Reef sharks, giant trevally, schooling jacks, tuna and even manta alfredi can be spotted here. Cross the channel to the opposite south side where there is a

Above The view over Gili Lawa Laut in Komodo is spectacular all year round.

Left This dolphin shark was pictured in the Komodo Marine Park, a frequent sight.

Below Komodo is not just for big fish. There is a huge diversity amongst smaller species too.

rubble plateau at 12 meters. Settle down and watch schooling yellow back fusiliers, jacks and larger predators. Follow the plateau back to where it tapers to a point with an upwards channel in the cleft of the wall from 12 up to 5 meters. Water runs across the plateau and is funneled up the cleft at an astonishing rate, giving this feature its name, the Shot Gun. This section needs to be approached with caution. Look ahead for your next hand hold and enjoy the exhilarating feeling of traversing up the shoot from one grip to the next. Once you have reached the top of the cleft, the currents can be strong as they rush over the reef top, but there is nothing that equals the rush of 'flying' over the reef before coming to a stop in the calm back eddying shallow waters on the south side of Gili Lawa Laut. It is an incredible ending to a challenging roller-coaster ride!

FLORES: SABOLAN KECIL

Located to the north of Flores Island, this site boasts a decent variety of coral, good macro opportunities and frequent schools of larger fish. It is particularly suitable for beginners and for those who do not favor strong currents.

Start on the south side of Sabolan Kecil at the east end, heading west. Two

Reef Manta Rays *Manta alfredi*

The ventral (belly) side of a manta ray has dark markings which are unique to individuals, just like fingerprints.

Manta rays are amongst the most majestic, enigmatic and unique creatures of our oceans. Historically, little has been known about them and it was only relatively recently that scientists discovered there are two distinct species: reef mantas (*Manta alfredi*) and giant or oceanic mantas (*Manta birostris*). Both harmless, reef mantas are smaller, with pectoral fin spans of up to 5.5 meters, whilst oceanic mantas have fin spans up to 7.5 meters. Mantas have spot patterns on their ventral sides (underside) which act much like fingerprints and make it possible to identify individuals as each spot pattern is unique.

Both species of Manta are seen around Indonesia but the majority of sightings are reef mantas. Reef mantas are non-migratory, they live in relatively large populations and they inhabit specific areas where they clean and feed. They are plankton feeders and their unique cephalic fins (the two fins that spiral down on the front of the manta's head) make them very efficient feeders. The fins can be moved

independently of each other to direct and maximize the flow of plankton into the mouth. In areas where there is a particularly rich concentration of plankton, the mantas are often seen barrel rolling (turning somersaults). This enables them to stay in the same spot collecting large quantities of plankton whilst dispersing as little of it as possible.

The manta ray's size, body shape and method of propulsion make it incomparable to other rays, and its cloaked appearance as it gracefully flies through the water is a humbling sight to behold. During mating, one female will be pursued by up to 25 males which will emulate her movements with precision (known as a mating train) until one male manages to catch onto her pectoral fin with its teeth. When mating, the mantas move into a belly to belly position and after mating they immediately separate. Mating is the only time when male mantas use their tiny teeth, known as denticles.

Manta rays in Indonesia are threatened by both targeted fishing, fishing lines and nets which they become entangled in, irresponsible tourism and injuries from boat propellers. As manta rays take years to reach sexual maturity, an entire population can become threatened very easily and in an astonishingly short time.

If you are visiting an area known for manta rays in Indonesia, read the guidelines for diving with manta rays in the Bali chapter, page 59.

small seamounts are to the south of the main sloping reef rising up from the sand at the point where the sloping reef bottoms out. Dive along the slope, around the two mounts and back onto the slope.

The reef starts at 5 meters with medium density coral coverage sloping down to white sand densely populated by garden eels at 30 meters. Coral species include gorgonian fans, black corals, barrel sponges, boulder and leather corals and soft cauliflower corals. Schooling fusiliers, surgeonfish and batfish cruise through the blue and pygmy seahorses occupy the fans. In the shallows, aggregations of damselfish crowd close to the reef and bottom dwellers, including scorpionfish, crocodilefish and nudibranchs, sit on the occasional rubble patches.

The seamounts peak at 16 and 18 meters and feature picturesque anemones. Schooling bannerfish hover in the blue and blue spotted stingrays nestle on the sand. Schools of barracuda are also known to pass through. Heading back to the slope, there is a bommie at 18 meters which is entirely shrouded by glassfish weaving in and out of one another with the synchronization of a well-practiced ballet. This is a great site for variety and a break from stronger currents.

FLORES: SABOLAN BESAR

This is an easy sloping reef site with good macro and critter life, giant clams and turtles in the shallows, and is suitable and enjoyable for all levels.

Above right These bright, colorful soft corals were pictured with the sun overhead in Komodo.

Right It is not unusual to find huge schools of glassfish around coral bommies across Komodo.

The site is a gentle drift along the east side of Sabolan Besar. The sloping reef extends down to 18 meters where it peters out to white sand with sporadic coral bommies. The reef displays a good mix of corals: leathers, plates, sponges, whips and various other soft corals. In the blue, neon fusiliers cruise by through clouds of red toothed triggerfish. Angelfish, damsels, scissortail gobies and Moorish idols all swim in and out of the corals adding splashes of color to the sloping reef. Fish life is not abundant but it is varied and rubble patches and anemones make good homes for critter life. Anemone shrimps, porcelain crabs, nudibranchs, lionfish, moray eels and reef

octopus are frequently seen. Highlights of this site include a collection of giant clams and blue spotted rays, and as you progress up to the shallower water, turtles are seen foraging on the reef.

FLORES: SABAYOR

This fringing, sloping reef dive site lies on the north side of Sabayor Island which is located midway between Komodo and Flores. It features a rubble slope to the east, a white sand bottom which eagle rays frequent and, to the west, a plateau atop a curved wall that attracts schooling fish.

Above Blue spotted stingrays are a frequent sighting at Sabolan Besar in Komodo.

Below One of the draws of diving Castle Rock is that the deeper areas are patrolled by white tip reef sharks.

Check for current and dive the site in the direction of the water movement. Starting from the east, the reef top is at around 5 meters, giving way to a rubble slope which extends down to 25 meters. As you head west, the bottom deepens to around 45 meters at the base of the wall. The rubble slope is an excellent place for critters, and where the slope meets the sand bottom look out for garden eels waving in the current. Heading west, fish biomass, coral density and coral quality increase as the reef steepens into what is named the Mini Wall, which curves in and out forming recesses, ledges and overhangs for cleaner shrimp, glassfish and other shade dwellers. The wall boasts a good variety of corals, including large sponges, barrels (look out for hairy squat lobsters), plates and boulders. A variety of reef fishes cruise by along with impressively sized groupers and emperorfish. Schools of surgeonfish, yellow back and neon fusiliers stream by in the blue. Aim to stay along the top of the wall where a plateau at around 15 meter is a great spot for watching action in the blue. For those who prefer critters, there is a mix of coral and rubble harboring numerous creatures. From the plateau, there is a gentle slope to the shallows for the safety stop.

KOMODO AND FLORES
TRAVEL PLANNER

In the past, long boat rides deterred many divers from signing up with shore-based operations. However, Blue Marlin Komodo has introduced purpose-built speedboat trips to the area and Castle Rock and Karang Makassar are now a comfortable 50 minutes away. The entire Komodo National Park can be accessed on a daily basis, with three dive trips, returning by mid-afternoon.

Seasonal winds dictate which areas of the park are dived when. From May to October, winds blowing from the south mean that operators favor the central and northern sites. The southern sites are dived more from December to March when the prevailing winds are from the north. November and April are transitional months.

Diving in the park requires entry permits which are available for single days or three-day durations. Many operators include the marine park fee in their packages.

Annual temperatures range from as low as 20 degrees in the south up to 28 degrees in the north. A 5 mm long suit is recom-

mended. The visibility range is from 30 meters plus in the north to a minimum of 10 meters in the south. Most operators are open all year round.

For advanced divers wanting to experience some of the more challenging sites, a reef hook is useful but not imperative. An SMB should be considered a requirement for all.

Recommended Operators
Labuan Bajo Dive Operators

Blue Marlin Komodo (Authors Choice) Jalan Soekarno-Hatta. Facilities include speedboat operated 3 dive trips, PADI courses with designated student boat, accommodation, purpose-built dive training pool, equipment hire, restaurant, bar, dive and stay packages. They also operate the *Ikan Biru* liveaboard (see page 188). Boats are equipped with GPS and VHF radios. Tel: +62 (0) 81237757892. www.bluemarlin-komodo.com. Email: info@bluemarlin-komodo.com.

Blue Marlin Komodo in Labuan Bajo offer daily dive trips, training facilities and a full service dive center.

Above Blue Marlin Komodo's accommodation has stunning views over the harbor in Labuan Bajo.

Above right Blue Marlin operate a purpose-built speedboat which can access all areas of the park in day trips.

Right Accommodation at Blue Marlin Komodo is spacious, comfortable and tasteful.

Wicked Diving Jalan Soekarno-Hatta. Offers day trips, liveaboard and dive training. Tel: +62 (0) 81337182258. www.wicked-diving.com/komodo.

Dive Komodo Jalan Soekarno-Hatta. Day trips, liveaboard and dive training. Tel +62 (0) 38541862. www.divekomodo.com.

Liveaboards

Ikan Biru A modified traditional wooden *phinisi* boat catering for 8 recreational divers or 6 rebreather divers. *Ikan Biru* operates on a hop-on, hop-off basis with tailored packages and private charters available. Sleeping arrangements are on the comfortable upper deck under the stars. GPS, VHF radio, oxygen and life raft on board. Experienced professional team accommodating all levels. Tel: +62 (0) 8123766496. www.ikanbaru.com. Email: info@ikanbaru.com.

Seven Seas Traditionally built sailing schooner offering luxurious 12 to 14 night trips, 8 state rooms for up to 16 guests. Nitrox available, experienced sailing and diving crew. www.thesevenseas.net. Email: info@thesevenseas.net.

(See also Liveaboard Options for Nusa Tenggara, pages 158–9.)

Accommodation

Blue Marlin Komodo Well located on the main street. Comfortable rooms with AC, hot water, TV/DVD, private balconies, wi-fi throughout resort, swimming pool, bar, restaurant, breakfast included. $$.

The Bintang Flores Hotel Jalan Pantai Pede. Labuan Bajo's most luxurious hotel. $$$. Tel: +62 (0) 3852443755. www.bintangflores-hotel.com. Email: info@bintangflores-hotel.com.

A range of budget homestays and guest houses in Labuan Bajo are bookable on arrival. Many do not have websites.

Diving Timor
City Break Dives and Freshwater Caves

Timor Island's capital city Kupang offers a number of dive sites. Whilst they cannot compete with neighboring Alor, they are ideal for those staying in the city who want a day or two of easy diving. Marine life in Kupang is not abundant and there is some reef damage but blue spotted stingrays flourish here along with a range of critters and macro life. Inland, the Oehani and Kristal freshwater cave systems are the real highlight of the area and at present they offer the only known cavern diving opportunities in Indonesia. For cave diving enthusiasts, Kupang is a must.

Kupang has a population of under 400,000 (2010 census) and is developing rapidly with a collection of new hotels being constructed around the bay area together with an international hospital, restaurants and other facilities. Kupang historically was, and still is, a major trading port with a bustling harbor.

Timor has the driest climate of the East Nusa Tenggara islands and, depending on what time of year you visit, the landscape varies from being brown, parched and arid looking to surprisingly lush, green and fertile. Timor's largely limestone foundations provide for some rugged and craggy cliffs and limestone pavements. Bananas, coconuts and corn all grow well in Timor's arid climate.

As the provincial capital, Kupang employs many people in administrative positions. Cement production and the main commercial and passenger port are also major employers. Subsistence farming and fishing support many and fish is also exported internationally from Kupang.

Fish is the main dietary protein in Timor but chicken and beef are offered on most menus. Kupang fare is simple and spicy. A local specialty is beef or pork *se'i* composed of strips of meat flavored with

salt and spices before being smoked over an open fire. The result is a jerky-like product which is used in many dishes.

Travel around Kupang is by taxi or *bemo*. The town area is relatively small and follows the main coastal road that runs past the original harbor to the new port.

The people of Timor are a mix of Muslims and Christians who speak Bahasa Indonesia. English is generally not well understood but the local people are friendly and approachable. Foreign tourist numbers are low. Kupang attracts many domestic travelers and business people and is hoping to develop foreign tourism in the future.

Schooling fusiliers such as these are a common sight across Nusa Tenggara.

Yellow margin moray eels such as this one are frequently spotted around Timor Island.

HIGHLIGHTS Stingrays are regularly seen and divers can enjoy having dive sites to themselves. The Kristal and Oehani Cave systems in Bolok are a major attraction for cave diving enthusiasts.

LOGISTICS Timor's airport is located just outside of the East Nusa Tenggara provincial capital of Kupang, which offers a range of accommodation from international standard hotels to smaller homestays. Kupang Airport (KOE) is serviced by numerous domestic airlines. There are no international flights into Kupang and transit is usually via Jakarta or Bali. Diving is only available through Dive Kupang Dive (see page 196), who will handle all logistics.

DIFFICULTY LEVEL Timor's sites offer very easy diving conditions: little current, warm water and a range of topographies. They are ideal sites for beginners and learners.

TIMOR'S BEST DIVE SITES

RAY REVIEW

This is a good site for ray sightings and an opportunity to take in the stunning coastline of Semau Island. The site is located on the northern coast of Semau on the eastern extension that stretches out towards Timor. Entry is made in the center of the coastline in the shallows where the reef top is relatively flat at around 5 meters. The reef slopes from 5 meters down to around 25 meters where it levels out into a sandy white bottom. The dive follows the sloping reef heading east towards Timor Island. The main attraction here is stingrays, so staying on the sandy bottom where it meets the sloping reef provides for best sightings and also means an easy swim up the reef as your no-stop time decreases. As you progress to the east, the sandy bottom shallows up to around 18 meters, and as you follow the reef along, the density of corals and amount of fish life tends to increase. The sloping reef is predominantly hard coral at depth. It has sustained some damage, particularly on the western end at the start of the dive. The sand bottom has some interesting coral formations, particularly near the base of the slope, with a handful of good sized gorgonians, boulder corals, some tables and brain corals all interspersed with soft varieties. As you start to make your way gradually up the reef, continue heading east, and at around 12 meters the corals become increasingly soft, with healthy leather corals, tubers and ferns taking precedence. Fish life also increases as you shallow up. Moorish idols flit around the reef, long fin batfish are frequently seen here as

LUCKY DIP Keep an eye out above you at Ray's Review as eagle rays and mobula rays are occasionally seen 'flying' overhead.

are clown triggerfish, juvenile midnight snappers, parrotfish and groupers. Smaller reef fish, such as damsels and basslets, aggregate over table corals. Butterfly fish dart in and out of the reef and feather stars sit proudly on some of the larger coral bommies. Finish the dive by continuing up the reef to make your safety stop on the soft coral garden reef crest.

DONOVAN'S DELIGHT
☆AUTHOR'S CHOICE

This is a seamount site with an inverted wall and good critter life. The top of the seamount sits at around 5 meters and is visible from the surface. It is marked by a large, steel warning buoy. The site was named by Kal Muller after Donovan

Whitford, an Alor and Kupang diving pioneer and the only operator currently based on Timor. Entry is best made at the buoy, which also serves as a boat mooring and provides a descent line (chain). Follow the buoy chain down to the reef at 8 meters where it slopes to 12 meters before becoming a wall which drops to flat reef and sand at approximately 20 meters. As you swim west along the wall, the bottom becomes deeper until the wall base is 30 meters plus. The deeper section of wall inverts beyond vertical, creating an interesting overhang situation. Coral coverage is healthy with a mix of tubers and other short soft corals and sponges. Look out for giant frogfish here, numerous lionfish and schools of cardinalfish hiding out in the branches of black coral

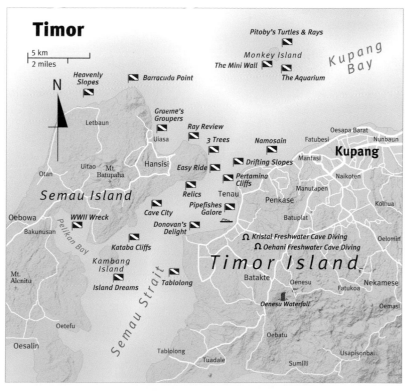

Kupang Cave Diving With Donovan Whitford and Dive Kupang Dive

Cave diving in Indonesia is hard to find, and it is possible that Kupang is the only place in the archipelago where divers can descend into the depths of caves as long as 500 meters. At the time of writing, two caves are available for diving but more cave sites are being explored on both Kupang and neighboring Semau Island by the pioneer of diving and cave diving in Kupang, Donovan Whitford. Australian-born Whitford, the owner of both Dive Kupang Dive and Dive Alor Dive is also a diving Instructor with over 1,000 dives in Kupang and 4,500 dives in Alor under his belt. He has been exploring the cave systems here since 1992.

Dive Kupang Dive offer two cave dives of differing difficulty levels, both of which have relatively easy access, wide tunnels and reasonably comfortable conditions. Both Kristal Cave and Oehani Cave offer divers up to 50 meters of visibility, a variety of limestone tunnels and passages, narrow swim-through points, air chambers, pools of glimmering light, shell-encrusted walls, crystal calcite stalactites and submerged tunnels up to 15 meters deep approximately 35 meters below ground level.

Oehani Cave is a 500-meter-long sink-hole with three air chambers whilst Kristal Cave is a 75-meter-long tunnel with one submerged chamber and one final air chamber (see page 195). Year round water temperature is approximately 27 degrees

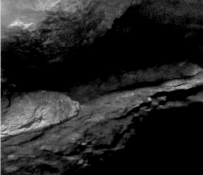

Above left Donovan Whitford is seen in the distance checking the entry point to Oehani Cave in Kupang.

Above right Kristal Cave is the easiest cave in Kupang but it still involves some steep inclines and narrow spaces.

Far right The underwater tunnels of Kristal Cave are studded with fossilized shells.

The cave pond of the Kristal Cave, when viewed from overhead, is truly crystal clear.

but a long suit is recommended for protection. Percolation, the process whereby divers' exhaust bubbles strike the ceiling or walls of the cave disturbing silt which then reduces visibility, is not a significant issue in either cave, making them both suitable for open circuit scuba. Both caves have haloclines within the passageways,

which is where waters with differing salinity levels meet, causing a surface-like mirage which, whilst being stunningly beautiful when viewed from below, can cause reduced visibility and disorientation. The dive profiles for the caves involves slowly progressing through the caves without stopping on the way in so as not to stir up the fine sediment that lies on the bottom and reduce visibility. On the way out, more time is spent stopping and looking at the walls and formations. Kristal Cave has fossilized shell-encrusted walls, physical evidence of historical tectonic actions forcing what was at sea level upwards and forming the island of Kupang and the numerous other islands of the Nusa Tenggara chain.

Kristal Cave is the easier of the two caves, with wider tunnels and easier access. Oehani Cave is more suited to experienced cave divers as access is more difficult and some tunnels are quite narrow. Side-mount equipment configuration would be beneficial but is not a necessity.

Dive Kupang Dive offers guided tours of both caves as well as dealing with logistics such as accommodation, transport, tanks, weights and equipment hire, if necessary, although bringing your own gear if you have it is strongly recommended.

Donovan has discovered a passion for cave diving which he says comes from 'the feeling of doing something unique and which can only be done in select areas of the world'. He has now led many divers through Kupang's underground passages.

that drape, web-like, from the wall.
Out from the reef, fish life is good, with schooling juvenile surgeons and fusiliers and mature yellow back fusiliers cruising through, injecting a ribbon of color to the blue. Follow the path of the wall whilst watching your no-stop time and gradually shallowing up. The top of the wall remains at 12 meters, and as you approach this depth start to move back onto the slope and flat area on the top of the seamount. Take some time to inspect the barrel sponges here, which are heavily laden with sea cucumbers living in symbiosis with the sponge, and look for lionfish lying well camouflaged against the barrels' outer edges. There are several rubble areas which are excellent places to find mantis shrimps and scorpionfish, and check for blue spotted rays hiding under some of the bommie skirts. The rubble patches are also home to some unusual nudibranch species, including several species of Flabellina, so look closely!

Clear cleaner shrimps like this one are found in recesses at the Pertamina Cliffs dive site.

PERTAMINA CLIFFS

This is a sloping reef dive with a lower wall section offering interesting folds and recesses that harbor good critter life. The upper reef sections have more abundant fish life and a reasonable variety of species.

This dive site is located on the eastern side of the channel that runs between the islands of Timor and Semau. It is slightly south of the Pertamina Port, from which it takes its name, just out from the cliffs. Entry is made in the shallow areas that are clearly visible from the surface as the sandy patches on the top of the reef are only 2 meters deep. Enter further out to the channel where the reef starts to drop away. The dive follows the slope of the reef east, with the reef on your right-hand side. This is a reasonably steep slope of 45 degrees which starts at 5 meters and continues down to 20 meters, at which point it becomes a mini wall down to 30 meters. The wall has some good recesses which are often bursting with cardinalfish that mask the cleaner shrimps, critters and pipefish hiding in the shade behind.

Above Ray's Review dive site lives up to its name and is home to many blue spotted stingrays.

Right The emperor angelfish is one of many angelfish species seen across Nusa Tenggara.

As you start to make your way east, slowly work your way up the wall and then back to the slope. Fish life here is good, with schools of juvenile fusiliers and mature yellow backs in the blue. The reef boasts some good gorgonian fans, whips and hard coral bommies that provide hide- outs for blue spotted stingrays, spiny lobsters, mantis shrimps and occasional turtles. On the sporadic rubble sections, look out for nudibranchs, gobies, phenomenal amounts of mushroom corals and juvenile batfish cruising in and out of the reef. There are some good sponge corals here, and as you shallow up the coral becomes predominantly staghorn coral with interspersed soft coral growths. In the 10 meter range, parrotfish, Moorish idols, damsels and butterfly fish brighten up the scene. When peering into the branches of the staghorns, look out for eyes peering back at you!

KRISTAL CAVE

Timor is one of the only places in Indonesia where cave diving is available: freshwater, 50 meters of visibility, occasional freshwater life, consistently stunning topography and a bit of an adventure!

Kristal Cave is a freshwater cave dive that begins from a cave pond at around 35 meters below ground level. After clambering down into the base of the cave, gearing up is done in the pond's surprisingly warm water. A guide line is in place, running from the entry pond to the final air chamber, which is around 75 meters away through a system of tunnels and submerged chambers. Once you have entered the cave, there are no air spaces

TIMOR TRAVEL PLANNER

Timor's dive sites are located around the channel between the islands of Semau and Timor with a few off Monkey Island to the north. The freshwater caves are 15 minutes driving time from Kupang town center in Bolok.

Water temperature ranges from 26 to 29 degrees and visibility from 10 to 20 meters. Reduction in visibility usually follows rainfall. Freshwater cave diving has a similar temperature range but visibility reaches up to 50 meters.

A 3 mm to 5 mm wetsuit is recommended and it is preferable to bring your own gear if you have it.

There is a public hospital in Kupang, Rumah Sakit Umung, which holds a good

supply of medical grade oxygen. An international hospital is currently being built. The nearest recompression chamber is in Denpasar, Bali.

Kupang offers a good mix of open water sites and freshwater caves. Whilst the diving here is reasonable, the quality of the reefs and fish numbers do not compare to nearby Alor. Kupang is excellent for beginners, those who do not want the challenge of Alor's currents or those who simply do not have the time to get over to Alor.

Recommended Operators

Diving

Dive Kupang Dive (Author's Choice) Based in Kupang since 1992, offers fun dive trips, PADI courses and freshwater cave diving. Hotel pick-up and drop-off service, domestic flight and accommodation booking (from basic to luxury), equipment hire available. Booking in advance is required, services available in English and Bahasa Indonesian. Tel: +62 (0) 8123960107. www.DiveKupangDive.com. Email: info@ DiveKupangDive.com.

Accommodation

Hotel La Hasienda Newly built hotel accommodation five minutes from the airport, nicely furnished rooms with AC and hot water, airport pick-ups, restaurant, wi-fi throughout, breakfasts included. $. Tel: +62 (0) 3808552717. www.Hotellahasienda.com.

Hotel On The Rock Jalan Raya Timor No. 2 Kelapa Lima, Kupang. International standard hotel situated five minutes from Kupang city center with ocean views, swimming pool, all rooms with AC, hot water, wi-fi, tea/coffee facilities and TV, business center, conference rooms, restaurant, fitness center and spa. $$$ Tel: +62 (0) 3808586100; www.ontherockhotel.com. Email: reservation@ontherockhotel.com.

Below Hotel La Hasienda in Kupang has a family feel and provides excellent service and comfortable accommodation.

Bottom Hotel La Hasienda offers conveniently located accommodation close to the airport—perfect for those transitioning to Alor.

The author exploring the final air chamber of Kristal Cave.

Kristal Cave's entry pond is so clear it almost creates a mirror-like illusion.

until the final air chamber as the entire tunnel system is within the water table. The initial descent is in the cave pond down to the opening of the first tunnel, which is at 5 meters. This first tunnel reaches a maximum depth of 12 meters and freshwater eels are sometimes spotted. After approximately a 20 meter swim, the tunnel opens up into a halocline chamber where two different salinities of water meet. This can cause visual disturbance. Continue through the chamber into the second tunnel section which slopes steeply upwards to a comparatively narrow opening, taking you up into the base of the air chamber pool. When navigating the narrow gap, be careful of your first stage hitting the cave ceiling. It helps to rotate onto your back as you swim through. Once into the base of the air chamber, the surface is visible overhead. The air chamber is approximately 20 meters in diameter and it is possible to exit the water here onto rocks. Occasional juvenile bats flit around in the

chamber, but there is no access to the outdoors. That is only possible by navigating back through the tunnel system to the entry point. On the way back, you can take more time. In the final tunnel on the exit route, look closely at the cave walls to see the fossilized shells and hanging crystals. This also makes for an excellent pass time during your safety stop before making the final ascent up to the entry pond. The pool of light overhead on the way out is quite spectacular! (See also Kupang Cave Diving, pages 192–3.)

Diving Alor
An Explosion of Life and Color

Diving in Alor is like opening the lid of a treasure trove and peering inside for the first time, a kaleidoscope of colors and a plethora of hidden gems that simply take your breath away. It may not be the easiest place to access, and facilities are very limited in comparison to other areas, but this is one of Indonesia's most stunning underwater archipelagos. Alor seems to have everything: sharks, critters, rays, dolphins, whale sightings, pristine reefs, adrenalin-pumping currents, astonishing visibility and not another dive boat in sight. Diving in Alor is well worth every bit of the journey to get there, and more.

The only town on Alor is Kalabahi which has a population of around 150,000. There are a couple of very basic local hotels, a local hospital and a range of small shops and *warung*. Facilities for tourists are extremely limited. If you cannot manage without luxury accommodation, this may not be the best destination for you. There are ATMs in Kalabahi and a handful of *warung* have wifi.

The people of Alor are predominantly Christian and the way of life is generally subsistence farming and fishing. The main industries on Alor are pearl farming in Kalahabi Bay and agriculture. Corn, coconuts, vanilla and almonds are grown here. Despite the phenomenal diving, tourism has yet to develop, perhaps due to the limited facilities currently available.

Bahasa Indonesia is taught in the education system but the main daily spoken language is Alor-Malay. Basic English is understood by some but not many.

Left Pearls from the Alor archipelago are sold in Jakarta as well as exported internationally.

Below The reefs of the Alor archipelago teem with spectacular life and color.

Left Local children in Kalabahi Bay are curious and start learning water skills early.

Below Kalabahi Bay is the entry point to diving Alor. It is millpond flat and used for pearl farming.

Alor is remote. The nearest hyperbaric chamber is in Bali, and whilst the public hospitals on both Alor and Kupang are capable of managing minor injuries, health care is not of Western standards.

DIFFICULTY LEVEL Alor is known for strong currents, making it best suited to experienced divers. However, some sites, if timed correctly, are suitable for divers of all levels but currents here are unpredictable and can change with little warning.

HIGHLIGHTS World class coral reefs, stunning walls, visibility in excess of 40 meters, abundant fish life and exhilarating currents with big pelagic opportunities. Dolphin pods are frequently seen and whales are known to pass through.

LOGISTICS Alor is approximately 2,800 square kilometers, which makes it the largest island of the Alor archipelago. Alor's Mali Airport (ARD) is currently only accessed via Kupang on Timor Island, which is only serviced domestically, so transiting through Bali or Jakarta is necessary. Flights from Kupang to Alor take 45 minutes and booking tickets from outside of Indonesia can be tricky. Many operators will handle this for you.

ALOR'S BEST DIVE SITES

THE FISH BOWL

The Fish Bowl is one site that definitely lives up to its name because of its abundant marine life, schooling fish and a kaleidoscopic coral wall.

The dive site, which runs from north to south, is situated off Alor Island to the north of the channel that separates Kepa and Alor. Currents can run quite fast here, making this an exhilarating drift. The reef slopes down from 8 meters before giving way to a vertical wall that is separated into two differing depth segments. The northernmost part of the wall begins at approximately 24 meters and extends down to 50 meters. The southern end of the wall begins at just 10 meters and drops to 18 meters. Where the two differing levels meet, there is a sharp fault that cuts up through the reef. To get the maximum allowable time on the wall, start on the north end and head south. This allows you to cover the deeper section first. Once you have covered both segments of the wall, move up onto the sloping reef and head back north, explor-

Traditional fishing traps are used in Alor by the local people who fish for subsistence.

Alor

10 km
5 miles

N

Half

Cave Poir

Bana
Pandai

Munasely

Pantar *Topsy Turvy*

The Arch

Pantar Wall

Bab

Wai Lawar

Kabir

Symphony #9

Pleasant Surprise

Pantar Timur

Paradise Point

The Backyard

Pura

Mt. Tuntuli

Mike's De

Bandar

The Boardroom

School'

Pantar Island

Current Alley

A Breeze

Sharks Ga

Abang Iwang

Neverland

Sla City

Tamalabang

Kelelaka Point

Sea Apple Slopes

The C

To'ang

Bay Watch

Pantar Strait

2 B (

Tama

---

ing the slope. Gradually shallow up as you go. The deeper wall is a vertical drop with a dense covering of short-cropped hard corals, small barrels and a range of sponges. Neon fusiliers stream past in flowing ribbon-like formations in the blue along with lone titan triggerfish and midnight snappers. As you traverse onto the shallow wall, look out for scorpionfish nestled down in soft corals, small fans, branching black corals and oversized ribbon sweetlips gathered around the base of the wall where it inverts beyond vertical. The slope is a good mix of soft and hard corals of intense density and color. Schooling fairy basslets and blue yellow damsels swim into the current close to the reef adding flashes of brightness to the already vibrant scene. Red toothed triggerfish school in the blue and Moorish idols, angelfish and butterflyish flit by, adding more layers to this stunning reefscape.

From 12 meters up, soft corals dominate, including patches of elephant ear corals, whips, ferns and tubers. The light here on sunny days is phenomenal and the rays penetrating through the crystal clear water make for some excellent photography opportunities.

This dive clearly demonstrates just how alive a reef can be. There is a good chance of passing pelagics also, but even in their absence this stands out as a top class site.

KAL'S DREAM
☆ AUTHOR'S CHOICE

This seamount, located in between the islands of Kepa and Pura, was named after Indonesian diving pioneer Kal Muller in the early 1990s when he first explored the Alor area with Donovan and Graeme Whitford. The schooling fish, passing large pelagics, sweeping currents and diversity of marine life that appealed to him back then still make this site a dream today.

The seamount can be subject to strong currents sweeping over the top, so stay

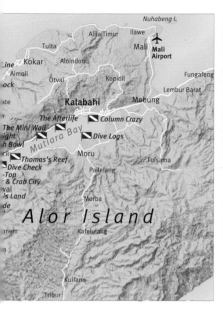

Bushy feather stars often attach themselves to sea fans to obtain a better position in the current.

close to the reef, descend quickly and be prepared to hold on.

The top of the seamount is a rock pinnacle which peaks at just 5 meters. When the currents are running here, a negative entry is necessary to ensure that you hit the top of the mount. If the currents are fast, enter upcurrent of the pinnacle and start descending down the west side of the mount's sloping reef straight away. Once you have descended onto the sheltered slope, the current slackens off but can still be a powerful force. Follow the reef as it drops away to the northwest to around 30 meters and look out to the blue. Spanish mackerel, various shark species, giant trevallies, dog tooth tuna, barracuda and schooling jacks are frequent visitors amongst the densely populated schools of red toothed triggerfish, fusiliers and surgeonfish. Watch your no-stop time and make your way back up the slope. There is a 12 meter plateau around the southern tip of the pinnacle which is a combination

of rocky boulders and formations covered with algae, plate and other close-cropped corals. The plateau makes an excellent area for observing hunting blue fin trevally as well as boasting some interesting critter life hiding in the crevices between the rocks. Look out for a variety of moray eels, reef octopus, scorpionfish, nudibranchs and shrimps. Work your way back up the pinnacle for the safety stop. The pinnacle is subject to strong currents coming over the reef so finding a suitable place to hold on may be necessary.

MIKE'S DELIGHT

A sloping reef drift dive on the east coast of Pura Island with a range of topographical features including bommies, boulders, ledges, drop-offs and beautiful staghorn coral fields.

The reef starts at around 8 meters and slopes initially down to 15 meters where there are large boulder formations. Visibility here can range up to 40 meters and the reef is bursting with life and

Branching corals hide all manner of life, Alor such as this scorpionfish and a spotted guard crab.

color. Hard and soft corals decorate the slope and their colors are accentuated by the contrasting silhouetted red toothed triggers, glimmering neon fusiliers and bright pyramid butterfly fish out in the blue. The reef is a display of barrels, anemones, brain corals, branching corals and plates all interspersed with soft coral clusters. From the entry point, mid-Pura Island, follow the current south towards the tip of the island. On days when the currents are strong, it is actually possible to round the tip of the island.

Descend down the reef to 25 to 30 meters. Passing pelagics and dolphin pods are seen at these depths. As you drift south, start to work your way up the reef. From 30 meters to 12 meters, the reef is a mix of healthy hard and soft corals and there is plenty of fish life in the blue. In the 12 meters and upwards range, the reef base is mainly soft corals with vertically protruding hard coral bommies and formations. Parrotfish, sweetlips, angelfish, Napoleon wrasse and yellow damsels all occupy reef space, while random schools of jacks sweep past defying the current in their streaming formations. At around 7 meters, there is a healthy field of staghorns that are seemingly draped with schools of antheas hovering above them. Stay tight to the reef and relatively shallow (above

7 meters) as you round the tip of the island. If you are deep, the currents push out and away from the island into the blue water and swimming in can be challenging.

A great dive for variety, abundant fish, good coral diversity and health and potential pelagic sightings.

PARADISE POINT

Situated on the northwest corner of Pura Island, this is an exhilarating deep drift dive around a sloping ridge that extends west towards Pantar Island. A great site for reef sharks, eagle rays, schooling batfish and, when dived at the right time, some adrenaline-pumping currents.

Enter in the shallow waters close to the small stone jetty where the bottom composition is predominantly black sand littered with small corals. Descend down heading west until the main coral reef comes into view. Follow the edge of the reef as a guide down to around 25 to 30 meters to where you start to drift along the south side of the ridge. Follow the ridge and round the tip before beginning the ascent back up the north side's sloping reef, which finishes up in the shallow waters of Pantar's upper west coast.

Both sides of the ridge are affected by the currents sweeping over the top, causing up and down drafts at either side.

The north side of the ridge boasts densely packed short-cropped hard and soft corals, sea squirts bursting with color and barrel sponges that have grown with a permanent lean due to the prevailing current. Fish life is abundant with impressive biomass. Schooling damsels swim with persistent determination in order to stay stationary over the reef, whilst in the blue there is a carnival of color as neon fusiliers stream overhead of cruising batfish, yellow back fusiliers intertwine in an upwards progression and midnight snappers hover close to the reef. Rounding the tip at 30 meters, look out to the blue and don't forget to pay attention to overhead action. Eagle rays are well known to cruise through here. Making your way up the northern slope, there is still good coral coverage but it is not so densely packed. From 20 meters upward, soft coral takes precedent, including elephant ears, sponges, barrels and anemones. There are some hard formations which are worth investigating for critter life taking shelter.

Keep a permanent eye out to the blue. You never know what will pass through. An exhilarating dive from start to finish.

SYMPHONY NO. 9 (PANTAR WALL)

A picture perfect slope and a deep wall drift dive with layers of overhangs, faults and inversions that leave you hanging in the blue with nothing below you aside from streaming, densely packed schools of fish. An upward glance is no less impressive as clouds of antheas, sergeant majors and damsels glimmer in the sunlight overhead.

The site is on the east coast of Pantar Island on a north–south axis. The wall is to the south and offers phenomenal coral density: tightly packed colorful soft and hard corals which do not appear to peter out with depth. At 30 meters, coverage is still excellent with light rays filtering through and highlighting the barrels, sponges, soft tree corals and tubers which adorn every surface. At depth, watch the blue for passing pelagics and numerous schools of fish that stream past. Start the dive on the wall section and head north to the slope, or if you prefer more time on the wall, zigzag your way back up it. The shallow waters offer conditions similar to that of a seriously overstocked aquarium with fish and corals glittering like jewels in a treasure trove. As you approach 15 meters, there is an overhanging ledge with an inversion below it. Hanging suspended under the ledge gives you a view straight down into the bottomless blue. Follow the ledge north to where the wall meets the slope and continue along the slope as you shallow up. Sergeant majors cluster around the reef, corals become increasingly soft with sporadic hard formations and bommies that attract numerous schools of sweepers, damsels and basslets all moving with the synchronization of a well-conducted orchestra, the basis of the site's name. Due to the currents on the wall, this is a deep dive for more experienced divers but it is possible to dive the wall shallow or just dive the slope, giving less experienced divers the opportunity to witness what can only be described as quite remarkable numbers of fish and world class corals.

It is not unusual to see large schools of jacks at Mike's Delight in Alor.

The Napoleon or Humphead Wrasse

Cheilinus undulates

The Napoleon wrasse, often called the humphead wrasse or Maori wrasse, is the largest member of the wrasse family (Labridae). Males reach up to 2.3 meters and reportedly weigh up to 190 kg. The Napoleon is not only distinguishable because of its size but also its thick fleshy lips and a humped forehead that becomes increasingly pronounced with maturity. The Napoleon's blue colored head is patterned with maze-like markings whilst its olive to dark blue-green body is characterized by dark vertical streaks. Juveniles range in coloration from red and orange to red and white.

Mature Napoleons prefer open coral reef environments, such as sloping reefs and channel walls, where they are found at depths of up to 100 meters. Their preferred places to settle include hard and soft branching corals and sea grass, whereas juvenile Napoleons tend to shelter in staghorn corals and deeper into the reef.

Napoleon wrasses feed on crustaceans, molluscs, small fish, sea urchins and sea stars. They are the only predators of several toxic species of marine creatures,

Above The Napoleon wrasse is the largest species of the Labridae family.

including boxfish, the sea hare mollusc and the crown of thorns sea star.

Napoleon wrasses tend to be solitary, with individuals most frequently being spotted, but it is not unusual to see male and female pairs. They are also commonly seen at dive sites where other large predators and pelagics are known to frequent. Despite being a relatively shy species, when it comes to divers they show little concern for other larger fish species.

Napoleons are long-lived. Life expectancy ranges from 25 to 50 years with females living longer than males. The do not reach sexual maturity until 4–6 years of age and are slow breeders. Due to their low reproduction rates and other factors, including habitat loss and degradation, unregulated and over fishing, destructive fishing practices such as cyanide and dynamite fishing, which they often fall victim to, and their high value in the luxury live fish trade, their numbers have been steadily decreasing and they are now listed as an endangered species on the IUCN red list.

ALOR TRAVEL PLANNER

The numerous dive sites of Alor are spread over a relatively small sea area encompassing the islands of Alor, Pantar, Pura, Kepa, Ternate and Crocodile. The sites are predominantly walls and slopes but there are also seamounts, ridges and pinnacles.

Alor is renowned for its incredible visibility that can reach 40 meters and beyond. At its worst during the wet season (January to March) it rarely drops below 15 meters.

There are currently four operators in Alor. Dive Alor Dive offers tailor-made fun diving packages, PADI courses and Kupang diving combos; Alor Divers is a French-operated resort on Pantar Island; Alor Dive operates daily fun diving boat trips and La Petite Kepa offers backpacker accommodation and diving from Kepa Island.

Operators sell diving packages ranging from two to four boat dives per day. Equipment hire and sizes should be arranged in advance but it is generally recommended to bring your own. Diving courses are possible in Alor but check availability with your operator.

Water temperature ranges from 26 to 29 degrees but thermoclines of 20 degrees are not unusual, so a 5 mm long suit is advised. Reef hooks are not essential but an audible signaling device and an SMB are strongly recommended. Strong currents are often present on the surface and there are not that many boats to find you if you drift.

Operators limit dives to 30 meters and maximum dive time to 60 minutes. Decompression diving is not recommended. For photographers, the stunning reefs, pelagics and unbeatable visibility are a wide-angle dream!

Recommended Operators

Diving

Dive Alor Dive Operated by Donovan Whitford since 1990. Tailor-made packages including a range of accommodation in Kalabahi, up to four boat dives per day, equipment hire, domestic flight booking service, pick up service in Kupang, PADI courses available in English and Indonesian. Kupang and Alor combo packages are also available. Tel: +62 (0) 8123960107. www.divealordive.com. Email: info@divealordive.com .

Alor Divers More upmarket French-managed dive eco resort on Pantar Island offering full board dive and stay packages. www.alor-divers.com. Email: info@alor-divers.com.

La Petite Kepa Budget accommodation and diving situated on Kepa Island. www.la-petite-kepa.com. Email: la_petite_kepa@hotmail.com.

Accommodation

The Pelangi Indah Jalan Diponegoro No. 34, Kalabahi. Tel: +62 (0) 38621251. Local hotel offering basic rooms with AC. $.

Alor Divers European resort on Pantar Island with 7 beach bungalows, full board basis. $$. (See above.)

The lives of the people of the Alor archipelago are dependent on the waters around them.

Maluku Islands

200 km
100 miles

N

Mapia Islands

Mt. Irau
2582m
Gunung
Meja
Reserve
Ambon
Tamrau Mts
Manokwari
Mt. Mebo
2940m
Numfoor I.
Ransiki
Kamundan R.
Wosian R.
Timofono R.
Mt. Umsini
2970m
Woinui Strait
Rumberpon I.
Papua
Mioswaar I.
Cendrawasih
Marine Reserve
Roon I.
watan
Bintuni Bay
I.
Berau Bay
Wondiwoi Wandamen
Mountains Reserve
ng Pt
Fakfak
ir Putih
Semai I.
Gusawi R.
Karas I.
Tongeram Pt
Kumafa Mts
Kaimana
Lengguru R.
WEST PAPUA
Aiduma I.
MALUKU
Adi I.
Nambima Pt
Papisol Pt
ela
Omboar R.
s
Kai Islands
Kai Besar I.
Aru Islands
Wokam I.
Kai Kecil I.
Pasir
Panjang
Maikoor I.
Kobror I.
Koba I.
Baun Reserve
ate I.
Trangan I.
Warkai I.
arat I.
I.
Southeast Aru
Nature & Marine
Reserve

Arafura Sea

MALUKU

The Maluku Islands offer divers a range of options, from muck diving in the Ambon Bay for weird and wonderful critters amongst desolate sandy slopes to picture postcard coral walls and white sand beaches around Weda Bay in Halmahera. The Malukus are all too often overlooked but, in fact, they have some of the most unique dive sites in Indonesia and are becoming increasingly more accessible. If you are looking to combine reefs and critters, then this is a perfect destination choice.

Ambon Bay is still building up a name for itself and, as such, dive sites are far quieter than those in Lembeh. Weda Bay only has one operator, so diving is exclusive with no other boats on the horizon. Weda does not have the same impressive fish numbers that are found in Raja Ampat but, given its proximity to the area, there are striking similarities in the species found, including epaulette sharks and occasional hammerheads, and the diving is considerably more affordable. These are two areas that are still just starting out in terms of dive tourism, but they look to have very healthy futures ahead of them.

Maluku at a Glance
Indonesia's Eastern Spice Islands

The Maluku islands, formerly known as the Spice Islands, sit between Sulawesi and West Papua and the northeast of Timor. They boast volcanic mountains, primary rainforests, stunning beaches and bountiful coral gardens. Underneath their beauty lies a volatile base. The islands are spread over the meeting point of four geological plates and two continental blocks. As a result, this geological foundation results in volcanic eruptions and frequent earthquake tremors.

The Maluku Islands are relatively young islands, approximately 1 to 15 million years old. They are thought to be the product of tectonic plate movements and collisions, hence the huge sea depths between them. This has resulted in numerous endemic species that are effectively imprisoned on individual islands.

Maluku's political and economic past largely revolves around exotic spices—nutmeg, cloves and mace—which were historically only found in this region of the world and were highly prized by Europeans. Prior to the 1600s, the islands were under Portuguese control, and named Moluquo, until they were expelled when the Dutch arrived in 1599. Eventually, the Maluku Islands became part of the Dutch East Indies until Indonesia gained independence in 1945,

though that was not until after the Dutch gave Manhattan Island to the British in return for the tiny island of Run so as to gain full control over nutmeg production!

Following Indonesian independence in 1945, the Maluku Islands were declared one province, but in 1999 they were split into two: North Maluku and Maluku.

North Maluku includes Ternate, Sofifi (the administrative capital), Tidore, Bacan and Halmahera. Maluku's administrative capital is Ambon and the area covers the Lease Islands, Seram, Buru and the Banda Islands. North Maluku is predominantly Muslim whilst Maluku has a larger Christian population. These religious differences led to conflicts from 1999 to 2002. Despite this relatively recent struggle, today the people of the Malukus focus on day to day life in peace.

Run Island in Maluku was traded for Manhattan Island in order to secure nutmeg production rights!

The Malukus are home to approximately two million people, which accounts for less than one percent of the population in Indonesia. Bahasa Indonesia is commonly spoken, and in areas visited by foreigners some English is understood. When traveling in more rural parts, it is best to be armed with some basic Indonesian.

The Maluku Islands cover approximately 850,000 square kilometers, 90 per cent of which is sea. There are about 1,030 individual islands, many of them uninhabited. Halmahera and Seram are the largest islands whilst Ambon and Ternate are the most developed despite being comparatively small.

Above Gunung Api, still an active volcano, rises up from the calm waters of the Banda Sea.

Left Small traditional fishing boats remain a common sight around the Maluku Islands.

Due to the vast area covered by the Malukus, there is a climatic range which becomes drier as you near Timor. In general, however, there is a healthy annual rainfall which supports these fertile islands. Each island group has its own climatic characteristics, but across Maluku as a whole the dry monsoon is from October to March and the wet monsoon from June through September.

Maluku's agriculture is not limited to spices. Rice, sago, cassava, coffee, cocoa and a variety of fruits are also grown. The local diet varies from island to island but most people rely heavily on fish for protein, whilst *papeda* is a common carbohydrate. This is sago flour cooked with water until it coagulates into a gluey, starchy consistency. Traditional local cuisine includes *papeda kuah ikan*, which is *papeda* made with a yellow fish soup flavored with turmeric, lime and other regional spices.

The main entry points to the Malukus are Ambon's Pattimura Airport (AMQ) and Ternate's Babullah Airport (TTE). At the time of writing, both airports are serviced by domestic flights only, though numerous daily flights arrive from Jakarta, Manado and Makassar. There are limited flights (operated by Express Air) linking Ambon and Ternate directly. Transit between the two is usually via Makassar. A departure tax of IDR30,000 is payable upon leaving the Malukus.

Taxi cars and sea taxis are widely available and haggling over the price is standard. *Angot* (small people buses) are common in towns and cities. Boat crossings are inevitably less reliable during the wet monsoon, leading to delays and cancellations. For longer journeys, there are numerous public ferries, and boat captains can be paid for private charters. Most dive resorts will offer pick-ups and transfers and this simplifies travel time and reduces stress considerably.

Diving Maluku
Remote, Colorful and Full of Surprises

Diving in the Malukus requires a little bit more planning than if you opt for one of the more developed diving destinations in Indonesia, such as Bali, where you can book things on a walk-in basis, but it is well worth the effort. There is a wide range of diving opportunities and divers and dive boats are few and far between, which guarantees some quality, uninterrupted dives.

When flying into the Malukus, airlines are becoming increasingly strict on baggage allowances, so if you are bringing your own equipment, which is recommended but not always necessary, be either conscientious when packing or bring enough cash to cover excess charges. Liveaboards generally require you to have a full set of your own gear. The few dive resorts that exist do offer gear hire but they will need size requirements in advance.

Water temperatures are warm all year round with an annual range of around 27 to 30 degrees. Long suits are recommended for protection. Currents are rarely strong, which makes the Malukus a good place for beginners. Topographies vary, from deep sea atoll walls in the

Above Diving around Halmahera promises divers phenomenal coral variety and colors.

Weda Bay of Halmahera to shallow muck diving slopes in Ambon Bay. The Malukus offer everything from pristine reefs with passing pelagics to rubble and dark sand with some of nature's weirdest species! Macro fanatics will be in their element in Ambon Bay, whereas a wide-angle enthusiast will have dives of a lifetime in Halmahera with its vast walls, gigantic gorgonians and variety of sharks and pelagics. Maluku truly has something for every diver!

Many operators in Maluku close for diving from June to September, so if you are planning to travel in these months check in advance for availability with

operators. Visibility during this period can be reduced due to the wet monsoon.

There are a limited number of dive resort operators in Maluku but most offer dive and stay packages which include one to four dives per day and full board accommodation. As currents and tides do not significantly affect conditions, diving is scheduled throughout the day, generally starting with a two-tank trip in the morning and additional dives in the afternoon. Nitrox is available through some operators.

Dive courses are available in Maluku but should be booked prior to arrival to ensure availability.

The nearest recompression chamber is in Manado and so conservative diving practices are advised and most operators limit dives to a maximum depth of 30 meters and 60 minutes bottom time. Decompression diving is prohibited. Divers should carry at least one audible and one visual signaling device (SMB).

Diving insurance is required by some operators and is strongly recommended for all divers.

There are no diving equipment stores in Maluku but most operators stock Aqualung equipment for hire, can handle minor equipment repairs and sell some small items. If you need to buy equipment and are transiting through Bali or Jakarta, it is best to make purchases in one of these locations prior to heading out to Maluku. Both Ambon and Ternate airports are serviced by Garuda Indonesia, Lion Air, Sri Wijaya Air and Express Air, together with some smaller carriers. At the time of writing, Express Air is the only airline flying directly between the two with other carriers transiting through Makassar.

This white variety of leaf scorpionfish was pictured on a reef top in Weda Bay, Halmahera.

Getting to Maluku

The two main diving areas in the region are Ambon in Maluku and Weda Bay in Halmahera, North Maluku. Ambon is accessed via Ambon's Pattimura Airport and Weda on Halmahera is best accessed through Babullah Airport on Ternate Island. Direct flights from Ambon to Ternate are available but only with Express Air. If you are not able to book a direct flight, then you will need to transit via Makassar. Both Sriwijaya Air and Garuda offer flights back and forth through Makassar to both Ambon and Ternate.

If you are entering Indonesia through Jakarta, you can fly direct to Ternate with Garuda or Sriwijaya Air in just under 4 hours. Direct flights to Ambon are available with Lion Air, Batik Air and Garuda and take 3.5 hours.

If you are entering Indonesia through Bali, all flights to Ambon and Ternate are through Makassar. The flight from Bali to Makassar takes 1 hour 25 minutes and then from Makassar to Ambon is another 1 hour 40 minutes. From Makassar to Ternate it takes just over 2 hours.

Considerations

The number of dive operators based in this region is very limited and they become fully booked very quickly, so advance booking is essential. Most operators will provide airport pick-ups and drop-offs either in the price or for a surcharge. Make use of these services as it will save you a lot of time and effort, especially in Halmahera where the diving region is a good five hours from Ternate airport and requires a combination of speedboat and car transfers. Weda Bay is incredibly remote and the resort is literally bordered by ocean on one side and nothing but rainforest on the other. If you are hoping to dive through the day and go out and socialize in the evening, this may not be the best place to visit. Ambon does have numerous local villages

around the edge of the bay but there is no tourist infrastructure here either. Again, if you are looking for shopping and nights out, you may find Bali a more suitable destination.

Combining Your Trip With a Cruise and a Liveaboard

There are a number of liveaboards that cover the Ambon Bay area as part of larger trips heading either further east in Indonesia (Raja Ampat) or further west (North Sulawesi). It is possible to use Ambon Bay as a point of embarkation or disembarkation for one of these trips either before or after diving the bay with an Ambon-based operator. Check with your liveaboard operator when booking for what options are available.

10 Day Itinerary for Ambon and Halmahera: Ambon Bay Critters and Weda Bay Walls

This is a 12 day itinerary that provides for 5 days of diving in Ambon Bay and 5 days of diving in Weda Bay. This itinerary is suitable for all levels of divers and will appeal particularly to photographers (both wide-angle in Weda and macro in Ambon). The itinerary requires either one or two domestic flights.

Day 1 Arrive in Ambon and transfer from the airport to Ambon Bay. Dive operator to provide airport pick-up. Check in to resort. Depending on arrival time, either afternoon or night dive. If arriving by liveaboard arrange for either a boat or shore pick-up.

Days 2–6 Diving in Ambon Bay. Up to 4 dives per day. Night dives also available.

Day 7 This is a non-diving day to allow for equipment drying and sufficient surface time prior to flying the following day.

Day 8 Fly direct from Ambon to Ternate with Express Air (if no direct flights are available, then transit through Makassar). Arrive in Ternate. Pick-up provided by Weda Bay Resort, speedboat to Sofifi and

Weda Resort in Halmahera is located amid rainforest and reef.

then 4 hour car journey across Halmahera to Weda Bay. Check in to Weda Bay in the afternoon/early evening.

Days 9–13 Diving in Weda Bay. Up to 4 dives per day plus night dives. On Day 13, aim to finish diving by lunchtime to allow sufficient surface time prior to flying the next day.

Day 14 Transfer back to Ternate for after-noon flight to next destination.

Useful Contacts

Recompression Chamber
Malalayang Hospital (Rumah Sakit Malalayang), Manado. Tel: +62 (0) 811430 913.

Pattimura Airport (Ambon) Jalan Doktor Leimena, Laha, Ambon. Tel: +62 (0) 911323 770.

Babullah Airport (Ternate) No contact information available. Contact airline operators direct.

Sultan Hasanuddin International Airport (Makassar) Jalan Rays Airport No. 1, Makassar. Tel: +62 (0) 411553183.

Garuda Indonesia 24 Hour Call Center Tel: +62 (0) 8041807807 or +62 (0) 2123519999. www.garuda-indonesia.com.

Sriwijaya Air Call Center Tel: +62 (0) 2129279777 or +62 (0) 8041777777. www.sriwijayaair.co.id.

Lion Air Assistance Line Tel: +62 (0) 216379 8000. www.lionair.co.id.

Express Air 24 Hour Call Center Tel: +62 (0) 21500 890. www.xpressair.co.id.

Diving Ambon
A Critter Hot Spot with a Superb Wreck

In recent years, Ambon Bay has been garnering fame for its critter and muck diving sites which range from true muck sandy slopes to more heavily coral populated reefs and a number of jetties and piers. The marine life in Ambon Bay does not disappoint and some of Indonesia's most unusual creatures can be found here: blue ring octopus, flamboyant cuttlefish, rhinopias, mimic octopus and many more. The *Duke of Sparta* shipwreck in the heart of Ambon Bay, an almost pristine wreck which is seldom dived and still relatively unexplored, is a major highlight for wreck enthusiasts.

Ambon Island is just 775 km square (51 km long) and sits on the north side of the Banda Sea to the southwest of the larger island of Seram. Ambon has a mountainous topography with predominantly tropical rainforest-covered highlands, which ensure a good rain supply and fertile lands flourishing with coconut palms, nutmeg and cassava. The island itself is an odd shape as it is almost divided in two from northeast to southwest by a large bay. Ambon city is located on the waterfront at the north end of the east bank of the bay. As you travel south from the city, the area becomes more rural, much like the west bank, which has several small villages along its coastline but no major city development. The airport, Pattimura (AMQ), is located to the southwest of the island, and most hotels, liveaboards and dive resorts provide airport pick-ups.

Above The *Duke of Sparta* wreck remains in great condition and is still relatively unexplored.

Left The short head fang blenny is commonly seen in hiding places. This one chose a bottle in Ambon Bay.

Traditionally, farming and fishing have been the main industries in Ambon, particularly the farming of nutmeg and cloves for which the island is famed. Nowadays, these industries still provide many with their main source of income and fishing boats moored at jetties still punctuate the coastline of the bay. Ambon also continues to be a strategic port for boats traveling to further eastern parts of Indonesia. Tourism has yet to develop and facilities for travelers are basic outside of the few international hotels. Bahasa Indonesian is widely spoken together with local dialects in

Ambon city, and when dealing with dive crews basic English is understood.

There is a mixture of Christian and Muslim villages in the area and relations between the two are smooth and positive despite historical conflict.

There are local hospital facilities in Ambon which are able to deal with most minor injuries and they also hold oxygen supplies.

HIGHLIGHTS Ambon Bay is gaining fame as a top Indonesian muck diving destination and a macro photographers' wonderland with its resident mandarinfish, mimic and blue ringed octopus, wunderpus, various frogfish species, flamboyant cuttlefish, rhinopias and a vast array of nudibranchs and shrimps. That's not all though. If you are looking for a change from sandy slopes and critters, the east side of Ambon Bay offers coral reef walls and the *Duke of Sparta* wreck.

DIFFICULTY LEVEL Suitable for beginner upwards, with little current. Most marine life is found in the 15 meter range.

As well as excellent muck diving, Ambon Bay offers coral reefs and several mini walls.

LOGISTICS Ambon is surprisingly easy to access, with direct flights from Jakarta or, if you are traveling from Bali, then via Makassar. Many liveaboards will pick up and drop off guests in Ambon who are combining a resort stay with a liveaboard diving trip.

AMBON'S BEST DIVE SITES

MALUKU DIVERS RESORT TO TAWIRI

From the Maluku Divers Resort heading north to Tawiri, in front of the Sultan Khairun Jamil Mosque, are as many as nine small sites offering similar topographies. The dark sand slopes characterized by small rock and hard and soft coral forms in the shallow waters become less closely grouped as you head down the 45 degree slope. The sand on these slopes is incredibly fine, so be aware of your buoyancy and your fins when you swim. Any stirred-up sediment does take time to settle. These sites are for real muck diving. Don't be fooled by the sandy slopes which initially may seem desolate and inhospitable to marine life as there is a treasure trove of critter life to look out for. Some of the residents include painted and clown frogish, thorny seahorses, ribbon eels, flying gurnards, robust and ornate ghost pipefish, banded cleaner shrimps, nudibranchs and some of the more obvious bottom dwellers such as scorpionfish, moray eels and peacock flounders. Flamboyant cuttlefish, blue ringed and mimic octopus, rhinopias and wunderpus are also seen here. On the reef flat, just upward of 5 meters, bright blue and yellow damselfish school over coral formations providing a contrasting dazzle

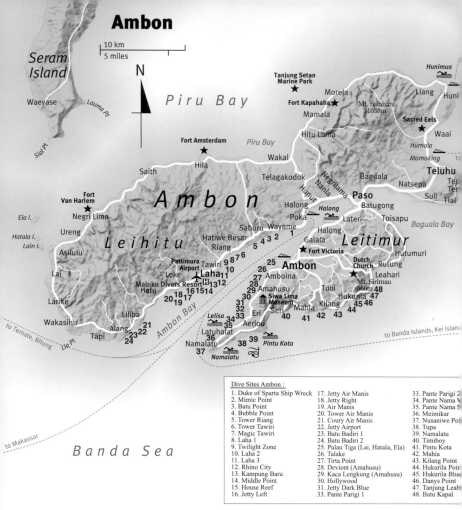

Ambon

10 km
5 miles

N

Seram Island

Piru Bay

Waeyase

Lauma Pt.

Sial Pt.

Tanjung Setan Marine Park ★

Piru Bay

Morela

Fort Kapahaha ★

Mt. Salahatu 1038m

Liang

Huni

Hunimua

Mamala

Sacred Eels ★

Waai

Fort Amsterdam ★

Hitu Lama

Hurnala

Momoking

Teluhu

Wakal

Piru Bay

Ela I.

Fort Van Harlem ★

Negri Lima

Hila

Saith

Telagakodok

Baguala

Natsepa

Suli

Ter
Ter
Tial

Negrilama
Nania

Hunut

Paso

Batugong

Ambon

Leihitu

Ureng

Asilulu

Lai

Hatala I.
Lain I.

Sahuru

Hatiwe Besar

Riang

Wayame

Halong

Halong

Poka

Lateri

Toisapu

Galala

Halong

Fort Victoria ★

Leitimur

Hutumuri

Baguala Bay

Larike

Wakasihu

Liliba

Pattimura Airport

Tawiri

Leke

Laha

Hatu

Maluku Divers Resort

9 8 7 6
5 4 3 2
1
25
27
26
28
29

Ambon

Amboina

Amahusu

Siwa Lima Museum

Dutch Church

Rutung

Leahari

+ Mt. Sirimau 666m

48

Tuni

Hukurila

47
45 46
44

Mahia

Kilang

Seri

Erl

Aerlou

40

41

42

43

Lelisa

Latuhalat

Namalatu

Namalatu

38 39

Pintu Kota

Alang

Tapi

Lia Pt.

Ambon Bay

to Ternate, Bitung

to Banda Islands, Kei Islan

Banda Sea

to Makassar

10
11
12
13
16 15 14
18 17
19
20
30
31
32
33 34
35
36
37

21
22
23
24

Dive Sites Ambon :		
1. Duke of Sparta Ship Wreck	17. Jetty Air Manis	33. Pante Parigi 2
2. Mimic Point	18. Jetty Right	34. Pante Nama V
3. Batu Point	19. Air Manis	35. Pante Nama S
4. Bubble Point	20. Tower Air Manis	36. Meimikar
5. Tower Riang	21. Coury Air Manis	37. Nusaniwe Po
6. Tower Tawiri	22. Jetty Airport	38. Tupa
7. Magic Tawiri	23. Batu Badiri 1	39. Namalatu
8. Laha 1	24. Batu Badiri 2	40. Timboy
9. Twilight Zone	25. Pulau Tiga (Lai, Hatala, Ela)	41. Pintu Kota
10. Laha 2	26. Tirta Point	42. Mahia
11. Laha 3	27. Deviont (Amahusu)	43. Kilang Point
12. Rhino City	28. Kaca Lengkung (Amahusu)	44. Hukurila Poir
13. Kampung Baru	29. Hollywood	45. Hukurila Blue
14. Middle Point	30. Jetty Dark Blue	46. Danys Point
15. House Reef	31. Pante Parigi 1	47. Tanjung Leah
16. Jetty Left	33. Pante Parigi 1	48. Batu Kapal

of color. The water here is generally clear and makes for some excellent blue backdrops for macro photographers. Whereever you drop in on this stretch, it is easy diving. Follow the slope with the current but go slow and give your eyes time to scour every surface as there is a lot here but you have to look, or have an excellent guide! It is worth dropping down to 20 to 25 meters to have a look around, but in general the best critter life tends to be sitting at around 15 meters. Make your way gradually shallower as you progress through the dive. The top of the reef

crest is an ideal position for your safety stop. If you are planning to cover a reasonable distance or if a current is present, an SMB is advisable due to boat traffic in the vicinity.

SOUTH OF MALUKU DIVERS RESORT TO AIR MANIS JETTY

South of Maluku Divers Resort to just beyond the jetty, known as Air Manis (No. 17, map), the area is divided into a number of small sites which offer similar topographies. These are also muck diving sites characterized by rich, fine,

Left The black tip grouper is often seen perching on reefs and underneath corals.

Below The Moyer's dragonet can be spotted across Maluku and is photogenic close up.

dark sand bottoms which slope away at a 45 degrees angle from the top of the reef flat which rests at about 5 meters. There is more shallow coral reef growth here than at the northern sites and, accordingly, more fish life, particularly in the shallows, where Moorish idols, butterfly fish and a variety of wrasses cruise by. Under the jetty at Air Manis, batfish hide out in the shade and schooling bannerfish can be seen on the drop-off. These sites have an abundance of bottom dwellers, such as scorpionfish and flounders, and various types of frogfish are not unusual together with hermit crabs, mantis shrimps, moray eels, cleaner shrimps and cuttlefish. On clear days with good visibility, the supports of the jetty are photogenic and are worth investigating for lionfish and other critters favoring the darkness.

Local fishing boats tend to be moored up at the jetty but are used to divers entering the water around them and do not cause any problems other than contributing to the amount of waste around the jetty.

The dive profile for these sites is straightforward, with an entry close to the shore, and then swimming down the slope to your maximum depth. The majority of critter

life tends to be upwards of 20 meters. Then start working your way back up watching your air supply and no-stop limits. If there is a mild current, it is possible to drift along the slope covering the width of 2 or 3 sites in one dive. Alternatively, pick a single site and work your way up by zigzagging back and forth. As you shallow up, the coral density increases as does the number of small rocky formations and occasional anemones. The safety stop is usually just below the top of the reef flat.

The white eyed moray eel is frequently spotted in Ambon Bay, often in pairs.

The thorny seahorse is one of the most commonly spotted species of seahorse in Ambon Bay.

The colorful Coleman shrimp lives in symbiosis with fire sea urchins and is often spotted in Ambon Bay.

DUKE OF SPARTA WRECK
☆AUTHOR'S CHOICE

The *Duke of Sparta* wreck (No. 1, map; see also page 220 for history), known for years simply as 'The Ambon Wreck', lies approximately 20 minutes north of the Maluku Divers Resort by small speed-boat and 50 meters south of the Perta-mina Harbor on the west bank. The entry point is clearly marked by a 2-meter-tall steel buoy attached to the deck of the ship by a mooring chain, which makes an excellent descent line. The site is a relatively deep one, with the top of the deck starting at 15 meters underneath the mooring chain and sloping down to 35 meters at the top of the bow. The ship is approximately 137 meters in length and, despite sinking over 50 years ago, is almost entirely intact with easily iden-tifiable features. If you enter using the descent chain from the moored float and are diving on air, it is advisable to limit

your explorations to the rear portion of the boat, which lies in the shallower water. It is a long swim to the bow and usually your no-stop time will run out on the way there. If not, it's almost guaran-teed you will be in deco by the time you return to the mooring chain. If you are using nitrox, however, a full exploration of the entire upper deck is possible. There are great technical diving oppor-tunities here and planned penetration dives appear possible.

The wreck lies stern to shore, with the bow facing the middle of the channel. The mooring chain is anchored on the upper deck between the engine room superstructure and the ship's main fun-nel, which has toppled, falling towards the bow and lying neatly along the center of the upper deck. The engine room is still a solid structure in the middle, with side beams branching out at either side, giving the appearance of spiders' legs,

The Flamboyant Cuttlefish *Metasepia pfefferi*

The flamboyant cuttlefish is a small species of cuttlefish measuring only up to 8 cm. Unlike other species, the flamboyant cuttlefish seldom swims and instead uses its lower pair of 'arms' and small paired flaps on its lower body to walk around (visible in the photo below). They are found in depths of 3 to 80 meters, are relatively easy to approach and will allow divers to get up close before they show signs of feeling threatened. Their bold colors appear to make them less shy than other cuttlefish species. Due to their habit of walking rather than swimming, they can be observed for long periods. When unthreatened, their coloration varies from white to a purple brown. Occasionally, hints of red and yellow are visible.

Flamboyant cuttlefish flash their impressive colors when they are under threat and these serve as a warning to any possible predators that their flesh is toxic. Colors range from bright reds and pinks to vivid purples and almost fluorescent yellow and orange around their skirts. The color flashes are often observed in tandem with the front tentacles being stretched upwards or forwards as another warning and perhaps as a way to make themselves appear bigger. Younger flamboyant cuttlefish are generally more colorful than older individuals.

Whilst these cuttlefish are small and colorful, they are definitely not to be underestimated. They hunt by day for smaller crustaceans and fish that dwell under the surface of the sand. Once they have iden-tified a target, their front pair of tentacles shoots forward with impressive speed and seizes the innocent and unsuspecting prey.

Flamboyant cuttlefish are seen in a number of locations around Indonesia, the most notable being the Lembeh Strait and Ambon Bay, where they are found on sandy flats and slopes. Due to their non-distinct colors when unthreatened, the best way to distinguish them from other cuttlefish species from a distance is by their size and method of movement. They are also commonly seen in pairs though individuals are not unusual.

The two individuals here were photographed in the Lembeh Strait, North Sulawesi, and it is possible to see the bright orange skirt, vivid coloration and extended tentacles.

This flamboyant cuttlefish is in defensive mode. Note its vivid colors, spiked appearance and outstretched tentacles.

The Duke of Sparta

The *Duke of Sparta* was a cargo ship built by William Gray and Company in Teeside, England, in 1940. She was 135 meters long, over 17 meters wide and weighed approximately 5,397 tons.

In 1951, she was sold to Grimaldi Brothers in Naples, and was renamed the SS *Aquiba*. In 1958, whilst moored in Ambon Bay, Maluku, she was targeted as part of a covert mission by the CIA and bombed by an unmarked Douglas B 26 Invader bomber piloted by Allen Pope. The CIA's goal was to cast a shadow over international trade with Indonesia, thereby destabilizing the Sukarno government of the day. The *Duke of Sparta* was badly damaged by the attack and sank shortly afterwards to the bottom of the bay, where she still rests to this day.

The existence of a wreck in Ambon Bay had been no secret for years. However, the *Duke of Sparta*'s identity was unknown and for over 50 years she was simply called 'The Ambon Wreck'. Her name, origin and even how she came to rest in the basin of the bay were one of Ambon's mysteries.

The bridge of the *Duke of Sparta* is easily penetrable and is still intact.

It was always rumored that the *Duke of Sparta* had been lost off Palu in Central Sulawesi.

In 2009, Maluku Divers, the pioneers of diving in the bay, made a planned penetration dive into the ship's engine room where they were able to locate a plaque on one of the water heaters that bore a manufacturer's stamp and serial number. It was by tracing back that individual mechanical part that a positive identity of the wreck as the *Duke of Sparta* could finally be made.

The *Duke of Sparta* wreck is a breathtakingly stunning dive. She is almost entirely intact and, incredibly, her mast head still stands upright from 32 meters. She has become host to a vast range of fish species and critter life. Encrusted with coral, she offers numerous swim-throughs and entry points. She has to be one of the most undived yet diveable wrecks in Indonesia, promising you the opportunity to have the entire wreck all to yourself.

The Clark's anemonefish varies in color from orange to almost black but always has two distinct white bars.

which make for very easy and open swim-throughs. If you are heading towards the bow, after you pass the funnel there is an area of open deck with only cross members in place. It is possible to drop down between the struts into a cavernous area with overhangs around the outer edge which are great to peer into with a torchlight. The next obvious structure is the bridge. There are swim-throughs here that are relatively easy but beware of your fins and look out for potential entanglements. Quite possibly the most awe-inspiring feature of this wreck is the colossal mast head, which still stands completely upright on the deck to the bow side of the engine room. After the mast head, you reach the bow area at around 35 meters.

The *Duke of Sparta* site is an obvious choice for wreck enthusiasts, but for the critter-loving crowd that Ambon attracts the site also has a lot to offer. The completely coral-encrusted superstructure provides a base for bubble coral, small fans, black coral and some good hard corals. These formations provide homes to a wide selection of ghost pipefish, lionfish, coral shrimps and nudibranchs, whilst the dark sand covered deck areas are ideal for stonefish, scorpionfish and other bottom dwellers.

As with many wrecks, fish life in general is more abundant here, especially in comparison with some of the predominantly sandy sites. Batfish and huge trumpetfish lurk in the shadows, fusiliers, snappers, damsels and surgeonfish school around the decks and Moorish idols, angelfish and butterfly fish add a beautifully contrasting layer of color.

JETTY DARK BLUE

If you are looking for variety, this site (No. 30, map) has it all: sloping coral reef, true muck diving sandy slopes, a great jetty and a great variety of critters. The site is situated in a small harbor with accompanying jetty on the east bank of Ambon Bay almost directly across the water from the Maluku Divers Resort. The entry point here can be anywhere in the vicinity of the jetty/harbor but get in close as the reef drops away steeply. To the north side of the jetty, there is good coral density sloping

The common marble shrimp is nocturnal but it can be seen during daytime in reef crevices.

Left This blenny found an excellent hiding hole in a hard coral formation.

Below The painted frogfish species has many color variations. This bright red one was spotted in Ambon Bay.

steeply down to sand at 20 meters. Fish life is much more abundant here and schooling fish are not uncommon. The coral section is a good place for a range of shrimps, leaf scorpionfish and other relatively common critters. If you head south along the sand at around 20 meters, look out for various types of frogfish, nudibranchs, octopus and cuttlefish amongst the sporadic formations and mooring lines. Work your way up the slope towards the jetty where schooling juveniles congregate out of the sun, frogfish and dwarf lionfish blend into the jetty stilts and crocodilefish lie camouflaged on the sand. A safety stop under the jetty itself is possible but be wary of where you come up here as there are boats in the harbor.

PANTE NAMA WALL

Pante Nama Wall (No. 33, map) boasts both good coral and fish life and is a nice change from the west bank's sandy slopes.

The site is on the east side of Ambon Bay, south of Jetty Dark Blue. At the northern end, the wall extends down to around 30 meters. Moving south, it shallows up to 10 to 15 meters and features some large overhangs above recessed caverns. The wall also has some top quality hard and soft corals ranging from fans and bubbles to branching and stone corals. Pyramid butterfly fish school out in the blue, with Moorish idols, spotted puffers, sea squirts, tubers, feather stars, nudibranchs, lionfish, angelfish and sponges giving variety and color to the reef. Amongst these typical wall dwellers, mantis shrimps, coral shrimps, jawfish, frogfish, gobies and cuttlefish are frequently sighted. This site is sometimes subject to current, but when possible try to start at the north end and drift south so that you progress from deep to shallow. The wall eventually peters out to the south, turning into a sandy sloping reef, so it is possible to cover a stunning wall and then complete the dive with some classic muck diving. A good second dive to do after Jetty Dark Blue, if walls and coral are not your thing, is to drop in at the end of the wall and cover the muck diving slope only.

AMBON TRAVEL PLANNER

Ambon Bay is best dived between November and May as July and August are the major monsoon months when many operators close. Year round water temperature is between 27 and 29 degrees and visibility ranges from as low as 5 meters directly after the monsoon season to 20 meters plus in the dry season. The bay is tidal but tidal exchanges are generally small. For better visibility, dive on a rising tide.

Dive sites are accessed by small local boats modified for diving or tenders from liveaboards. Shore diving would definitely be possible here and may develop if more resorts open along the coast.

The nature of the muck diving here—mainly nitrox diving photographers combined with relatively shallow dives—means dive times tend to be longer than 60 minutes and time is usually dependent on air consumption. Diving in a shortie is possible, but with longer dive times and occasional stingers in the water, a long suit offers more comfort.

Ambon has yet to develop an efficient waste disposal system and a lot of rubbish from the city and villages finds its way into the bay. If you are hoping for crystal clear, clean waters, Ambon may not be the destination for you.

Recommended Operators

Maluku Divers (Author's Choice) Centrally positioned on the west side of Ambon Bay which is renowned for the best muck diving sites in the area. Access to the east side for walls and reef is just a 10 minute boat ride. Diving packages available with up to four dives per day plus night dives, nitrox, equipment hire, camera room, camera processing desks and lights in all rooms, full board accommodation, tailored packages available. Airport pick-ups and drop-offs included. Courses and equipment hire available but should be booked in advance. Tel: +62 (0) 9113365307. www.divingmaluku.com. Email: info@divingmaluku.com.

Below The restaurant at Maluku Divers resort serves divers three set meals a day.

Bottom Maluku Divers Resort has purpose-built dive boats which also offer camera storage facilities.

Diving Weda Bay (Halmahera)
Spectacular Atolls, Reefs and Walls

Weda Bay and its reefs are natural wonders. Mid-sea atolls stretch down hundreds of meters and hard coral walls are of staggering immensity and scale. On land, primary rainforest stretches as far as the eye can see, its green slopes disappearing into the horizon. Everything natural around Weda Bay seems to be on an oversized scale, which makes it all the more breathtaking. It is not just about the diving or the landscape, it's a complete package and a place to relax and enjoy an area of true natural beauty.

Halmahera is predominantly rainforest, and on first sight the enormity of it is difficult to comprehend. Never ending steep mountainous peaks and ridges are carpeted in deep green, textured with folds and creases. Weda Bay is the large bay on the southeast of Halmahera which opens up into the Halmahera Sea. Outside of Ternate and Sofifi, most people in Halmahera live in small coastal fishing villages and fish and farm for subsistence. Mining companies are major employers in many regions and bring work to areas otherwise without employment opportunities. Some mining companies are replanting areas of forest once work is completed but, unfortunately, illegal logging is still an issue in places.

The land of Halmahera is rich and fertile, with the main agricultural crops including coconuts, bananas, sweet potato, sago, nutmeg and cassava.

Transport around Halmahera is by both sea and road. In more remote areas, the road conditions vary from excellent through to rough tracks requiring four wheel drive vehicles.

English is taught in schools, but with so few tourists it is not frequently practiced. Knowing a few Indonesian phrases can be invaluable when getting around.

There are local hospital facilities in both Ternate and Weda which have both oxygen and basic supplies. The nearest international hospitals are in Manado and Makassar.

In Ternate, the population is predominantly Muslim but outside of the city religion is a mix of Christian and Muslim. Visitors should try and dress conservatively, with women keeping their shoulders covered.

HIGHLIGHTS Immense walls with world class coral diversity, mid-sea atoll reefs, passing pelagics, an endemic species of epaulette shark, easy conditions and not another dive boat in sight.

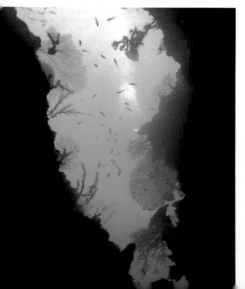

Opposite above These two feather stars have attached themselves to a sea fan for better positioning in the current.

Left Elmoos reef has some beautiful swim-throughs which offer stunning views out to the blue.

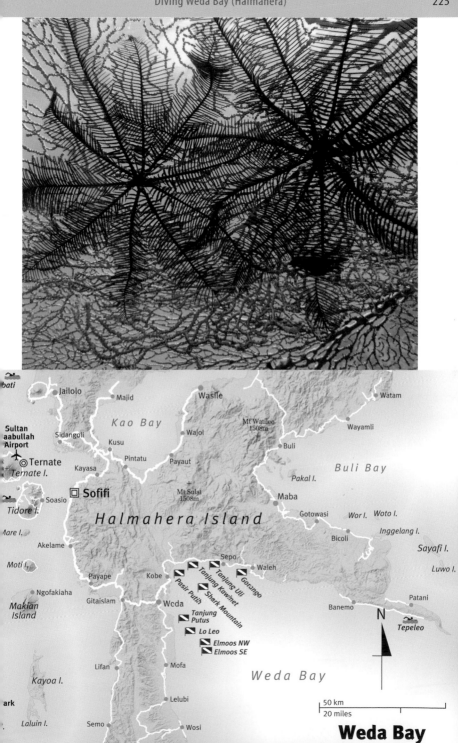

Weda Bay

50 km
20 miles

TIP BOX Weda Resort offers bird watching tours. An early morning trip into the rainforest to witness the standard wing bird of paradise in its display tree is a once in a lifetime opportunity and you can be back at the resort in time for breakfast and the first dive of the day.

DIFFICULTY LEVEL Easy diving conditions, warm water and very little current make Weda Bay suitable for beginners upwards. Plus an awe-inspiring range of corals and phenomenal topographies.
LOGISTICS The main airport in Halmahera is Ternate. If diving with Weda Resort, airport pick-ups are available (and advisable), with transfers to the resort that involve a 30 minute speedboat crossing to Sofifi and a 4 hour drive through stunning primary rainforest.

WEDA BAY'S BEST DIVE SITES

ELMOOS REEF
☆AUTHOR'S CHOICE

Phenomenal walls of world class hard corals, incredible visibility and simply staggering topography. This is an open sea atoll reef about 30 kilometers south, southeast of Weda Resort, an hour away by small speedboat. The outside walls of the atoll reef offer a breathtaking display of color, diversity of coral species and sheer volume of coral that is difficult to match. From the drop-off at just 3 meters down to 25 meters, the reefscape is a candy box patchwork of brain corals,

Batfish have highly distinctive body shapes best viewed from side on.

plates, tables and stone corals competing fiercely for space on the reef. Branching out like outstretched fingers from the wall are vast gorgonians in a variety of colors, sea fans, whips and tubers. The wall itself offers small ledges, overhangs and areas of inversion. Towards the north of the reef, there is selection of caverns which start from 15 meters and extend down to around 25 meters. These huge hollows with cathedral-like ceilings offer shady recesses and swim-throughs for juvenile batfish, sweetlips and larger reef predators, such as giant trevally and large groupers.

Whilst the reef is literally teeming with coral to around 25 meters (and beyond still has by no means mediocre coverage), the most abundant fish life is within the top 15 meters. Small schools of juvenile fusiliers, cardinalfish and curtains of glassfish aggregate just out from the reef, swaying in synchronization. Damsels dart in and out of the reef and brightly colored fairy basslets swarm over coral outcroppings like jewels against the clear blue back-drop. The currents are minimal here with almost still water and excellent visibility.

Gorango Reef in Weda Bay, Halmahera, has stunning and immense hard coral walls.

In the shallow portions of the reef, the soft corals take precedence. Undulating colorful folds of leather corals ripple in the sunlight interspersed with a variety of other soft species.

Lo Leo Reef is similar to Elmoos Reef, with excellent walls of dense and abundant hard corals.

SHARK MOUNTAIN

This is an incredible deep seamount, the summit of which sits at around 32 meters. A mooring buoy with descent line is in place, but is strategically positioned 5 meters below the surface. GPS is essential to find the right spot. Descent is made down the line which, if there is current present, divers should keep hold of until reaching the reef. The line is anchored just off center of the ridge's summit, which has a rocky, undulating composition with a smattering of small hard and soft corals.

Because of the depth of this site, time actually spent on the ridge is short. You want to make your way down the line as fast as possible to give a little longer no-stop time on the ridge. From the anchorage, it is a few meters swim to the top of the ridge from where you can peer down the other side at a frenzied mass of juvenile, mature, small and medium sized plankton feeders in the blue being patrolled by black tip, white tip and grey reef sharks and other large predatory pelagics, from giant trevally and Spanish mackerel to schools of jacks. With at least a few of minutes no-stop time left, head back to the anchor point for the descent line and begin the ascent up. It is worth stopping on the way. Almost half of this dive can be spent on the line where the show continues in the water column. Large schools of jacks will hover in the blue around divers on the line. Rainbow runners have also been seen in schools here and giant trevally and barracuda hover below the surface waiting for you at the safety stop. Again, divers should maintain contact with the line

The White Tip Reef Shark *Triaenodon obesus*

The white tip reef shark is a species of requiem shark of grey to brown coloration on top, a white underbelly and distinctive white tips to the anal and caudal fins. It is a small member of the shark family, ranging from just 52 cm as a newborn pup to around 1.6 meters when fully mature. Physically, the white tip has a relatively slender body and a short head, both ideal for forcing itself into small crevices and hollows whilst hunting for the crustaceans and bony fish on which it feeds. White tips are predominantly nocturnal hunters and sleeping fish inside corals are easy targets. By day, white tips spend most of their time resting underneath ledges or on sandy bottoms and they are commonly found in caves. As the white tip does not rely on ram ventilation as a method of breathing (a process which requires constant swimming), it can lie still and is able to pump water over its gills whilst stationary in order to breathe.

Despite the white tip reef shark being one of the most common shark species in the Indo-Pacific region, females only give birth to 1 to 6 live pups in each pregnancy,

White tip reef sharks are one of the more common species of shark seen in Halmahera.

and in a lifetime a female white tip may only produce up to 12 pups. It is no surprise, then, that with unregulated shark fishing in the area their numbers are in decline. They have a low reproductive rate and do not reach sexual maturity until they are approximately 1.1 meters, at around 8 or 9 years of age. Their gestation period of 11 to 13 months is biennial.

White tips are an unaggressive species of shark which are seen solitary and in pairs or small schools. They are non-migratory and individuals tend to stay in the same locales for long periods. Whilst they may move from place to place, the distances they travel are small.

White tips prefer coral reef environments and relatively clear water and are usually seen at between 8 and 40 meters. However, they can also be spotted on sandy flats in lagoons close to reef areas.

Life expectancy for white tips varies from region to region but could be upwards of 25 years in some areas.

all of the way up. Due to the depth of this dive and the descent in the blue (even though it is with a line it can be disorienting), it is recommended for more experienced divers only, particularly when there is current.

PASIR PUTIH

A few minutes from Weda Resort lies Pasir Putih, a shallow sandbar visible from the surface, which gives way to a white sand slope decorated with coral formations, bommies and small but high density patches of reef.

This is a great dive for people who want to go and find things, as it is a shallow, pretty reef which provides opportunities for spotting all kinds of sand and bottom dwellers, ranging from the field of garden eels starting at just 2 meters and extending down to 5 meters to crocodilefish, scorpionfish, lionfish, a variety of nudibranchs, giant clams, leopard solefish and schools of glassfish and sweepers in amongst the reef. The corals here are varied, but what stands

out in the clear, shallow water are the impressive barrel corals and sporadic giant gorgonians. The main coral section lies at between 5 and 18 meters. This is a very easy dive site which is highly recommended for both beginners and for experienced divers making a third or fourth dive of the day because of its shallow sloping nature.

GORANGO REEF

This site comprises immense walls towering out of the depths of the Halmahera Sea. The overwhelming topography and the sheer enormity of the site as well as the seemingly more abundant fish life here make it a must see.

Gorango Reef, meaning Shark Reef, is located around 50 minutes east of Weda Resort off the northern coastline

Right Tanjung Putus in Weda Bay has an exquisite variety of soft and hard coral species.

Below These schooling jacks were photographed from the descent line on Shark Mountain, Weda Bay.

Numerous species of cuttlefish are found across the Maluku archipelago.

sized parrotfish and sweetlips are found at shallow depths and schools of brightly colored damselfish dance in the light over small table corals branching out from the shadows of the wall into the sun. Huge gorgonians decorate the sides of the reef, providing habitats for feather stars which look as though they are trapped in spiders webs. Schools of cardinals and glassfish also take shelter behind these giant branching fans. Unlike Elmoos Reef, which is almost pristine, there are some areas of broken coral on Gorango and it is here that the sheer drop of the wall, together with the forces of nature are visible. The broken corals appear as landslides down the wall. Most areas of damage are small strips that are on faults in the wall. The rubble mass left behind provides good areas for scissor tail gobies, scorpionfish and nudibranchs. Despite these strips, the reef is almost entirely intact on the south side and makes for an excellent dive with numerous wide-angle photo opportunities.

of Weda Bay. It is a large offshore atoll, which is easily big enough to be divided into several sites. The southern side of the reef offers good fish life and staggering walls stretching down as far as you can see and beyond. Marine charts show that the waters here drop down to almost 900 meters, and although the actual depth of Gorango's walls has yet to be determined, it is safe to assume they are deeper than diving limits allow. The reef is composed of hard coral, with huge plate, boulder and brain corals forming the main part of the walls, offering an interesting mix of both sheer vertical drops and rugged areas featuring ledges, recesses, overhangs and outstretched branching corals, which make for a unique side profile against the blue.

The reef begins from just below the surface and the dive is along the southern walls. If there is a current present, and it is possible, begin by swimming into it for better fish sightings. Keep an eye out to the blue for schools of both juvenile and mature yellow back fusiliers and passing pelagics, such as sharks and barracuda. There is a healthy population of medium sized fish here. Midnight snappers hang out from the reef, good

OLD WEDA RESORT

This is a black sand muck diving site in complete contrast to other sites in Halmahera. It also plays home to some of the area's more bizarre looking creatures. Macro photography opportunities here abound. This is also one of the only muck diving sites in Indonesia where you will not find man-made muck (trash)!

The site is in the bay of Old Weda Resort, close to the Weda Bay Nickel Mining Base. The black sand site runs from east to west with a small jetty on the eastern side. The main dive area is in the center of the bay, although most

A Better and Brighter Future for Halmahera

The Sawai Eco-Tourism Foundation (SETF) is a registered Indonesian foundation working to improve the living standards and educational opportunities of the people of the Sawai Itepo village and to maintain and protect both the terrestrial and marine environments of the Weda region in Halmahera, an area rich in natural beauty and diversity and yet surprisingly poor in so many other ways.

The Weda area is one of vast, dense, primary rainforest. In 2011, it attracted the attention of Rob and Linda Sinke, the founders of SETF, as a site for an eco-tourism operation. SETF was not pre-planned. It came into being after the Sinkes discovered the standard wing (bird of paradise) in the rainforest close to their planned Weda Resort. The birds' *lek* (display trees) were in an area scheduled to be logged. The Sinkes immediately bought the area surrounding the *lek* to protect the bird but discovered later that natural rainforest could not be owned by private individuals. SETF was thus created and the land promptly donated to it. What began as a 25 hectare purchase to protect a single species has now grown to 600 hectares of forest, protected from logging, hunting and poaching, providing sanctuary to numerous species of birds and animals.

Later in 2011 it became apparent to the Sinkes that the people of Sawai Itepo village lacked educational opportunities; 70 percent were illiterate. With a background in teaching, Rob Sinke decided to use the foundation to develop a village kindergarten. SETF now pays for two full-time teachers in the kindergarten, has furnished the classroom, provided books and uniforms and awards certificates for students at the end of each year. By giving education status and the students recognition, the popularity of the kindergarten has increased and the students who are alumni are excelling in primary school compared to those who did not attend. They are also educated about the environment around them and its importance.

The Sawai Foundation has also installed an 85-meter-deep well to feed six main water taps in the village. Three public toilets have been installed and the foundation pays for a janitor to maintain them.

The foundation aims to continue improving the lives of the people of Sawai and to grow its expanse of primary rainforest to protect the wildlife within it. Marine tourism is also on the Sinkes' priority list. As dive operators, they are well aware of the damage that deforestation has on reefs. With the continued support of Weda Resort, SETF, the local community and the Sinkes' passion for this part of Halmahera, Weda Bay and its reefs stand a good chance of staying as pristine and enchanting as they are now for a long time to come.

To support SETF or to find out more, go to www.sawai-ecotourism.com.

The SETF kindergarten is helping to improve the education of children in Sawai.

Estuarine stonefish are often spotted at the black sand sites in both Weda Bay and Ambon Bay.

parts of the bay can be dived. It can also be dived as a shore dive after a surface interval break on the beach. Start close to the shore and make your way to the start of the slope at around 4 meters. The slope is gentle, less than 45 degrees. Head down to your maximum depth and then gradually work your way back up the slope using the current or zigzagging back and forth to cover more area. There is really no coral here, only sand and occasional rocks. Look out for sand hollows, driftwood, branches and leaves on the sand as these pieces of natural debris provide habitat, shade and food for many of the site's inhabitants and come to form mini ecosystems on the desolate sandy slope. Be aware of your fins here as the sand is very fine and silty and once disturbed it takes time to settle. The site provides excellent opportunities for spotting an impressive range of critters, including estuarine stonefish, mimic octopus, flamboyant cuttlefish, frogfish, ghost pipefish, pygmy pipefish and a range of shrimps. On the shallow areas of the slope, look out for unusually large blind gobies and shrimps working symbiotically to dig out huge tunnels and holes.

TIDOR KECIL AND TANJUNG PUTUS

Tidor Kecil and Tanjung Putus are two more wall sites that differ slightly to the ones mentioned above as they are not as deep, bottoming out at around 20 meters to sand and rubble. Both of these sites have healthy fish numbers and interesting bottom dwellers. Sharks are frequent visitors to both these wall sites and Tidor Kecil, in particular, offers good shallow life on the reef top. Octopus, small stingrays and moray eels are often spotted in amongst the soft and hard coral formations.

Tidor Kecil is best dived on the north side where schools of red toothed triggerfish are scattered in the blue along with fusiliers which cruise through in ribbon-like formations. The healthy fish numbers here also attract hunting predators, such as black and white tip reef sharks and barracuda.

Tanjung Putus also boasts a healthy biomass, with pyramid butterfly fish brightly punctuating the blue and large sea whips and gorgonians harboring schools of cardinal and glassfish. Look out for large boulder corals adorned with numerous, brightly colored Christmas tree worms ranging from blue to orange, fuchsia, yellow and white. Whilst they are shy and quick to retract, their colors are impressive. On the base of the wall, at around 20 meters, check for bottom dwellers. Crocodilefish, flat worms, scorpionfish and nudibranchs all enjoy the camouflage of the rubble and sand composition.

WEDA BAY TRAVEL PLANNER

Weda Bay's annual water temperature ranges from 28 to 30 degrees and visibility ranges from 15 meters after rainfall to 40 plus meters. The diving operation closes from June until September for the monsoon season, so check in advance if planning to travel around this time.

Weda Bay hosts numerous mid-sea atoll reefs which can be kilometers from land. Sites are located using GPS. These sudden eruptions of coral reef surrounded by turquoise water are like small oases in the big blue!

At the time of writing, there is only one dive operator in Weda Bay and, as such, diving here is very much an exclusive experience, with not a single other dive boat on the horizon. Dive sites range in depth from shallow sandbars like Pasir Putih to walls such as Gorango, which reach down to almost a kilometer in depth. Maximum advisable depth is 30 meters for most sites and decompression diving should be avoided. The nearest recompression chamber is in Manado, North Sulawesi.

Weda Bay offers just about every diving topography imaginable, including immense walls, shallow white sand reefs, caverns, black sand muck diving, slopes and deep seamounts. This pristine and relatively unexplored area boasts some of the easiest and most diverse diving in Indonesia, and with further exploration anything is possible here! Marine diversity is not only limited to topography. The range of coral species found at any one site is nothing short of staggering.

Recommended Operators

Weda Resort (Author's Choice) Weda Resort sits towards the north end of the west coast of Weda Bay and offers diving, birding and eco tours. The resort has six cabins overlooking the bay, with solar powered hot water bathrooms and private terraces. Full board dive and stay packages are available. The resort operates two speedboats that are able to access sites within 30 kilometers, and are equipped with GPS and oxygen. Equipment hire and courses should be requested in advance. Cabins are almost entirely constructed from sago trees and the resort has been constructed with minimal effect on the environment. Tel: +62 (0) 8124433754 or +62 (0) 81340044758. www.wedaresort.com. Email: info@wedaresort.com.

Below Weda Resort operates speedboats purpose-built for diving.

Bottom Comfortable cottages at Weda Resort were constructed with minimal impact on the environment.

RAJA AMPAT, WEST PAPUA

Raja Ampat is fast becoming every discerning diver's mecca: uninhabited islands, dive sites with no other boats in sight, plenty of places still to explore, warm water, stunning coral reefs, numerous species of rays, including mantas, sharks, a plethora of critters and turtles and an abundance of fish that is simply hard to believe. The region lends itself very well to liveaboard diving but there are island-based operators for those who prefer their evenings on the ground. Numerous efforts are being made to preserve this area as it is one of phenomenal marine biodiversity. Thankfully, these efforts appear to be working and some of the protected reefs are going from strength to strength.

Raja Ampat is not an easy place to access in Indonesia but do not let this put you off as the effort is more than worth it. The island landscapes are as stunning as the underwater reefs. Rock pinnacles surrounded by white sand beaches and shallow water corals make it the picture postcard trip of a lifetime. Diving in Raja Ampat is every diver's dream for many reasons.

Halmahera Sea

Piai I.
Sayang I.
Waya
Wa
Uta Island
Kapaleo
Yu Island
Omnial
Gebe
Fau I.
Island
B
Gebe Airport
Umera
Gag Isla

Klaarbeek I.
Miosyepban I.   Komme

Ettom I. Taudore I.   Jailolo I.   Deer I. Hebe
Boo   Eftorobi I.
Besar I.   Boo   Kofian Isla
Yef   Kecil I. Gebe Is
Beto I.   Walo I.   Ayuan I.
Tabek I.

Ga
Senyu I.
Fafan I.   Kane
Nanisa I.
Nampale I.
Kanari I.   Waigama
Fet Dom Point   Adua
En

Raja Ampat

20 km
20 miles

N

Bougainville Strait

Ayau Island

Island
Uranie I.
ville I.
Schun Is.
Sepatu I.
Go
Missigit
Manuran I.
Lam Lam Kabarei Warkori
Worai Point
Bone I.
Roibe I.
Mey I.
Salio
Wairemah
Wagailom
Wagailon
Waigeo Island
West Waigeo
Nature Reserve
Wauyai
Rabia
Mumos
Waigeo Island
Poeper
Warai Pt
Yenbekaki
yel I.
Pt
ele
ng Pele I.
Waigeo
Gof
Besar I. Gemin I.
Kabui Bay
Wurai I.
Wakre
Mansikor Po
Mamiyai I.
Urbinasopon
minyalfuin I.
Tsiep I.
Pef I.
Walpriren Bay
Gam I.
Yenbesar
Tapokreng
Saonek Kecil I.
Saonek
Waim I.
Yenbekwan Poi
ar I.
Yeben I.
Gaman Bay
Airborek I.
Kri Island
SEE KRI MAP
Dampier Strait
Sausapo
m Besar I.
Keruo I.
Mansuar Island
Merpati I.
Malaworsai
esar I.
Fambemuk I.
Waai I.
Dore Point
Uore Hum Bay
Mega
Dela
Salewok
Inus I.
Makbon
Klawasi
Sceleber
Kemin
Wawesi
AMPAT
RESERVE
Marandanweser
Wensawai
Makoi Point
Kossari Pt
Sorong
Dum I.
Jeffman Airport
Serikoberi
Khadas
Yorbes
Mabo Point
Batanta Island
West Batanta
Jodlo
Weiyaar Bay
Sayosa
Sailala
Klatim
Wailebet
Sagewin Strait
Matalamagi
Dadi Point
Warangke
Waijaar
Waiwo
Flaur
Waiji I.
Yawya I.
West Papua
Kulual
North Salawati
Nature Reserve
Waiboe
Klamono
Tarsa
Klamit
Kapot Bogin Pt
Igiem I.
Salawati Island
Kampung Samodir
Jeflio
Klamono
Kebu I.
Sapraan
Sele Strait
Sorong Daratan
Airport
Biakarlf
Wanurian
Yef Danga I.
Sailolof
Matugu
Salebam
Serebau
Loslos I.
Mara
Yefasim I.
Teminabuan
Fuilu I.
Lopon I.
Deni I.
Kasim
Kampung Baru
Jemur I.
Seremuk
Konda
an I.
Yapdio I.
Efwai I.
Mesluput I.
Sele Point
Seget
Klasafet
Klarion
Komanggaret
Weeim I.
Dua Is
Kalukedi
Wakamoek
Gisim
Sira
M.
Segun Bay
Yamtup Point
Kaibus Bay
Lawat I.
Gewie I.
Kabu I.
Bakoi Point
Waromge Bay
alies I.
Yamtu Point
SEE MISOOL MAP
Oni
Ebo I.
Len Malaas
Nukari Bay
Suabur Point
ol Island
eserve
Folley
Winsop Point
Johadian
I Island
Tamulol
Kalalio
Mustika I.
Biga
Yabatano I.
Farondi Is
ol
Lelintah
Gemut I.
nka Is
Yellit I.
Kalig I.
Daram I.
Pelee I.
Wayilbatan I.
Warakaraket I.

West Papua at a Glance
The Land of the Four Kings, Raja Ampat

From tropical beaches with crystal clear lagoons, lush green rainforest and mangrove coastlines to alpine grasslands and mountainous peaks, the diversity of nature is nowhere more apparent than in West Papua.

Previously known as Irian Jaya, the region was divided into two provinces in 2002: Papua and West Papua. West Papua is also known as the 'Bird's Head Peninsula' because of its shape. It encompasses both the peninsula and the islands of Misool, Salawati, Batanta and Waigeo, collectively known as Raja Ampat, literally 'Four Kings'. The predominant religion is Christian (approximately 60 percent) whilst the other 40 percent is mostly Muslim.

Historically, West Papua was under the control of the Dutch, forming part of the Dutch East Indies, and this continued after Indonesia's independence in 1949. It was not until 1969, after much turmoil and conflict, that the Dutch handed the region back to Indonesia, a move that was not welcomed by a large proportion of the inhabitants of West Papua.

Local children in Raja Ampat have beautiful big smiles for visitors and photographers.

There is still a movement within the region for freedom from Indonesia, but this is for the most part peaceful.

West Papua's climate is hot and humid all year round. The region's dense rainforests combined with the elevation of the Maoke Mountain range, which runs through the region, ensure a tropical environment with a good supply of rain.

West Papua lies in the Asia Australian transition zone and, in fact, shares the same tectonic plate as Australia, which explains the Australian character of the fauna here, including marsupials such as tree kangaroos and wallabies. It was the collision of the Australasian Plate with the Pacific Plate that resulted in the mountainous islands of Raja Ampat being thrown upwards out of the sea, forming the craggy rock pinnacles and islands that provide homes to an abundance of both underwater and terrestrial species of flora and fauna. The naturalist Alfred Russel Wallace was both shocked and overwhelmed when he stepped foot in West Papua to hunt for the mystical bird of paradise and found species that were so different to those present in the west of Indonesia. It was these discoveries that contributed to his theory of the evolution of species and, more famously of the Wallace Line (see Alfred Wallace and the Wallace Line, pages 8–11).

Green pinnacles rising out of the blue, the Wayag Islands in Raja Ampat are simply stunning.

Given that historically New Guinea was joined to Australia by a land ridge, it is not surprising that the plants and animals here bear Australian traits. Ever since sea levels rose and divided the land masses, numerous endemic species have evolved specifically suited for survival in this area. West Papua showcases natural biodiversity like nowhere else on earth and is fast becoming a place of pilgrimage for naturalists and marine enthusiasts the world over.

Many traditional tribes continue to live in the coastal rainforest where they are faced with issues of deforestation. Many tribes have already become extinct and many continue to die out. Outside the two main cities of Sorong on the west coast of West Papua and Manokwari, the capital, to its east, the majority of people live in the west of the province, spread out across villages around the coast of the Raja Ampat Islands where they survive on fish, limited fruits and vegetables and their main carbohydrate, taro.

West Papua has huge natural resources. The main industries in the area are now oil production, mining and logging, the latter being the reason behind much of the deforestation. Fishing remains a large industry, with overfishing a problem in many areas.

The main airports in West Papua are in Sorong and Manokwari and are relatively easy to access from other major cities in Indonesia. Direct flights to Sorong are available if you are coming from Jakarta, but if you are traveling from Bali you will need to come via Makassar. Be aware that excess baggage fees are usually charged on flights into and out of Sorong, so travel light or bring enough money to cover the costs. Sorong does not operate flights outside of daylight hours.

When traveling to West Papua, keep in mind this is not a major tourist spot and some modest clothing is advised. Long trousers and covered shoulders should prevent any offense.

Diving Raja Ampat
A Supreme Showcase of Biodiversity

Pristine coral, diverse reefscapes, phenomenal biomass, endemic species, pelagics and warm clear water set amidst tropical islands combine to make this one of the most stunning areas of natural beauty on earth. It is no wonder that Raja Ampat features on every discerning diver's top five places to visit.

Raja Ampat, with walls, slopes, canyons, seamounts, drifts and calm lagoons, has something to offer everyone, from beginners to seasoned divers. The quality of the coral and the sheer volume of fish are difficult to match and, when coupled with the fact that its remoteness means few divers at each site, you have the right ingredients for some rewarding dives. Gorgonian fans grow meters across, soft corals provide kaleidoscopic colors and, when looking up the reef, it can feel like you are underneath a fish expressway as schools of juvenile fusiliers, sweepers, cardinalfish and glassfish stream overhead. Taking a look out to the blue, the scene is no less dynamic. Schooling triggerfish, mature fusiliers, surgeonfish and bannerfish persistently swim into the current, only interrupted by the passing of patrolling pelagics: sharks, tunas, trevallies and barracudas.

Advance booking is imperative. There is a capped limit of 40 liveaboards in the area and only a handful of reputable

Above Raja Ampat is home to some of the world's most diverse coral reefs.

shore-based dive resorts, which fill up in advance. The best time for travel is between October and June. Only operations in the north of the area run outside of these months due to the monsoon season in the south. The starting point for liveaboards and access to island resorts is via Sorong, which is served domestically by Express Air, Sriwijaya and Lion Air. Operators have limited equipment for hire and generally require guests to have at least fins, mask and wetsuit. If you require BCD and regulator hire, state this when booking. There are no dive equipment stores in Sorong.

Raja Ampat is remote. The plus side of this is that the reefs and islands have escaped the mass tourism found in other areas, such as the Gili Islands and Bali. The reefs are amongst the most pristine in the world and, with the assistance of several NGOs, approximately 45 percent of Raja Ampat is covered by a marine park. In 2007, the government of Raja Ampat introduced a tag system similar to that used in North Sulawesi. Divers purchase a tag, which is valid for one calendar year. At the time of writing, the tag fee is IDR250,000 for Indonesians and IDR500,000 for non-Indonesians. The revenue generated is divided up as follows: local government (30 percent), conservation/patrols (28 percent), administration costs (14 percent) and community initiatives (14 percent). Individuals can purchase tags from the Raja Ampat Marine office in the Je Meridien Hotel in Sorong, but usually your operator will arrange this for you. A passport sized photograph and photocopy of your passport are required.

The remoteness of Raja Ampat does have some drawbacks. There are few facilities for visitors in Sorong and standards are basic. Access to emergency medical services is limited. Although there are local hospitals in Sorong with oxygen supplies, the nearest internationally recognized recompression chamber is in Manado, North Sulawesi. It is strongly advised that divers dive within the no decompression limits. Operators should have medical supplies, but it is best to be well prepared and pack enough of any prescription medications for your trip. Telephone communication in some areas is impossible, and whilst access to the Internet can be purchased from many operators, it is very slow and connections are not always successful.

Whilst Raja Ampat is an area of extreme beauty, boasting some of the world's richest and most diverse reefs, there have been destructive fishing practices in the past and some areas have been overfished. That said, with the growing number of conservation efforts in the area, extensive community work by organizations such as the Raja Ampat Research and Conservation Centre (see pages 268–9), the support of local government and the success of no-take zones, such as that established by the Misool Eco Resort, shark numbers are increasing and biomass is flourishing.

Dense schools of fish are not uncommon in Raja Ampat where biomass is excellent.

Kri and Misool:
18 Days of Remote Reefs

If time allows, then diving in both Kri and Misool offers a stunning range of dive sites on some of Indonesia's most pristine reefs. Transfers from one to the other will be via Sorong and require an overnight stay there, as outlined below. Divers can start in Kri and finish in Misool, or vice versa.

Day 1 Arrive in Sorong and overnight there ready for transfer to resort the following morning.

Day 2 Transfer to either Kri Island or Misool Eco Resort in the morning using operator's transfer boat. Afternoon dives or a check out dive if required.

Days 3–8 Diving in either Kri or Misool; 3 to 4 dives per day plus night dives if desired.

Day 9 Transfer back to Sorong with operator's transfer boat and overnight in Sorong.

Day 10 Transfer to either Kri or Misool Eco Resort in the morning using operator's

Right The *Tambora* liveaboard features a large saloon area for guests to relax and enjoy the cuisine.

Below *Tambora* looks stunning under sail but is also well equipped with motors for when winds are not in her favor.

transfer boat. Afternoon dives possible.

Days 11–16 Program for these days is as for Days 3–8. On Day 16, consider if you are flying on day 17 and curtail dives to ensure 24 hours of non-diving prior to flying.

Day 17 Return to Sorong with operator's transfers for either afternoon flight or morning flight on Day 18 or transfer to liveaboard (see below).

Land and Liveaboard

It is possible to combine a trip to either Misool or Kri with a liveaboard trip. If this is your intention, there are two options for transferring from your shore-based operator to the liveaboard. The first is to return to Sorong and transition there, but this will probably require a one night stay in Sorong. Alternatively, you can arrange for your

chosen liveaboard to either drop you off at your shore-based resort or pick you up from there. Most liveaboard operators are happy to accommodate divers, but it does mean that when scheduling your trip you need to find out the date when the liveaboard will be in the same area and then work out the dates for your shore-based diving from there. Make sure that both the shore-based operator and the liveaboard are clear about pick-up and drop-off arrangements and who is taking responsibility for which.

Liveaboards

(See also Liveaboard Diving in Indonesia, page 272–7, for more options.)

Tambora A purpose-built upper mid-range liveaboard with 8 spacious ensuite cabins catering for 16 passengers. *Tambora* offers a high level of comfort, excellent dive facilities, including nitrox and gear rental (upon request), as well as being well equipped with two tenders, modern safety and navigation technology and an experienced crew. Tours include Raja Ampat, Komodo and others. Tel: +62 (0) 213920918. www.tamboradive.com. Email: info@tamboradive.com.

Arenui The *Arenui* offers divers some of the most high-end liveaboard facilities in Raja Ampat. With 8 cabins catering for up to 16 guests, the *Arenui* provides 5 star service and luxurious accommodation. Tours include Raja Ampat, Komodo and others. Tel: +62 (0) 361750 034. www.thearenui.com. Email: info@ thearenui.com.

Shakti The *Shakti* liveaboard is a popular choice for those looking for a more affordable option, offering bi-monthly 12 day tours around Raja Ampat. Shakti is a 32 meter schooner which caters for 10 guests with shared bathrooms. Stationed permanently in Raja

Ampat since 2002. Tel: +62 (0) 8124838873. www.shakti-raja-ampat.com. Email: info@ shakti-raja-ampat.com.

USEFUL CONTACTS

Je Meridien Hotel Jalan Basuki Rahmat Km 7, across the main road from the airport.

Recompression Chamber Prof. Dr Kandou Hospital, Jalan Raya Tanawangko 56, Malalayang Satu. Tel: +62 (0) 431838305. Dr Hanry Takasenseran Tel: +62 (0) 81340000840.

Sorong Hospital Kartini Hospital, Sorong, Dr Russel Tel: +62 (0) 8124835614.

Tag Purchase www.diverajaampat.org or email info@diverajaampat.org.

Sorong Airport (SOQ): Tel: +62 (951) 32769.

Sriwijaya Air Call Center Tel: +62 (0) 21 29279777 or 08041777777. www.sriwijayaair.co.id.

Lion Air Assistance Line Tel: +62 (0) 21 63798000. www.lionair.co.id.

Xpress Air 24 Hour Call Center Tel: +62 (0) 21500890. www.xpressair.co.id.

Master Selam Aqualung retailer with outlets in both Bali and Jakarta. www.masterselam.com.

The *Arenui* liveaboard is staffed by a friendly, experienced and professional crew.

Misool Filling Station

The Misool Filling Station (MFS) is a joint venture by the folks at Misool Eco Resort and their registered marine conservation foundation, Misool Baseftin. The cafe/shop is located directly across the street from the entrance to Sorong Airport. MFS offers chic air-conditioned café-style surroundings, Internet access, a range of coffees, iced drinks, juices, smoothies, cold beers and homemade treats to enjoy whilst you wait for your flight or pick-up. MFS also sells dive books, toiletries and other adventure provisions you may have forgotten to bring, locally made handicrafts and cruelty-free souvenirs (no dolphin teeth necklaces or turtleshell bracelets). A wealth of information about related conservation projects is also available. Depending on the item, between 3 and 100 percent of the proceeds go to the Misool Baseftin Foundation, so you can rest assured that you are helping the marine life and people of Raja Ampat whilst you relax in comfort. Jalan Basuki Rachmat Km. 8, Ruko No. 8. Tel: +62 (0) 9513160388. www.misoolfillingstation.com.

Left The friendly team at Misool Filling Station are ready to welcome you to Sorong.

Below Misool Filling Station offers great refreshments in comfortable, stylish surroundings.

Diving Misool
Exceptional Diving at Iconic Dive Sites

From Magic Mountain to Boo Windows, Misool is home to some of Raja Ampat's most iconic dive sites. With the Misool-Daram no-take zone created by Misool Eco Resort now covering an area twice the size of Singapore, it is easy to see why this is one of the world's most prestigious diving areas. Sharks and rays, including mantas, patrol the reefs and keep the prolific fish life in check. Shallow water soft corals in a profusion of colors sway in the sunlight, and deeper down the reefs display high-density coral coverage and are home to a diverse range of species. Turtles, wobbegongs, reef sharks, epaulette sharks, stingrays, mantas, schools of jacks and trevallies, barracuda and Napoleon wrasse are all found on Misool's reefs. If macro life and critters are more to your liking, the pygmy seahorses, huge range of nudibranchs, shrimps and ghost pipefish will not disappoint. Misool is an exceptional destination, and whilst it is not the most accessible region in Indonesia, the effort it takes to get here is rewarded by diving in one of the archipelago's most untouched areas. As the development of conservation zones continues, Misool only stands to get better and better.

Whether you are staying at the Misool Eco Resort or sailing by liveaboard, this is a very remote area so think ahead when it comes to packing as there are no opportunities for heading out to buy snacks or supplies. Alcohol is expensive but most operators have no objection to guests arriving with duty free. Due to the large Muslim population, pork is not readily available but most dietary requirements can be met. Let your operator know any specific needs in advance.

Packages/liveaboards in Misool are all-inclusive covering meals, snacks, soft drinks and hot beverages while alcohol is billable as is laundry and phone charges.

There is an ATM in the Je Meridien Hotel in Sorong which accepts most major cards.

HIGHLIGHTS Stunning, remote islands with white sand beaches. Pristine reefs with world class soft coral, gorgonian fans of impressive proportions, abundant marine life, epaulette sharks, manta rays, wobbegongs, white tip and black tip

reef sharks and turtles, all of which are increasing in numbers largely due to the marine park's no-take zone.

DIFFICULTY LEVEL Misool has a range of dive sites that can be suitable for all levels of divers. There are currents here but operators time dives and select dive sites according to tidal changes. Some seamount sites do have stronger currents, such as Magic Mountain. If currents look strong at the surface, there are many other sites to choose from.

LOGISTICS Misool is the most southerly of the Four Kings and there are only really two options for diving here: liveaboard

The Misool Eco Resort is set around a crystal clear, tranquil bay.

The halimeda ghost pipefish is camouflaged to look almost identical to *Halimeda macroalga*.

or staying at the Misool Eco Resort. For both, the starting point is Sorong. Usually divers will overnight in Sorong before being met by their operator and depart to either the resort or to their liveaboard the following morning. At the time of writing, most operators use the Je Meridien Hotel as it is close to the airport and harbor and Sorong currently offers few other alternatives.

MISOOL'S BEST DIVE SITES

WHALE ROCK

Craggy and rugged above the water but with layers of schooling fish, Whale Rock is full of color and life beneath. The entry point is usually on the south side of the rock and the dive begins by heading west. The topography is a mix of wall and steep sloping reef with a shallow water soft coral garden. Both coral and fish are abundant. The reef is a good mix of soft and hard coral species, and as you reach the western end of the rock there are a couple of interesting undulations in the 20 to 22 meter range. If the current allows, it is possible to circumnavigate the entire rock in one dive. If this is not possible, it is still a beautiful dive heading west along the south side and then back to the east as you make your way back up. Large green turtles are often seen here as are vast schools of red toothed triggerfish in the blue. The wide variety of corals on the reef means that macro life is plentiful and similarly varied. Look out for orangutan crabs and nudibranchs and sporadically scattered fans. Damsels and brightly colored antheas adorn the shallow water soft corals against the backdrop of the blue.

FIABACET

Fiabacet not only has interesting topography but also abundant soft corals, a variety of mixed fans and impressive schools of juvenile fusiliers, surgeonfish and damsels glittering like colorful gems in the sun. This site typifies some of the best traits of Misool diving. The soft corals grow densely and a wide array of species is showcased. The site starts from Fiabacet Rock. If you enter on the north side, start by heading east, towards Whale Rock. Make your way down to around 20 to 25 meters, keeping an eye out into the blue for passing pelagics. Depending on the current, you can either cross the ridge to Whale Rock or simply traverse Fiabacet. Fiabacet wall on the south side has numerous recesses and overhangs so a light is worth bringing along. It's possible to find nudibranchs, scorpionfish and a variety of shrimps. In the shallow water, Fiabacet really comes to life. Colorful tubers, fans and sea squirts cover the reef crest whilst damselfish and fairy basslets catch the light from the sun as they dart in and out of the reef. Breathtaking scenery with an abundance of life that is hard to match.

Note that Fiabacet is also the name given by some operators to the underwater ridge that connects Tank Rock and Nudi Rock.

SIXTH SENSE

This is a sloping reef and wall dive with huge macro diversity, phenomenal light-blocking fans and an abundance of healthy soft corals for which the Misool area is famed. The site is around a rocky island on a steeply sloping reef to the east with predominantly soft corals, tubers and small fans growing from sandy ledges, which harbor pygmy seahorses and coral shrimps. On the north side of the rock, the reef topography changes and becomes more of a vertical wall. The wall supports much denser coral growth and the gorgonians here cast shadows as they block out the light from above. Huge black coral ferns hang out from the wall, providing shelter for schools of cardinals and sweepers. Recessed caverns are scattered across the wall in the 20 meter and upward levels and are good for checking out crustaceans. If the current allows it, continue making your way up the wall until making a safety stop on the reef crest. If the currents are strong, it may be necessary to double back the way you came as you progress to shallower depths. In the shallows, the sunlight brightens the reef and creates a soft coral patchwork in a variety of colors and textures. Keep an eye out to the blue for schooling batfish and fusiliers, and don't forget to look overhead as the sheer volume of fish life is astonishing.

THE BIRTHDAY CAKE

A topographical melting pot based around a seamount featuring sloping reefs, walls, ridges and pinnacles that give the birthday cake its 'candles'. The site is renowned for shark and pelagic sightings, remarkable biomass, extreme coral diversity and kaleidoscopic colors.

The Birthday Cake is a submerged seamount around 50 meters out from the south side of the largest island of the Boo chain. The entry is made over or slightly

Above The Misool area is well known for its variety of colorful soft corals.

Left Manta rays are frequently spotted at cleaning stations around Misool.

up current from the top of the seamount, less than 10 meters. Descending down the mount, there is a wall to the west and a sloping reef to the east. Following the sloping reef east at around 20 to 25 meters, the coral is an even mix of soft and hard species interspersed with sandy ledges. The sloping reef bottoms out at around 25 meters. The sheer volume of biomass here makes this dive an awesome experience. On a good day, both vertical curtains of glassfish and horizontal ribbons of juveniles stream past. Keep an alert eye out to the blue. Sharks patrol the mount and turtles are also frequently seen here. Looking into the reef, there are numerous vertical faults and crevices and horizontal ledges that create shadowy areas for critters and nocturnals to hide out in. As you head east, look out for the start of the ridge that forms the spine of the seamount. This will guide you back up to the entry point, taking you around an array of pinnacles and formations stretching upwards to just below the surface. The most stunning part of the Birthday Cake has to be heading back up the ridge to the shallows: pinnacles adorned with soft corals and small barrels and table corals taking up the spaces in between. The shallow water and sunlight make these pinnacles truly the icing on the cake. Vivacious colors are made even more intense by the surrounding contrasting blue water. It is an amazing locale for your safety stop, but watch for currents here, though, sweeping over the top of the mount!

Misool Dive Sites

Dive Sites :
1. Kalig Wall
2. Fiabacet
3. Whale Rock
4. Nudi Rock
5. Tank Rock
6. Boo West
7. Birthday Cake
8. Boo Windows
9. Cape Boo
10. Southwest Batbitim
11. Misool Eco Resort
12. Sixth Sense
13. Epaulette City
14. Warakaraket Wall

10 km
5 miles

N

Seram Sea

MAGIC MOUNTAIN (SHADOW REEF)
☆AUTHOR'S CHOICE

This is a site that really lives up to its name. Anything is possible around this seamount and its ridge: manta rays, patrolling white tips, sheltering wobbegongs, big tunas and hunting trevallies. It is definitely a site for looking into the blue!

Magic Mountain is an underwater seamount characterized by a plateau area ranging from around 5 to 12 meters with an extending ridge on the west side which drops down to around 23 meters before rising back up again to 19 meters at its tip, which forms a manta ray cleaning station.

This white tip reef shark was pictured patrolling the blue, off the side of Magic Mountain.

As the site is relatively small and requires an entry in the open ocean, a negative entry may be necessary if the currents are running fast. Drop down to the plateau and head west to find the arm of the extending ridge. Usually one side of the ridge will be subject to current but the other side is comparatively sheltered. Head out along the ridge to the raised cleaning station but approach with care. Mantas will continue to clean despite divers being present, but if spooked unexpectedly, they may leave the area. The cleaning station attracts mainly reef manta rays but passing oceanic rays (*birostris*) are not unheard of. Keep an eye out to the blue of the current side of the ridge as the currents attract schooling fish and patrolling white tips in numbers. Giant trevally and tuna also hunt here. Watch your air and no-stop time. Bear in mind that ideally you want to make it back to the top of the plateau for the safety stop, which means allowing enough time to traverse back along the ridge and up the slope. The plateau does not fail to impress either, with rugged, brightly colored coral-encrusted pinnacles that attract schools of fairy bass-

lets, juvenile fusiliers, golden sweepers and cardinalfish sheltering from the current. Around the base of the pinnacles are craggy boulders that wobbegong sharks hide underneath. Mantis shrimps, stonefish and morays inhabit shaded crevices and dugouts.

This is a site not to be missed for its mantas, sharks, big predators, some decent currents and a kaleidoscope of colors.

TANK ROCK (BATU KECIL)

A rock pinnacle rising up from the sea with an underwater topography of walls and sloping reefs that host impressive critter life and abundant schooling smaller fish and juveniles. The entry point for this site can be on the north or south side of the pinnacle depending on the current direction. If you enter on the south side, follow the ridge east down to around 15 meters from where the wall begins. Following the wall west at 20 to 25 meters, the coral is a mix of hard and soft with an array of smaller fans, sea whips and black corals with schools of golden sweepers taking shelter behind them. The wall has a mix of small ledges,

Allied cowries have intricate markings and are found on sea fans and soft corals.

overhangs and shelves. Sea squirts on the reef and Christmas tree worms growing on stone corals are abundant. Blue triggerfish school in the blue along with fusiliers, and there is a possibility of bigger predators. Macro life does not fall short here either. Ornate ghost pipefish and ringed pipefish are known to find camouflage on the wall. Making your way up the wall towards 15 meters, the coral density increases and schools of smaller fish dart back and forth overhead. Green turtles are frequent visitors here. At 10 meters, the soft corals create a candy shop display of colors and textures. Damselfish and fairy basslets swim persistently into the current just above the reef and a variety of reef fish, from Moorish idols and coral groupers to sweetlips, add to the vibrant mix.

GORGONIAN PASSAGE (WAYILBATAN)

A stunning wall with impressive corals dominated by enormous sea fans that really make this a breathtaking site.

Gorgonian Passage is a narrow passage running north to south between the islands of Wayilbatan and Walib. The site can be dived from either end depending on the current, but it's usual to dive the wall of Wayilbatan on the west side of the passage and start at the northern end as this is the deeper end of the canyon which bottoms out at 32 meters. As you head south through the canyon, the depth gradually decreases to around 20 meters. The fans are the reason for diving this site, and will impress even the most seasoned of divers, particularly in the 10 to 20 meter range on the north end where they stretch almost 3 meters across. As when any body of water is pushed between two narrow points, there is usually some current here running from one end of the canyon to the other, so stay relatively close to the wall. The vertical curtains of sweeperfish and glassfish gathered against the walls are good indicators of current changes! At around 25 meters where the sand begins, look out for bottom dwellers such as scorpionfish and forests of garden eels. Make your way up the wall as you progress along the channel. Whilst the fans are clearly the highlight of this dive, there is other notable marine life: bat and sweetlips can be found under many of the ledges of the wall, schools of glassfish hide out behind and in the fans and macro marine creatures, including ghost pipefish, coral shrimp and nudibranchs, can all be found here too.

NUDI ROCK

The site is given its name due to the shape and appearance of the rock pinnacle, which is visible from the surface. Do not be mistaken though. This is definitely a site for larger pelagic lovers!

The rock pinnacle is on an east–west axis and the dive is best started on the north side heading east, if the current allows, as this is the steeper and deeper side of the site. Do not be surprised if the wall is not your focal point here. From the surface down, there can be schools of fish in the blue water column, from fusiliers to triggers and schooling banners. Don't forget to look up as great barracuda often school below the surface. Patrolling pelagics are often a little further out, keeping the smaller swimmers in check. White tip reef sharks are frequent visitors. Heading east along the wall at around 22 meters, a ridge is formed which runs from Nudi Rock to nearby Tank Rock. After crossing the ridge, there is a rubble and sand area at 25 meters which extends around the eastern tip and then meets the sloping reef on the south side of the rock. Over the sand, yellow tail barracuda and batfish cruise through, while the south side

sloping reef is home to green turtles, nudibranchs and other smaller critters. Make your way up the slope to the safety stop on the wall crest. The shallow waters are also full of life and a variety of hard and soft corals. Table corals, boulder corals and plates provide ledges for scorpionfish, a variety of shrimp and eels and hoards of Misool's colorful reef fish.

EPAULETTE CITY: NIGHT DIVE

A small seamount site which epaulette sharks are known to frequent at night, plus some other interesting nocturnal marine life.

The top of the Epaulette City seamount ranges in depth from around 9 to 15 meters and is littered with various formations and pinnacles. The plateau

The Birthday Cake dive site is home to many dense schools of glassfish.

This green turtle was pictured during a night dive at Epaulette City.

drops away on all sides to a sloping reef beginning at around 15 meters. The top of the mount is predominantly a hard coral mix of tables, other branching corals and some boulders and plates with a smattering of small soft corals filling the spaces in between. Epaulette sharks are the primary reason for diving here, and whilst they are a non-swimming species of shark, they still move fast, particularly when under torchlight, which will send them looking for cover. The sides of the seamount provide a hunting ground for larger species, including black tip sharks, so a look over the edge is worthwhile. Aside from shark life, the site is a good one for sleeping turtles and a range of crustaceans. Look out also for schooling batfish overhead that seemingly follow divers around the mount. The descent to the top of the plateau is made via the mooring line and the dive itself is a case of navigating the circumference of the seamount in decreasing circles back to the mooring line. Due to the steep sloping sides around the plateau, navigation here is easy as the top of the seamount is relatively small.

The Pygmy Seahorse

Hippocampus bargibanti

The *Hippocampus bargibanti* was the first species of pygmy seahorse to be discovered, as late as 2000. There are now known to be several species of pygmy seahorse, which rarely grow to more than 2 cm in length, including the tail. Pygmy seahorses are not found worldwide and the majority of them inhabit the area of Asia known as the Coral Triangle, which encompasses parts of Indonesia, Malaysia and the Philippines. They are part of the Syngnathidae family, which includes seahorses, pipefish and weedy and leafy sea dragons, whose distinctive features include tubular mouths into which they suck their food and very short snouts. The males carry their young inside their trunk as opposed to inside a pouch on the tail like other seahorse species. The majority of pygmy seahorses, including the

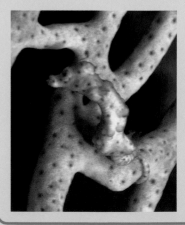

Bargibanti, are found on sea fans although some species also attach themselves to algae and soft corals.

The three main species of pygmy seahorse found in Indonesia are Bargibanti's pygmy seahorse, Denise's pygmy seahorse and Pontoh's pygmy seahorse, with the Bargibanti being by far the most widespread.

Bargibanti's pygmy seahorses (*Hippocampus bargibanti*) live on Muricella gorgonian fans between 16 and 40 meters and are able to match their skin color and appearance to that of the fan almost exactly. Combined with their tiny size, this makes them very difficult to spot. Their camouflage ability is no coincidence. They appear to live in symbiosis with the fan, which leads to them reacting and developing tubercles that mimic the bulbous textures of the fan corals. The most common color variations are pink, yellow and light purple. The maximum length of a Bargibanti is 2.7 cm, including the tail, which makes them the largest of all the pygmy seahorse species.

Denise's pygmy seahorse (*Hippocampus denise*) is smaller than the Bargibanti and measures only up to 2.4 cm in length and it tends to be less fleshy. Denises are found on different species of fans rather than just being limited to one particular host. The

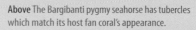

Above The Bargibanti pygmy seahorse has tubercles which match its host fan coral's appearance.

Above left This tiny Denise species of pygmy seahorse was pictured clinging to its coral host.

Opposite below Numerous species of pygmy seahorse are found in Raja Ampat.

Denise species have considerably fewer tubercles, which gives their skin a much smoother appearance. They also have a number of color variations, including red, yellow, brownish and orange. Denise's pygmy seahorses have been sighted at depths of up to 90 meters.

Pontoh's pygmy seahorses (*Hippocampus pontohi*) do not live on gorgonian fans but instead are found on algae such as halimeda algae and various sea grasses. Unlike other species, they do not stick to one host and are seen moving from place to place in depths of 3 to 25 meters. The Pontoh lacks tubercles and ranges in color from white with pink to yellow patches.

Whilst pygmy seahorses are seen across the archipelago, Raja Ampat is one of the best places to view a number of different species of these tiny creatures.

Top Scorpionfish are known to yawn, revealing their huge, cavernous mouths.

Above The ceratosoma nudibranch is one of numerous species found across Raja Ampat.

BOO WINDOWS (JAMUR BOO)

With phenomenal topography, schooling marine life, hoards of fish, critters, pelagics and swim-throughs, Boo Windows is an iconic Misool site that has it all!

The site is situated around the two small rocky outcroppings on the most eastern tip of the Boo Island chain. Entry is best made to the south with the current to the north. The site is very susceptible to surge in the shallows so is best dived when sea conditions are relatively flat and calm. The two rocks are connected underwater by a ridge with a sloping reef dropping away to each side. Swim down the sloping reef in front of the larger rock heading south, then progress around the smaller rock. In good conditions, you can make it back to the larger rock on the opposite side to your entry area. The name Boo Windows comes from the two swim-throughs just below the surface on the larger rock, which make it possible to swim through the rock and back to your drop in point without having to swim around the northern tip.

The topography of this site is what makes it remarkable. Aside from the swim-throughs, which appear as aquamarine windows in the rugged rock, there are boulder formations and pinnacles around the southern tip of the ridge that are completely encrusted with short, bright soft corals and sea squirts. As you round the smaller rock, the sheer volume of fish can make it hard to see your buddy, it is that abundant! Schools of sweepers, glassfish, juvenile fusiliers and damsels stream past in the current, whilst in the blue triggerfish, barracuda, trevally and other predators hover menacingly. The shallow waters are sublime, with scorpionfish, shrimps, lionfish and sweetlips adding to the rainbow of colors. This is a site which could keep you occupied and wanting more, dive after dive.

MISOOL TRAVEL PLANNER

The Misool area is characterized by literally hundreds of small, rocky islands and pinnacles that were formed when layers of rock were thrust upwards when the Asian Indo-Pacific and Australasian plates collided. The islands vary in size from small rocks only a meter or two above the surface to much larger islands that tower overhead and support an abundance of tree and shrub life. The islands are long and narrow and generally lie along an east–west axis.

The best way to dive the pinnacles is to enter mid-island on the side that the current is hitting first, swim into the current towards the tip of the Island, then either drift back or around the tip and continue on the other side. This type of profile gives the best fish sightings. The small size of the islands means that drifting with the current is not practical. By swimming into the current, you maximize time on the reef and at the tip of the islands, which is where you will see abundant fish life, large schools of smaller fish and possible bigger pelagics in the blue.

Water temperature is 28 to 30 degrees year round and visibility ranges from 15 to 25 meters. A long suit is advisable to protect against stingers. As Misool is very remote, depths are generally restricted to 30 meters and dive times to 60 minutes with at least one hour surface interval in between. Diving with an SMB is recommended.

Liveaboards and the Misool Eco Resort offer similar diving schedules with a morning dive followed by breakfast, mid-morning dive, afternoon dive after lunch, late afternoon dives and night dives. Nitrox is available and recommended if you are planning three or more dives in a day.

Much of the area around southeast Misool falls under the Misool-Daram Conservation

Top The Misool Eco Resort is surrounded by shallow reefs that can be enjoyed by the whole family.

Above A snorkeler watches a school of barracuda near the Misool Eco Resort.

Area. Liveaboards contact the resort ahead and check dive schedules to ensure there is no more than one boat at any one site.

Recommended Operators

Misool Eco Resort (Author's Choice)
Luxury resort situated on Batbitim Island, full board dive and stay packages with stunning water bungalows over an exquisite aquamarine lagoon boasting a population of juvenile black tip sharks. Dive center, conservation center, daily fun diving, 4 dives per day and night dives, nitrox available, equipment hire and PADI courses available on request in advance, spa, speedboat transfers from Sorong. www.misooleceresort.com. Email: info@misooleceresort.com.

MISOOL ECO RESORT

A Shining Example of an Eco-Friendly, Sustainable Marine Resort

Misool Eco Resort (MER) is based on the tiny island of Batbitim in the Misool area of Raja Ampat, West Papua. Whilst the resort itself is small, the reaches of its no-take zone and many conservation projects, including its 1,220 kilometer Marine Conservation Area, are anything but.

The concept of a conservation center in southeast Misool was first mooted by Andrew Miners in 2005, and since then he and his wife Marit have worked tirelessly to not only construct the resort but to create a marine conservation area approximately twice the size of Singapore, which prohibits fishing of any kind, including longlining, turtle egg collecting and any other invasive or destructive practices. The entire zone is patrolled by MER Rangers who ensure that the terms of the zone are being upheld and who also work on many of the other conservation projects underway.

The resort itself is a prime example of how construction can be managed to produce the smallest possible footprint on the environment. The bungalows are constructed entirely from reclaimed timbers, all of which came from Batbitim or neighboring islands and, amazingly, not a single tree was cut down to build the resort or furnish the interiors.

Misool Eco Resort Rangers patrol the resort's huge no-take zone daily.

Andrew and Marit Miner have succeeded in creating an operation which, first and foremost, serves to protect the natural environment of southeast Misool and works in tandem with the local people to improve education and employment opportunities. It also demonstrates that sustainable tourism can provide a more ethical and longer term source of income than shark finning, mining, logging or destructive fishing.

So why has Misool been so successful in a field where so many others have had only limited results? There are several answers to this but the most notable has to be determination. The Miners did not just oversee the resort's construction, they lived it, literally. Sleeping in tents on the north beach and with no fresh water, limited food and even scarcer finances, they milled timbers, sailed to nearby islands to access wells, dug foundations, set cement, worked side by side with local laborers and craftsmen despite language and communications problems, and all of this on modest food rations, no telephone reception and being up to six hours away from the nearest major town, Sorong. Their success, in part, also comes from two local communities: the Yellu from which MER leases the reefs covered by the No Take Zone and the Fafanlap. The people of these communities have a tradition of *sasi*, which involves opening and closing fishing seasons on reefs in turn so that no one area is ever significantly depleted of fish. In the early 2000s, several fishing rights had been sold to outsiders who began shark finning in concentrated areas, in direct conflict with the concept of *sasi*. This paved the way for the granting of the lease for the No Take Zone, which was received as a return to traditional values. Finally, MER is based in the province of West Papua where the laws regulating the ownership of reefs are markedly different from those in the rest of Indonesia where ownership of reefs is not recognized.

Misool Eco Resort is now a successful enterprise offering guests high-end resort accommodation and the opportunity to dive the protected zone around them. Since the creation of the No Take Zone, biomass has increased by a phenomenal 250 percent. The lagoon, which was a shark finning camp, now hosts juvenile black tip reef sharks that swim to the steps of the onlooking bungalows. The Raja Ampat Shark and Manta Sanctuary is well underway, monitoring both activity within the zone and across all of Raja Ampat. Another initiative, the Misool Manta Project, was instrumental in establishing the national ban on manta fishing in Indonesia.

The improvements which can be attributed to the Misool Eco Resort and its associated registered charity Misool Baseftin, are not just marine based. Local workers who helped to construct the resort were taught English so that they could remain in employment as resort staff after construction was complete. The resort employs over 120 local staff and Baseftin has built a kindergarten in the local village of Fafanlap and supports local school libraries.

With its far-reaching projects and the continued support of the local community, Misool Eco Resort is carving out a future for the continued protection and preservation of this unique area and its people and setting an example for other operators to follow.

For more information about Misool Eco Resort, see page 253.

Above left The Misool Eco Resort employed local workers in its construction, many of whom still work in the resort.

Left Black tip reef sharks swim in the bay of Misool Eco Resort, once a shark finning camp.

Diving Kri
Diversity Beyond Compare

With scenery that looks as though it has come straight out of a travel magazine and dive sites to match, Kri has to be one of Indonesia's most picturesque destinations both on land and underwater. The reefs around Kri boast a wealth of diverse marine life, from numerous shark species and manta rays to tiny pygmy seahorses and macro critters. This stunning area can be explored from either a land base operated by one of a handful of shore-based operators or by liveaboard. Whichever option you choose, you will not be disappointed by Kri's truly world class dive sites.

Of all the main Raja Ampat islands, Waigeo is the one with the most going on. It has a range of local stores and *warung* for buying supplies. There is also a local hospital on Waigeo, a recompression chamber and a number of clinics and pharmacies. There are several local budget homestays around Waisai, the administrative capital of Raja Ampat, a handful of which offer diving. If you are hoping to travel to Raja Ampat on a budget, this is where you will find the cheapest diving, but be aware that you are in a very remote area and not all operators follow safety conscious protocols. Equipment and tanks may or may not be serviced regularly, guides are not necessarily trained and dive schedules can be disorganized. Diving with a more reputable operator is strongly recommended.

Cell phone reception and Internet access in the area are very limited and in some places non-existent. Check what facilities your operator has in advance and ask which service provider offers the best coverage in their area before buying a local SIM card.

The local people of Kri mainly fish and farm for both subsistence and trade and a small number of locals are employed in tourism-related positions in resorts and homestays and on transfer boats.
DIFFICULTY LEVELS The diving in Kri Island ranges in difficulty from easy to advanced depending on the site and the

Below Manta Sandy is one of Kri's most renowned dive sites for seeing manta rays.

Right Epaulette sharks, also known as walking sharks, are a nocturnal species seen on night dives.

This small broadclub cuttlefish was displaying changing colors and textures.

time you dive. Most sites can be timed to minimize currents but there are some which generally have stronger currents and occasional down drafts. If you are hoping to see schools of fish, some current diving is necessary.

HIGHLIGHTS Picture perfect islands surrounded by turquoise waters. Stunning reefs with prolific fish life and diversity, various reef sharks, epaulette sharks and wobbegongs, manta rays, turtles, large schools of fish and a whole host of critters.

LOGISTICS The small island of Kri is positioned approximately two hours to the west and slightly north of Sorong on the western tip of West Papua. The larger island of Gam sits to the north and Batanta to the south. There are two resorts based on the island of Kri itself: Kri Eco Resort and Sorido Bay Resort. Both are owned by Papua Diving and offer different experiences and cater to different budgets. Kri Eco Resort was

the first shore-based resort to open in Raja Ampat and offers traditional wooden Papuan bungalows built on stilts over the water. It is the cheaper option of the two and is generally more basic. Sorido Bay is the more upmarket of the resorts, offering private cottages and high-end service. Liveaboard diving is also a popular choice for diving in the area (see pages 272–5.)

Liveaboard guests and those staying with Papua Diving resorts are met in Sorong and transported to the harbor to board either their liveaboard or transfer boat to Kri. Transfers are included in Papua Diving's prices providing you meet their scheduled transfers. If you are making your own way, there is a daily public ferry from Sorong to Waisai on Waigeo Island, but unless you are staying on Waigeo you will need to charter another boat in Waisai to take you to your chosen island or have your operator pick you up. Ferry crossings to Waisai take 2 to 3.5 hours depending on sea conditions and on which ferry is making the trip.

KRI'S BEST DIVE SITES

CAPE KRI AND SORIDO WALL
☆AUTHOR'S CHOICE

Cape Kri is the site where Dr Gerald Allen set a new world record when he counted 374 species of fish in a single tank dive. Once you have dived here, it is easy to see how! Cape Kri offers excellent biomass, phenomenal diversity and some interesting currents.

The entry point is on the southeast side of Kri island where the top of the reef offers a picturesque shallow coral garden interspersed with sandy patches. It is also a great place for watching passing hawksbill turtles feeding on the reef. The drop-off is a little further out and gives way to a steeply sloping reef offering a mix of both soft and hard corals down to 40 meters. As you descend over the drop-off, head east along the reef towards the tip of the island and the channel that separates Kri from Koh. Currents here can be both strong and tricky as the water is split when it hits the tip of Kri. As with many Raja Ampat dive sites, where the current hits the reef is where you find the majority of the fish, and Cape Kri fits the formula. Schools

Around Kri every coral head and bommie harbors a profusion of reef fish.

of fusiliers dart back and forth whilst hoards of damselfish glitter against the reef. Everything seems alive and the colors in the shallows are spectacular, even on the cloudiest of days. Depending on your air supply and the current, aim to spend some time in the current stream as it is a great place to watch the marine food chain in action. The schools of smaller fish here bring in numerous predators. Look out to the blue for patrolling giant trevallies, Spanish mackerel and hunting tuna. On good days, white tip, black tip and grey reef sharks are also seen. On the sandy bottom below the slope at 35–40 meters, there is a scattering of bommies which are shrouded with glassfish and schools of ribbon sweetlips. Between the bommies, look out for resting sharks (black and white tips) on the sand. Keep an eye on your depth and no-stop time and start to zigzag your way back up the reef to the plateau for the safety stop. The gradual ascent, working your way along the reef, provides for numerous macro and critter opportunities. Scorpionfish, nudibranchs and fans with pygmy seahorses are just some of the smaller highlights amongst the multitude of reef fish that flit in and out of the corals.

Sorido Wall is actually located further east of Cape Kri but is usually dived on an east to west current, which makes the dive end on the reef top of Cape Kri. Sorido Wall is a mix of steeply sloping reef with large steps, resulting in smaller wall portions. The wall has decent coral coverage, mainly short-cropped corals

due to the currents that run along here. As you work your way up the slope, look out for schools of pick handle barracuda, huge Napoleons, nudibranchs under the wall's overhangs and white tip reef sharks patrolling the blue. Finishing on the reef top at Cape Kri is really the crowning glory of this site.

Cape Kri promises a bit of everything and delivers on all counts, but check current strength before you dive here. When the currents are running fast, it is a site best suited to divers with some current diving experience behind them.

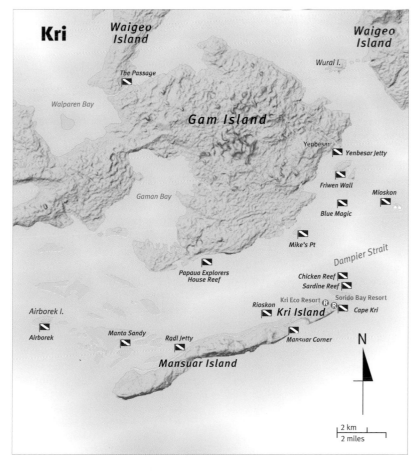

THE PASSAGE (KABUI PASSAGE)

The Passage is an iconic and unique Raja Ampat dive site, situated between the islands of Waigeo and Gam and running roughly on an east–west axis. The stretch of water between the south coast of Waigeo and the north of Gam ranges in width from 20 meters to 40 meters with a maximum depth of just 15 meters and an average depth range of only 5 to 10 meters, but this site is extraordinary. The banks of the Passage are dotted with outcroppings of mangroves, and the larger trees lean over the Passage forming, in places, a canopy over the narrow stretch of water. The Passage resembles a jungle river far more than it does a dive in the sea, but that is the exquisite nature of this site. It is almost like a melting pot of rainforest and reef. The Passage itself is almost 1.6 kilometers long, and in places the coral and rock formations almost breach the surface. The dive is best after 10 am, tides permitting, as then there are spectacular sunbeams filtering through the leafy canopy, which make for some excellent photography opportunities.

Currents can be brisk in the Passage, so you do have to be aware of coral and rock formations coming up ahead, but as soon as you reach either end, the

The Sorido Bay Resort jetty is visible in the center (bottom) and the Kri Eco Resort jetty on the right (middle) of Kri Island.

currents abate as you drift out into either the Halmahera Sea on the west or Kabui Bay on the east. The numerous bommies within the passage also make superb sheltering places if you tuck in behind them. Along the way, there are also two main caverns on the Gam side which, again, lend themselves to some wonderful photography.

The dive is usually from near to the caverns to Kabui Bay, or vice versa, depending on current flow and your operator, but in most cases you dive the Gam side of the stretch as it offers stunning soft corals and some interesting rock formations. The limestone walls of the Passage are completely encrusted with orange soft corals, tunicates, sea squirts, bright orange and candy pink fans and soft corals which, when contrasted with the river-like silt bottom, are nothing short of breathtaking. In the Passage itself, there is a mixture of fish life and critters. Flatworms, nudibranchs and octopus are frequently seen as well as blue spotted rays on the sand and rubble patches. As you leave the Passage, look out for larger schools of bigger fish waiting in the open water. Schooling jacks and chevron barracuda are often lying in wait, along with reef sharks and tuna.

When the currents are not running so fast, take your time and look under rocks and ledges, as anything from cuttlefish to wobbegongs could be hiding underneath. Diving the Passage really is a special experience, and when timed right is suitable for all levels.

SARDINE REEF

Sardine Reef is a dive best suited to divers with a little more experience, particularly in currents, and especially when diving around new moon or full moon when currents tend to run faster. For those who dive Sardine Reef, though, it is a rewarding dive with schools of fish so dense that they can block out the sunlight from overhead.

Sardine Reef is a small submerged seamount, the top of which sits at around 5 meters before dropping off into a sloping reef which extends down to about 30 meters. The mount is best dived on a falling tide when the current is running from east to west. Drop in with a negative entry on the east side, to the point where the currents are hitting the mount. This will ensure the best sightings of schooling fish for which this site is renowned. A negative entry and quick descent down to 25 meters then gives you the remainder of the dive to zigzag your way back up the eastern side. Whilst diving where the current hits the reef may mean holding on or swimming hard into the current to maintain your position, the rewards make it worthwhile. Numerous species of schooling fusiliers, trevally, chevron barracuda and jacks are

Top The Passage is a dive site where the ocean and rainforest truly merge into one.

Above Melissa's Garden boasts stunning shallow water soft corals with spectacular colors.

amongst the chaos in the blue. Predators are drawn to the flocks of smaller fish, and grey reef sharks and both white tip and black tip reef sharks are frequently seen here in numbers, as are Spanish mackerel, large Napoleon wrasse, pick handle barracuda schools and passing hawksbill turtles.

The corals at the Sardine Reef site are a healthy mix of hard and soft coral. There are also good numbers of sea fans providing homes to pygmy seahorses. It is possible to spot Bargibanti, Denise and Pontoh species all in one dive. The coral on the south and east sides is more impressive than that on the west and north sides, so when currents are running, aim to drift around the south, although for those with a keen eye all sides of the mount harbor excellent critters, provided you can spot them!

Progressively shallow up as you make your way around the reef. The safety stop is on the top of the seamount. Currents on the top of the mount can be strong as the water flows over the top of the reef. Be prepared to hunker down. On good days, tasseled wobbegong sharks are often seen under rock formations and it is not uncommon to see the resident school of bumphead parrotfish cruising across the shallow reef top. The reef top itself is damaged in many areas but do not let the rubble mislead you. There is a lot of life to be found amongst it!

This is an excellent dive for sheer biomass and for those who like current diving. When timed right, this is an exhilarating dive with numerous large schooling fish sightings.

Dense groups of schooling fish are a frequent sight at Sardine Reef.

BLUE MAGIC

This submerged seamount is located just under 10 kilometers northeast of Kri Island. On a day when the current is running, it provides for excellent biomass, pelagics, including a range of shark species, oceanic manta rays in the season, barracuda, trevally and tuna. Not only is there an action-packed scene in the blue, but the mount's plateaued top boasts healthy and diverse corals alive with smaller critters to please macro fanatics.

The site can be dived on both a rising and falling tide, but a reasonable current is best if you are hoping to see big fish and larger schools. The entry is ideally negative, with a quick descent down to the top of the mount, which ranges in depth from around 10 to 14 meters before sloping

This pleasing flatworm is one of numerous flatworm species found around the Dampier Strait.

make for excellent current breakers to duck behind if the currents are strong. Be careful, though, as you may find that your intended resting place is already occupied by one of the many tasseled wobbegong sharks that hide out here during the day or a school of hundreds of glass-fish or sweepers, or, some-times, all of the above!

If smaller sea life is more to your liking, the plateau is also home to painted frogfish, Bargibanti pygmy seahorses, which are found on the small fans on the slope, mantis shrimps, scorpionfish, several species of nudi-branch and shrimps.

The Blue Magic site can be a thrilling dive from start to finish, and with the possibility of manta rays, sharks and hunting pelagics, combined with a range of critters, it is hard not to get excited about diving here.

MIKE'S POINT

Mike's Point is located around 8 kilometers north of Kri Island and to the southeast of Gam. This is another iconic Dampier Strait site that is typically situated around a small rock island. This site boasts unique topographical features, stunning soft coral colors in the shallows and, with a little current, excellent fish biomass. The site can be dived from east to west, or vice versa, depending on the direction of the current, but it is best to traverse around the south side to see some of the incred-ible reef formations that are on offer.

The vast majority of the reefscape is owed to the US Air Force who, during

away gently around all sides. The slope peters out to a sandy bottom at around 25 to 30 meters. On good days, divers need not venture below 15 meters as all of the action is happening on the plateau where, from December to April, oceanic manta rays come for cleaning. These huge mantas, reaching up to 7 meters across, hover seemingly effortlessly over the reef top in even the strongest of cur-rents. Take time to look up, though, where the schooling fusiliers can be so dense at times that they literally shroud parts of the mount.

The dive is basically a circumnaviga-tion of the mount, making your way pro-gressively shallower. Whilst the area is not huge, the range of marine life cer-tainly is. Keep an eye out to the blue for patrolling grey tip reef sharks, hunting barracuda and passing tuna. On the reef itself, the coral coverage is excellent and encompasses a mix of hard and soft spe-cies, including brain, table, branching and leather, small gorgonian fans and large coral bommies carpeted with tuni-cates, hydroids and other colorful soft varieties. The bommies themselves also

This bearded scorpionfish is particularly well camouflaged against the reef.

World War II, mistook Mike's Point for a disguised Japanese ship and so set about repeatedly bombing the island. As a result of the bombings, large portions of the island were blasted away and fell into the surrounding water. These are now the huge bommies that are carpeted in soft corals, tunicates and a profusion of fans. In the deeper sections of the dive site, the bombing resulted in craters, overhangs, ledges and shelves, which are patchworked with crevices and swim-throughs.

Mike's Point is best dived on an out-going tide when the current is running from east to west. Make your entry on the northeast corner and traverse the east side heading south. Continue around and along the south side, gradually shallowing up as you go. Many of the caves, swim-throughs and overhangs are in the 24 to 30 meter range, but even up to 5 to 10 meters the features of the reef are clear to see, with large overhangs casting shadows and big bommies strewn

around the base of the island like giant shrapnel. Despite the relatively recent history associated with this site, the coral coverage is excellent, with hard and soft corals adorning every available surface. Soft coral growth is most prolific in the shallows. On the reef top plateau, there is a stunning array of fans.

Biomass here is healthy, particularly when the current is running. On the south side, it is not unusual to see large schools of sweetlips, fusiliers, batfish and barracuda. Macro life here can be exceptional. Nudibranch and flatworm species are numerous, and the many shady areas created by the reef's profile provide habitats for an array of shrimps, octopus, crocodilefish and other crustaceans.

CHICKEN REEF, SLEEPING BARRACUDA, CHICKEN BAY, SURGEON FISH SLOPE

These four sites are basically the names given to each of the four corners of one roughly four-sided reef. Chicken Reef occupies the east side, Sleeping Barracuda is on the northwest corner, Chicken Bay is on the southwest corner and Surgeon Fish Slope lies to the south. The diving here is dependent on the current direction. If it is running from east to west, it is best to dive Chicken Reef and head west. If the current is from west to east, then starting at Chicken Bay and finishing at Surgeon Fish Slope makes for an excellent dive.

Chicken Bay, on the eastern side of the island, is a sloping reef that drops away at around a 45 degree angle. Coral coverage here is excellent, but you should aim to start the dive on the sandy area of the slope as this is where the current hits the reef and there are large aggregations of fish in the blue: fusiliers, surgeons, schooling bannerfish, blue triggerfish, passing barracuda and also patrolling white tip, black tip and grey reef sharks.

On the sand itself, there is also a dense forest of garden eels and resting white tips are not uncommon. Drifting from the sand slope to the coral reef, heading to the south side, the reef is a packed mix of fans, soft corals, brain, plate, branching and table hard corals and sponges and whips. Fish life is healthy and reef dwellers such as scorpionfish, moray eels, mantis shrimps and other critters are all found here. As you progress along the slope, start shallowing up as you near Surgeon Fish Slope. The name of this site is not without reason! Just below the reef crest at around 10 meters, it is not unusual to see a dense aggregation of surgeonfish that hang suspended in the blue just up from the reef in a wall-like formation. Around the reef crest and on the reef plateau, the action starts again. Usual sightings here include a school of resident bumphead parrotfish, some of which have reached gargantuan proportions, schools of pick handle barracuda, black tip reef sharks cruising through, darting schools of fusiliers, inordinate amounts of damselfish glittering in the sunlight and giant trevally patrolling from above. The reef top is one that would rival almost any Dampier Strait site in terms of biomass, and regardless of which site you dive around this reef, all are equally impressive.

MANTA SANDY

As one of the Dampier Strait's more popular dive sites, this can be a busy site so you should aim to dive here early before the liveaboards and snorkel boats start to arrive. The site is basically a sand slope that starts from just a meter under the surface. From 5 to 10 meters, there is coral coverage and below that a sand slope down to a relatively flat bottom at 15 to 18 meters. On the sand bottom, there are a couple of large bommies that form cleaning stations for the reef manta rays (manta alfredi) resident in the area. Operators have constructed a narrow 'wall' around 20 centimeters high out of coral rubble and divers must stay behind this wall. Crossing over this line is seriously frowned upon, and if divers attempt to do so they should not be surprised if they are pulled back. Staying behind the line and low to the bottom prevents the manta rays from being scared away from the cleaning stations prior to the cleaning process being completed. (For more guidelines regarding diving with manta rays, see page 59.)

Whilst this makes the site sound a little like a tourist attraction, it does enable all divers to have good manta sightings. The mantas are in the area year round, but if you are diving from December to April when the water is most plankton-rich, then the sightings are more consistent and the numbers of mantas are usually higher. However, due

Cape Kri is home to this resident school of ribbon sweetlips.

to the high plankton content in the water, visibility tends to be lower, in the 15 meter range rather than 25 meters which is not unusual from June to August.

If you are not a manta fan, or once you have had enough time with them, this site does have a lot more to offer. The sandy area is a great place for looking for critters and a variety of nudibranch and flatworms are found here, along with Pegasus sea moths, octopus and a range of crustaceans.

To end the dive, head back up the slope, making sure to give the cleaning stations some clearance. The corals in the shallows are also worth checking for critter and macro life.

If you are hoping to see manta rays, this site is a must, but with good critters too it offers a little bit for everyone.

FAM ISLANDS: MELISSA'S GARDEN

Melissa's Garden is located around three rock pinnacles in the Fam Islands region. It is about a 90 minute speed boat journey from Kri Island, but it is well worth the journey! The site was named by Max Ammer after his daughter, and it truly is an under-water garden. The three pinnacles sit atop a shallow plateau boasting a glorious array of hard corals, soft corals and huge fans. The shadows that are cast by the pinnacles make for some stunning photographic opportunities, as do the schools of glass-fish, hoards of damsels and huge tridacna clams that are found here. It is important to check the current before diving as you should aim to enter the water up current from the pinnacles. The shallow platform drops away on all sides to gently sloped reefs which have excellent coral coverage. The sloping reef extends down to only 20 meters, where it bottoms out to sand, and this is the best place to start the dive, where the currents split around the reef. In the blue, schools of fusiliers stream by, great barracuda hang out in the water column and glassfish and sweeper aggregations can be found behind most bommies. Make your way up and around the slope according to the current but allow plenty of time to explore the shallow reef top. It is definitely worth investigating around the base of each of the three pinnacles. Colorful fans catch the sunlight, antheas dart in and out of the branching corals, huge yet delicate table corals sit amid candy colored soft corals and everything looks alive and vibrant. For macro enthusiasts, soft coral crabs are frequently found here as are nudibranchs, cowries on the fans, flat worms and a whole host of marine treasures. With stunning scenery, vivid colors, staggering fish numbers and variety, Melissa's Garden is a dive not to be missed!

Batfish are frequently found just below the surface where they appear to bask in the sunlight.

The Tasselled Wobbegong *Eucrossorhinus dasypogon*

This is an unusual looking member of the wobbegong family of which there are 12 species. Wobbegongs are also often referred to as carpet sharks due to their bottom dwelling nature, flattened bodies and patterned skins. The tasselled wobbegong has a brownish orange to yellow body which is exquisitely decorated with light ringed dark spots, providing it with perfect camouflage against coral reefs. The tasselled name derives from its bearded looking mass of branching skin flaps that run the length of its jaw line. Whilst other wobbegong species also have similar skin flaps, none are as extensive as those found on the tasselled variety. Other distinguishing features include rounded pectoral fins, a broad head and a habit of resting with the tail curled rather than straight.

Wobbegongs are solitary and nocturnal in nature but they will feed opportunistically throughout the day. During daylight hours, they favor coral reefs where their camouflage is most effective and their flattened body allows them to maneuver under narrow ledges. The wobbegong relies heavily on its excellent camouflage when hunting. It will lie still and wait for small fish to approach its tasselled jaws. Wobbegongs have also been seen waving their tails slowly when larger fish are near-

This tasselled wobbegong shark was pictured around Kri. Note the curled tail position.

by as the caudal fin has a dark eye spot close to the base making it resemble small fish or prey. As the larger fish approaches, the tail of the wobbegong will strike. Tasselled wobbegongs have large mouths and can swallow reasonably sized fish whole, but for any large fish they are also equipped with some menacingly long, fang-like front teeth. Their diet mainly consists of schooling nocturnal fish such as squirrelfish, soldierfish and sweepers.

Mature tasselled wobbegongs can reach 1.8 meters in length, and whilst much is still unknown about their breeding patterns, they appear to give birth to live young and a litter can be of 20 plus pups. Despite this large litter size, the tasselled wobbegong is listed by the IUCN as near threatened due to a number of factors, including habitat loss and degradation, destructive fishing practices, fishing incidents involving long-lines and nets and, in certain areas, they are caught for human consumption and their skins can be highly valued.

Wobbegongs generally do not pose a threat to divers, but if they are stepped on or provoked, they have been known to react defensively.

Innovation, Education and Empowerment for Successful Conservation

The Raja Ampat Research and Conservation Centre (RARCC) is based on Kri Island along with Papua Diving's Kri Eco Resort and Sorido Bay Resort. Kri Eco Resort was the first shore-based diving operation in Raja Ampat and was opened by Max Ammer, the founder of Papua Diving, in 1993.

Ammer is frequently referred to as the Pioneer of Papua Diving, and this is a title that is not undeserved. Since he first visited Raja Ampat in search of World War II

Raja Ampat is an area of extraordinary beauty. A key aim of the RARCC is to empower local communities to ensure ongoing conservation.

wrecks and artifacts, he has not only discovered the majority of dive sites in the region but has made it his personal mission to raise awareness of the area, work with local communities and find ways, sometimes against all odds, to promote conservation and preservation of the place he now calls home.

In 2004, Papua Diving opened its second resort on Kri Island, Sorido Bay Resort. Sorido Bay offers upmarket bungalows and high-end service for guests who want to explore Raja Ampat without leaving behind the comforts of home. In the 20 or more years that Max has been based on Kri Island, his house reef, Cape Kri, has not

only set a world record for having the highest number of marine fish identified in one single tank dive but it has gone on to break its own record, which now stands at a staggering 374 species. In addition to proven world class biodiversity, shark numbers in the area are reported to be increasing every year, new species of fish continue to be discovered and the exceptional biomass and fish density are evident as soon as one peers below the surface.

How is it that whilst many areas globally are suffering from declining fish numbers and coral reef degradation, the Dampier Strait region appears to be flourishing? Successful conservation efforts have been pivotal in the development of the area, and with Kri Eco Resort being the first operator, tourism has been introduced with a focus on preserving the natural environment. After numerous projects and campaigns by a number of NGOs, Conservation International and Papua Divers, the Indonesian government has now declared seven marine parks across the Raja Ampat area, which cover over 45 percent of the reefs. There is a tag system in place and Conservation International remains heavily involved in protection and conservation efforts based on limiting liveaboard numbers, banning destructive fishing practises (both cyanide and dynamite), turtle egg poaching and longlining. Whilst these bans have certainly assisted protection of the area, Ammer's focus veered away from projects to ban practices that were destructive to the reefs to look behind the practices themselves and at the local people involved in them and their motives. If a man has a family to feed, he needs some form of employment, a skill or a trade, and in Papua where education and employment opportunities are limited, fishing, poaching, turtle egg collecting and shark finning all provide a man with means. Max recognized that

this was the crux of the problem, and thus his primary goal became to provide alternative employment opportunities for as many of the local Papuans as possible. This included training them in trade skills and English. Kri Eco Resort was not only constructed by local people but it also trains and employs Papuan dive guides and resort staff. When Sorido Bay Resort began construction in 2003, the same principles were applied and local people were employed for the construction and later for the resort and dive operations. Papua Diving now employs almost 100 Papuan staff across its two resorts, many of whom were previously fisherman, shark finners and turtle poachers. With both resorts fully staffed, the conservation initiatives now continue under the RARCC, which became an official PBO under Dutch law in 2010.

The RARCC consists of a small team spearheaded by Ammer whose time is now almost 100 percent devoted to conservation. The primary goal is to create more self-funding and sustainable initiatives that provide West Papuan people

Papua Diving train and employ local Papuan dive guides for both Kri Eco and Sorido Bay Resorts.

Kayak4Conservation is an RARCC initiative to provide training, employment and sustainable futures for local Papuan communities.

closely with local guest houses situated along the kayak routes. This has brought further economic benefits to the guest house owners and their local villages, including extending them interest-free loans to develop their own enterprises.

The Bell 47 helicopter project is one of the RARCC's most ambitious, involving importing and building two Bell 47 helicopters and a vast collection of spares, tools and all parts required for maintenance and servicing. The helicopters' primary duty is to conduct air patrols across the Raja Ampat region, looking out for illegal fishing boats and others employing destructive practices. Sea landings are possible as the helicopters are equipped with floats. They are also able to cover larger areas and are much faster than the boats used in the current patrol system, although both search mechanisms work in tandem. In addition to this, the helicopters are used to assist scientists, marine biologists and other researchers by allowing them to access some of the more remote islands and numerous areas in minimal time.

With more RARCC projects in the pipeline, including further educational and training workshops, not just for fiberglass but in woodwork and carpentry, it is hoped that their success to date continues well into the future. With their community-based initiatives, they are making a positive and empowering change to the people of West Papua and helping them to realize the importance of safeguarding the naturally unique and staggeringly beautiful habitat in which they live.

To keep up to date on RARCC projects, make a donation or find out how you can help, go to www.stichting-rarcc.org.

with both training and employment. Many RARCC projects center around tourism, which has the added benefit of educating local people about both the economic and environmental benefits of preserving the nature which exists in the Raja Ampat archipelago. The list of RARCC initiatives is impressive, but recent and ongoing projects include training Papuan people in fiberglass work and boat building. The trainees now have skills for a lifetime of employment, potentially even to set up their own boat building companies and train other local workers. A further benefit of the fiberglass project is that fibreglass boats use 40 percent less fuel than traditional wooden boats, a saving for both boat owners and the environment.

The fiberglass workers have also been utilized by Kayak4Consevation (www.kayak4conservation.com), another RARCC project, which hires sea kayaks and guides to tourists. Kayak4Conservation trains and employs local kayak guides and also works

KRI TRAVEL PLANNER

This area of Raja Ampat is quite possibly the most stunning in terms of natural beauty, with picture postcard white sand beaches and tiny tropical islands glittering in the aquamarine waters. Wildlife around Kri Island includes cuscus, monitor lizards, cockatoos as well as a range of other birdlife. On nearby islands, both the Wilson's and red bird of paradise can be seen.

Papua Diving explores the reefs around numerous Raja Ampat Islands as well as Kri Island.

Because of Kri's protected position between larger islands, there is good year round diving with visibility ranging from 10 to 30 meters (the lower end of the scale during periods of prolific plankton content in the water, most likely from December through to April). The best visibility is from May to September, but if you are hoping to see manta rays and other pelagic life, remember that they tend to come with the plankton! Year round water temperature ranges from 27 to 30 degrees. As Kri is positioned so close to the equator, there is no real wet and dry season but humidity is high and there are occasional tropical rain showers or storms.

There are currents in this area of Raja Ampat, but they vary in strength according to the time of the tide and the lunar cycle. If you are diving around full or new moon, you should expect currents to be stronger as there are greater tidal exchanges. If you are diving around neap tides, currents are minimal. Expect to dive with some current as it draws in the large fish aggregations that the area is well known for.

The diving in this region is stunning, diverse and prolific, but as the area is very remote, diving insurance is strongly recommended and some operators will require you to show proof of it.

Recommended Operators

Papua Diving Resorts Operate two resorts on Kri Island both of which offer a range of dive packages, full board accommodation, PADI courses, nitrox and equipment hire. Booking must be in advance. Papua Diving is also responsible for the Raja Ampat Research and Conservation Centre which is adjunct to Sorido Bay on Kri Island (see RARCC feature). Divers are encouraged to support this organization in order to safeguard the Raja Ampat area. Both resorts endeavor to employ local Papuan staff wherever possible to support the local economy, as well as undertake numerous marine and community projects. Ten percent of Papua Diving's profits are donated to RARCC. www.papua-diving.com. Email: info@papua-diving.com.

Kri Eco Resort Offers dive and stay packages in comfortable, rustic Papuan water bungalows with fans and choice of bathroom arrangements. Packages include up to 4 boat dives per day and unlimited House Reef diving.

Sorido Bay High-end dive and stay packages with luxury cottages and upmarket service. A truly remarkable resort with a range of facilities and exceptional service to ensure a comfortable stay. Dive packages can include up to 4 boat dives per day plus unlimited House Reef dives. Tailor-made packages are available on request.

Liveaboard Diving in Indonesia

Indonesia's thousands of tiny islands make for some phenomenal liveaboard opportunities, especially if you travel further east across the archipelago to where there are few shore-based operators. The vast majority of the liveaboards that are based in the Indonesian archipelago have been built in the same style as Indonesia's beautiful traditional *phinisi* schooners. *Phinisi*, or *pinisi*, are two-masted, timber-built sailing ships which were, and still are, used by the Buginese and Makassarese for fishing and cargo transportation around the archipelago. It was the Konjo people from South Sulawesi who played the most influential role in the design and construction of the early *phinisi*, which were hand-built using traditional methods. In modern times, the construction methods have changed very little and still include choosing the right trees for each part of the vessel and conducting numerous ceremonies and rituals at the beginning and completion of each stage of the building process.

The main and original boat building areas in Indonesia are Bulukumba on the

The *Arenui* has a stunning deck, perfect for after dive dining and relaxation.

tip of South Sulawesi and Sangeang in East Sumbawa where the villagers learnt their skills from migrants from Bulukumba. There are now also several boat construction yards in Kalimantan. The boat building was, and still is, started on the beach. Originally, this was because the craftsmen were close to the timber needed for a boat's construction, although today much of the timber has to be shipped in due to short supply.

Historically, teak wood was used for building *phinisi* vessels but it is now very difficult to source and is also poorly regarded by modern builders. Instead, other Indonesian hardwoods are used, the most popular of which is ironwood sourced from Kalimantan. Although it is a heavy wood, it is hard wearing. Bangkirai, another tropical wood, is used for planking and deck structures. Timbers are joined together with wooden nails, which resemble small pegs.

Suitability of Phinisis as Liveaboards

Phinisi schooners make excellent live-aboard vessels. They vary in size but the largest, which tend to be the most luxurious, are 40 meters long and up to 10 meters wide. Smaller *phinisi* can be anything from 20 meters long but these are rarer to find. The shape of the vessel makes it a smooth sailing boat capable of covering long distances. Whilst almost all *phinisi*-style liveaboards have full sailing rigs, they are now also equipped with engines, which means that they can sail into currents and wind and, for the most part, maintain schedules regardless of weather and sea conditions.

The *Indo Siren* under sail is a spectacular sight.

Boat Layouts

Whilst the hulls, keels and general body of the *phinisi* vessels have not been changed, their interior layouts have been adapted substantially for liveaboard purposes. Traditionally, these vessels were left as bare as possible in order to maximize the available space for cargo. Modern liveaboard *phinisi*, however, have been transformed to include guest cabins, dive decks, lounges, crew quarters, galleys and even sun-loungers and relaxation areas on deck. Most modern liveaboards are also designed to reduce engine and generator noise in the cabins, ensuring a good night's sleep.

Daily Schedules

Liveaboard schedules vary from operator to operator but most offer relatively intensive diving schedules. Pricing is based on an all inclusive daily rate, so understandably guests want to be able to make as many dives as possible. A typical liveaboard daily schedule is as follows:

Small breakfast followed by dive number 1, cooked breakfast followed by dive number 2 and then a break for lunch. After lunch is the third and (if possible) fourth dive (often a small snack is served in between these dives) and then a night dive followed by dinner.

The *Tambora* liveaboard operates across the archipelago.

Guests can join as many or as few of the dives as they choose. Naturally, doing the maximum number of dives possible makes the trip more cost-effective.

Services

The services and standards of service on liveaboards vary substantially. Video nights, photography clinics and marine life talks are popular evening activities across all operators. Many of the high-end vessels also offer massages and a range of other luxuries, whilst some carry paddle and surf boards for those looking for more active surface time. Operators offer some day trips to land-based activities as well for those not diving or needing a break from diving, whether it be caves or local villages. Check with your operator to see what is available.

Overnight Moorings

Liveaboards try to moor overnight in sheltered locations but be aware that if there are strong winds or big waves the boat will inevitably rock. Most modern liveaboards are built so as to minimize the effect felt by those on board, but be prepared for some movement.

Routes in Indonesia

By far the two most popular areas for liveaboards in Indonesia are Raja Ampat and the Komodo National Park. Most of the high-end vessels spend November through to May in Raja Ampat and July through to September in Komodo. In October and May, the boats are generally moving from one region to the other, and these are good months for those wanting to explore the places that lie in between. There are numerous liveaboards that are based in the Komodo National Park year round. However, most of the boats that work in Raja Ampat leave during July, August and September because of the monsoon season.

Durations

Trip durations vary but in general tend to be around 14 days for boats covering Raja Ampat or when touring numerous regions. If you are taking a liveaboard in the Komodo Marine Park, much shorter trips are available, anything from three days upwards.

Embarkation and Disembarkation

Most liveaboard operators will organize airport pick-ups for guests and arrange local hotel accommodation if you need to spend one night on shore before boarding the vessel. This may or may not be included in the package price. Upon disembarking, similar transport arrangements have usually been made by your operator for drop-offs.

Regulations in Raja Ampat

Currently, there is a capped limit on the number of liveaboards allowed to operate in Raja Ampat. The limit at the time of writing is 40. The Raja Ampat marine park regulations also state that there should only be one dive boat at a dive site at any one time. Liveaboards are allowed to enter the Misool Eco Resort no-take zone but they must radio ahead. Liveaboards in Raja Ampat are not allowed to drop anchor in water shallower than 40 meters.

Private Charters

Most liveaboards will accept bookings for private charters, but as bookings are made so far in advance, if you are intending to make a charter booking you need to be looking at making a reservation up to 12 months in advance (often more) for some of the bigger vessels. Some vessels only operate private charters.

Equipment Hire

In general, divers are expected to bring their own equipment on liveaboards. There is limited space on the vessels and carrying numerous sets of gear does not make sense. Some operators will hire BCD and regulators if you inform them in advance. All reputable liveaboards carry some spare pieces of equipment in case of breakages or malfunctions.

Bookings

Operators' websites generally display schedules for up to two years in advance and are updated regularly to show how many places are left or if the booking is for a private charter.

Above The *Aurora*'s cabins are comfortable and designed to maximize space.

Packing for the Trip

Liveaboards are well stocked but it is advisable to take a supply of seasickness medication and any small snacks and treats that you cannot live without. Soft drinks and tea and coffee are usually included but alcohol is not and is generally expensive, so a bottle of your favorite tipple is a nice addition to your luggage.

Below The *Seven Seas* liveaboard has a wealth of experience operating in Indonesia

Safety and Emergencies

As a bare minimum, liveaboards should be equipped with enough tenders or life rafts for everyone onboard as well as life jackets, flares, oxygen supplies, first aid kits, GPS, satellite phone and marine radios. For Raja Ampat liveaboards where the diving is extremely remote, safety and emergency equipment are essential.

Prerequisites

Before booking your liveaboard trip, make sure that you meet all of the prerequisites of the operator. Some liveaboards request that divers are of at least Advanced Open Water level. Others have only nitrox filling facilities and so a nitrox certification is required. Other prerequisites may include having DAN insurance (see page 25), having dived within the last 12 months or having taken a refresher course.

Courses

Courses are available on most liveaboards but they need to be booked in advance so that materials and instructors are available. Most liveaboards that are using nitrox offer courses on board for those not certified.

Costs

Whilst many liveaboard trips, particularly those in Raja Ampat, may initially seem expensive, remember that the cost includes all of your accommodation, full board meals and diving. Check with your operator exactly what is and isn't included in the package.

Linking Liveaboard and Shore-based Trips

It is possible to link liveaboard trips with shore-based trips, but it is essential to make sure that both operators know your plans and are clear about embarkation and disembarkation points and who is assuming responsibility for drop-offs and pick-ups.

Language Primer

Personal Pronouns

I **saya**
we **kita** (inclusive), **kami** (exclusive)
you **anda** (formal), **saudara** (brother/sister)
you **kamu** (for friends and children only)
he/she **dia**
they **mereka**

Forms of Address

Father/Mr **Bapak** (**Pak**)
Mother/Mrs **Ibu** (**Bu**)
Elder brother **Abang** (**Bang** or **Bung**)
    Mas (in Java only)
Elder sister **Mbak** (in Java only)
Elder brother/sister **Kakak** (**Kak**)
Younger brother/sister **Adik** (**Dik**)
Note: These terms are used not just within
    the family, but generally in polite speech.

Basic Questions

How? **Bagaimana?**
How much/many? **Berapa?**
What? **Apa?**
What's this? **Apa ini?**
Who? **Siapa?**
Who's that? **Siapa itu?**
What is your name? **Siapa namanya?**
    (Literally "Who is your name?")
When? **Kapan?**
Where? **Di mana?**
Why? **Kenapa? Mengapa?**
Which? **Yang mana?**

Civilities

Welcome **Selamat datang**
Good morning (7–11 am) **Selamat pagi**
Good midday (11am–3 pm) **Selamat siang**
Good afternoon (3–7 pm) **Selamat sore**
Goodnight (after dark) **Selamat malam**
Goodbye (to one leaving) **Selamat jalan**
Goodbye (to one staying) **Selamat tinggal**
Note: *Selamat* is a word from Arabic mean-
    ing "May your time (or action) be blessed."

How are you? **Apa kabar?**
I am fine. **Kabar baik.**
Thank you. **Terima kasih.**
You're welcome. **Kembali.**
Same to you. **Sama sama.**
Pardon me **Ma'af**
Excuse me **Permisi** (when leaving a
conversation, etc.)

Numbers

1 **satu**	11 **sebelas**
2 **dua**	12 **dua belas**
3 **tiga**	13 **tiga belas**
4 **empat**	20 **dua puluh**
5 **lima**	50 **lima puluh**
6 **enam**	73 **tujuh puluh tiga**
7 **tujuh**	100 **seratus**
8 **delapan**	600 **enam ratus**
9 **sembilan**	1,000 **seribu**
10 **sepuluh**	3,000 **tiga ribu**
1,000,000 **satu juta**	10,000 **sepuluh ribu**
2,000,000 **dua juta**	
half **setengah**	second **kedua**
first **pertama**	third **ketiga**
	fourth **ke'empat**

Time

minute **menit**	Sunday **Hari Minggu**
hour **jam**	Monday **Hari Senin**
(also clock/watch)	Tuesday **Hari Selasa**
day **hari**	Wednesday **Hari Rabu**
week **minggu**	Thursday **Hari Kamis**
month **bulan**	Friday **Hari Jum'at**
year **tahun**	Saturday **Hari Sabtu**
today **hari ini**	later **nanti**
tomorrow **besok**	yesterday **kemarin**

What time is it? **Jam berapa?**
(It is) nine thirty **Jam setengah sembilan**
    (Literally 'half nine')
How many hours? **Berapa jam?**
When did you arrive? **Kapan datang?**
Four days ago. **Empat hari yang lalu.**
When are you leaving? **Kapan berangkat?**
In a short while. **Sebentar lagi.**

Pronunciation and Grammar

Vowels

a	As in father
e	Three forms:
	1) Schwa, like the
	2) Like é in touche
	3) Short è; as in bet
i	Usually like long e (as in Bali); when bounded by consonants, like short i (hit).
o	Long o, like go
u	Long u, like you
ai	Long i, like crime
au	Like ow in owl

Consonants

c	Always like ch in church
g	Always hard, like guard
h	Usually soft, almost un-pronounced. It is hard between like vowels, e.g. **mahal** (expensive).
k	Like **k** in **k**ind; at end of word, unvoiced stop.
kh	Like **k**ind, but harder
r	Rolled, like Spanish **r**
ng	Soft, like fling
ngg	Hard, like tingle
ny	Like **ny** in Sonya

Grammar

Grammatically, Indonesian is in many ways far simpler than English. There are no articles (a, an, the). The verb form 'to be' is usually not used. There is no ending for plurals. Sometimes the word is doubled, but often number comes from the context. And Indonesian verbs are not conjugated. Tense is communicated by context or with specific words for time.

Useful Words

yes **ya**   no, not **tidak, bukan**
Note: Tidak is used with verbs or adverbs, bukan with nouns.

and	**dan**	better	**lebih baik**
with	**dengan**	worse	**kurang baik**
for	**untuk**	this/these	**ini**
from	**dari**	that/those	**itu**
good	**baik**	same	**sama**
very good	**bagus**	different	**lain**
more	**lebih**	here	**di sini**
less	**kurang**	there	**di sana**
to be	**ada**	to be able to	**bisa**
to buy	**membeli**	correct	**betul**
to know	**tahu**	wrong	**salah**
big	**besar**	small	**kecil**
to need	**perlu**	to want	**ingin**
to go	**pergi**	to stop	**berhenti**
slow	**pelan**	fast	**cepat**
to wait	**tunggu**	to continue	**terus**
to	**ke**	at	**di**
old	**tua, lama**	new	**baru**
full	**penuh**	empty	**kosong**
quiet	**sepi**	crowded, noisy	**ramai**
few	**sedikit**	many	**banyak**
cold	**dingin**	hot	**panas**
clean	**bersih**	dirty	**kotor**
entrance	**masuk**	exit	**keluar**

Small Talk

Where are you from? **Dari mana?**
I'm from the US. **Saya dari Amerika.**
How old are you? **Umumya berapa?**
I'm 31 years old. **Umur saya tiga pulu satu tahun.**
Are you married? **Sudah kawin belum?**
Yes, I am. **Yah, sudah.**
Not yet. **Belum.**
Do you have children? **Sudah punya anak?**
What is your religion? **Agama apa?**
Where are you going? **Mau ke mana?**
I'm just taking a walk. **Jalan-jalan saja.**
Please come in. **Silahkan masuk.**
Please sit down. **Silahkan duduk.**

Hotels

room	**kamar**	bed	**tempat tidur**
towel	**handuk**	bedsheet	**sprei**
bathe	**mandi**	bathroom	**kamar mandi**
hot water	**air panas**		

Where's a losmen? **Di mana ada losmen?**
good hotel **hotel yang baik**
Please take me to... **Tolong antar saya ke...**
Are there any empty rooms? **Ada kamar kosong?**
Sorry there aren't any. **Ma'af, tidak ada**
How much for one night? **Berapa untuk**

satu malam?
One room for two people.
   Dua orang, satu kamar.
I'd like to stay for three days.
   Saya mau tinggal tiga hari.
Here's the key to the room. **Ini kunci kamar.**
Please call a taxi. **Tolong panggilkan taksi.**
Please wash these clothes.
   Tolong cucikan pakaian ini.

Restaurants

to eat **makan**   to drink **minum**
drinking water **air putih, air mimun**
breakfast **makan pagi, sarapan**
lunch **makan siang** dinner **makan malam**
Where's a good restaurant?
   Di mana ada rumah makan yang baik?
Let's have lunch. **Mari kita makan siang.**
May I see the menu?
   Boleh saya lihat daftar makanan?
I want to wash my hands.
   Saya mau cuci tangan.
Where is the toilet? **Di mana kamar kecil?**
fish, squid, goat, beef, chicken
   ikan, cumi-cumi, kambing, sapi, ayam
salty, sour, sweet, spicy (hot)
   asin, asam, manis, pedas

Shopping

cheap **murah**   expensive **mahal**
Please, speak slowly.
   Tolong, berbicara lebih pelan.
I want to buy... **Saya mau beli...**
Where can I buy... **Di mana saya bisa beli...**
How much does this cost? **Berapa harga ini?**
2,500 rupiah. **Dua ribu, lima ratus rupiah.**
That can't be true! **Masa!**
That's still a bit expensive. **Masih agak mahal**
May I bargain? **Boleh tawar?**
Is there a discount? **Ada diskon?**
Thanks, I already have one/some...
   Terima kasih, saya sudah punya ...

Directions

here **di sini**   there **di sana**
near **dekat**   far **jauh**

inside **di dalam**   outside **di luar**
map **peta**   street **jalan**
north **utara**   south **selatan**
east **timur**   west **barat**
central **pusat**   middle **tengah**
left **kiri**   right **kanan**
straight **terus**   turn **belok**
I am looking for this address.
   Saya cari alamat ini.
How far is it? **Berapa jauh dari sini?**
Which area? **Daerah mana?**

Diving

dive **selam**   diving **menyelam**
diver **orang menyelam**
night dive **selam malam**
cave dive **selam goa**   Nitrox **nitrox**
coral **karang**   beach **pantai**
rock or stone **batu**   sea/ocean **laut**
fish **ikan**   big fish **ikan besar**
lots of fish **banyak ikan**

Conditions

wind **angin**
wave **ombak**
big wave **ombak besar**
current **arus**
strong current **arus kuat**
sunset **matahari terbenam**
moon **bulan**
full moon **bulan purnama**
shallow **dankal**
deep **dalam**
cold water (very) **air dingin (sekali)**
warm water **air hangat**
kondisi bagus **good conditions**
kondisi tidak bagus **bad conditions**

Useful Questions and Statements

How deep? **Berapa dalam?**
Are you ready? **Siap?**
Ready **Sudah**
Wait **Tunggu**
Is the tank already changed? **Sudah ganti
   tanki?**
This tank is empty **Tanki ini sudah kosong**

Please can you help me? **Bisa kamu tolong saya?**

How long? **Berapa panjang?**

When do we get there? **Kapan datang?**

I feel seasick. **Saya mabuk laut.**

I forgot… **Saya lupa…**

Be careful. **Hati hati.**

Do you have a smaller BCD? **Ada BCD lebih kecil?**

Do you have bigger fins? **Ada fin lebih besar?**

I am nervous. **Saya takut.**

I only want to dive for 40 minutes **Saya mau menyelam untuk empat puluh menit saja.**

Do you have an extra tank? **Ada satu tanki lagi?**

Equipment

Most equipment terms are the same in Bahasa as in English and guides understand most that are different. Here are a few that you may find helpful

mask **masker**

tank **tanki/tabung**

float or buoy **pelampung**

weight **berat**

torch **lampu**

ladder **tangga**

rope **tali**

anchor **jangkar**

boat **kapal** (or the type of boat, e.g. **speedboat, jukung, phinisi**)

engine **mesin**

Items that are described using English words include BCD, regulator, octopus, fin, booties, snorkel, weight belt, wetsuit. In Indonesia, SMB's are known as safety sausages, the Indonesian for which is *sosis*!

Certification Levels

In Indonesia, the levels of diver certification are referred to in English: Open Water, Advanced, Rescue, Divemaster and Instructor.

Left Photography-focused dive operator critters@LembehResort has a professional on hand to assist with repairs.

Below For those traveling with camera equipment, it is reassuring to book somewhere with camera room facilities.

Travel Practicalities

Visiting Indonesia is an exciting and unforgettable experience. For many people, it is the trip of a lifetime because of its stunning scenery, spectacular wildlife, remote areas which have yet to be explored and friendly people smiling at you wherever you go. For those who have never traveled in Indonesia or Asia before, a mild case of culture shock is not unusual in the first few days as there is often little around you that represents life back in your home country. Don't panic. Relax, go with it and embrace the Indonesian culture!

The following is a list of practicalities that you should consider before traveling to Indonesia. It is not an exhaustive list but is designed to cover the major points.

AIR TRAVEL IN INDONESIA

When taking domestic flights in Indonesia, most airlines require you to arrive at least one hour before departure time. Always allow extra time for traffic delays en route. For international departures, you should aim to be at the airport 2 to 3 hours prior to departure, but check for any additional time requirements on your tickets.

Departure taxes are payable at the airport for all domestic and international flights and must be paid in cash (rupiah). Current rates are as follows:

International flights departing from Bali (DPS) IDR200,000; international flights departing from Jakarta (CGK), Lombok (LOP) and Makassar (UPG) IDR150,000; international flights departing from Manado (MDC) IDR75,000.

Domestic flights departing from Jakarta (CGK) IDR40,000; domestic flights departing from Bali (DPS) IDR 75,000; domestic flights departing from Makassar (UPG) IDR50,000 and all other airports vary from IDR13,000 to IDR30,000.

Garuda Indonesia is the national airline in Indonesia, and one of the more expensive carriers, but it is currently the only operating Indonesian airline that meets the required safety standards to fly in EU airspace. Other major Indonesian airlines include Sriwijaya Air, Lion Air, Air Asia Indonesia, Xpress Air, Merpati Nusantara Airlines, Trans Nusa Airlines, Wings Air (a subsidiary of Lion Air) and Tiger Air Mandala. All of the operators listed above have websites, and tickets can be booked online. (See Booking Flights below.)

Unfortunately, flight delays and cancellations are relatively commonplace but services are improving, particularly in major airports such as Bali, Jakarta and Makassar. As you travel further east across Indonesia, airports become increasingly basic and flight times become a little more flexible.

BAGGAGE ALLOWANCES

Most domestic airlines allow a baggage allowance of 20 kilograms plus your carry-on bag. However, some airlines that operate smaller planes only allow 10 to 15 kilos, so consider your packing carefully. Overweight baggage fees are thankfully not so expensive and range from around IDR20,000 to IDR50,000 per kilo.

BARGAINING

In Indonesia, bargaining or haggling is part of everyday life and when visiting as a tourist there are plenty of opportunities to have a go at this. However, it is not appropriate in all circumstances. As a general rule of thumb, street vendors and markets are open for haggling but stores in major malls, etc. operate on a fixed price basis. Most upmarket hotels are also fixed rate, but if you are staying in smaller guest houses you may be able to negotiate a better rate, particularly in the low season. Quite often it will be the vendor who starts the haggling process. If you are not sure whether or not to haggle, it is best just to ask if it is a fixed price rather than to cause offence.

BOOKING ACCOMMODATION

Booking accommodation in Indonesia has become increasingly easy over the last couple of years, with many smaller hotels that do not have websites joining booking sites such as Booking.com and Agoda.com. Previously, only the high-end resorts had online booking services and webpages. These online booking sites have resulted in numerous small homestays and guest houses having an online presence.

BOOKING FLIGHTS

When booking domestic flights via the Internet, some Indonesian airline web-sites do not accept non-Indonesian credit cards. If you have problems processing an online payment, try using a different Internet browser. If you continue to have problems, it may be that your foreign card is not recognized. If you are traveling east of Bali, many operators will book domestic flights for you and add the price to your final bill. Check with your operator to see if they offer this service and if a surcharge applies. If you are booking a sequence of flights, try to use the same airline for all flights. Whilst this is not always possible, it means that if you miss a flight due to an earlier flight being delayed or cancelled, the airline will assist you to reach your final destination.

CURRENCY

See Money on page 282.

DUTY FREE

If you are planning to bring duty free into Indonesia with you, the current limits apply:

Tobacco: 200 cigarettes or 25 cigars or 100 grams of tobacco.

Alcohol: 1 liter of spirits

Perfume: A reasonable quantity

ELECTRICITY

Indonesia operates on a system of 220v/50Hz electrical outlets for two-pin plugs. Mains power supplies across Indonesia vary considerably. Most urban areas have 24/7 power. However, when you start traveling to smaller islands and further east, power becomes more of a problem. Some more remote islands are connected to the mains supply but for limited periods only, for example from 6 am to 6 pm, and in other areas such as Raja Ampat there is no mains power at all on most smaller islands. The majority of reputable operators in these areas have 24/7 power supplied by generators. Electricity should be used with consideration and visitors are urged to turn off AC units and lights when not in their rooms. It is worth noting that a few eco-friendly dive resorts have installed solar powers and wind turbines in order to reduce their generator usage and carbon emissions. Power cuts are frequent in comparison to Western countries and bringing a small torchlight for such occasions is recommended.

INTERNET ACCESS

Internet access is becoming increasingly available throughout Indonesia from large Internet cafes in towns and cities to free wi-fi at beachside local cafes. Many resorts and hotels have free wi-fi and you just need to ask for the password, but the range is often limited to areas such as the reception and restaurant. Larger international hotels will have wi-fi in the rooms. In more remote areas, you may be asked to pay a supplement for Internet access, while in other areas it is simply not available. If you need to check your emails whilst you are away, check with your operator before departure what facilities are available.

LANGUAGE

The official language of Indonesia is Bahasa Indonesia but there are over 700 indigenous languages in Indonesia that are still used today. Older generations, particularly in rural areas, have limited Bahasa and will rely mainly on their local language. Younger Indonesians and those in tourist areas have some basic English. Experienced dive guides usually have reasonable English and a few will be able to speak the basics of other European languages, most notably French and German. Western resorts tend to employ Western instructors, and courses are widely available in a range of European languages and in Asian languages such as Chinese and Japanese which are growing markets.

A well-stocked first aid kit is essential for traveling in Indonesia.

MEDICATIONS

If you are taking any prescribed medications, make sure you pack enough to last the duration of your trip. Depending on where you are, access to a prescribing doctor and the same medication may be limited. If you are planning to learn to dive and are taking medication, tell your operator beforehand.

MONEY

The currency in Indonesia is the Indonesian rupiah or IDR. It is possible to change money at numerous money changers across Indonesia but the best rates are usually found in more popularized areas, such as Bali and Jakarta. Many operators will request payment in advance, or at least part payment, and this would usually be made by bank transfer. Prices are quoted in various currencies depending on the operator, most notably Indonesian rupiah, American dollars and Euros. Outside of resorts, payment is almost always in rupiah. Payments by credit card are widely accepted but check with your operator prior to traveling. There is usually a bank charge on credit card payments, which can range from 3 to 8 percent. ATMs are widespread, but check with your bank about the charges you will incur. Travelers Checks are generally not accepted.

PACKING

Depending on where you are traveling in Indonesia, there can be limited opportunities for picking up supplies along the way, particularly if you are taking a liveaboard trip or traveling to the eastern parts of the archipelago. If you are traveling to more tourist-centric areas such as Bali where supplies are more readily available, you can rely on being able to pick up essentials but it is impossible to guarantee that you will be able to find everything on your list.

The following lists the most important items that you should consider bringing from home although it is not intended to be an exhaustive list.

Sunscreen, factor 50 plus
Photocopies of passport information page and visa page
Clothing: lightweight and light colored long pants and sleeves for evenings
Insect repellent
Medications
Snacks and treats
Alcohol: a bottle of your favorite tipple
Rechargeable batteries and charger
Batteries (take dead batteries home with you)
Torchlight/headlamp
Mosquito net, if not provided at your accommodation
Sea sickness medication
Dive certifications and Log book
Insurance documents
Anything requested by a resort, e.g. passport photographs, etc.
Polarized sunglasses
After sun lotion
Books
Chargers, camera, phone, kindle, tablet, laptop and extra batteries
Minor first aid kit including alcohol swabs, plasters, betadine, Panadol, antibiotic powder, paracetamol, ear drops, rehydration salts
Contact lenses and solution
Credit cards and ATM card
Two-pin plug adaptor
Folding raincoat

RELIGIOUS HOLIDAYS

Indonesia recognizes multiple religions and, as such, there are numerous public holidays for a multitude of religious days. Most operators, particularly Western-owned ones, do not close for religious holidays, but for the following holidays check with your chosen operator if you are staying in one of the areas listed. It is also worth noting that the dates of Muslim and Balinese Hindu holidays change from year to year:

Christmas: 25 September. In North Sulawesi, resorts are open but may be operating with reduced staff.

Idul Fitri: Dates change from year to year. Operators in Java and Lombok, which are predominantly Muslim areas, may close during this time.

Nyepi: Dates vary year to year. This is Balinese New Year, which is deemed a day of silence where everything closes, including the airport, and people are required to stay within the bounds of their homes or hotel. No resorts on Bali, including Nusa Lembongan and Nusa Penida, will dive on this day and hotel services will be limited.

TELEPHONE COMMUNICATIONS

If you are planning to call local numbers in Indonesia, by far the cheapest option is to invest in a local SIM card rather than use your phone overseas. Pay-as-you-go SIM cards and top-up vouchers (known as *pulsa*) are available from most street stalls and are very cheap. Check if your cell phone is able to accept other networks or if it is locked prior to departure. If you are planning to pick up a SIM card, check with your dive operator which network providers have the best coverage in their area. When traveling to remote parts of the archipelago or traveling by liveaboard, do not be surprised if there is no network coverage. Operators in these areas should have satellite phones for emergencies but it is best to advise friends and family prior to traveling that you will be out of reach for a week or so.

TIME ZONES

Although the Indonesian archipelago geographically stretches across four times zones, the government recognizes only three: Indonesia Western Time, Indonesia Central Time and Indonesia Eastern Time. Indonesia Western Time, locally known as WIB, is GMT+7. It covers Sumatra and Java and western and central Kalimantan. Indonesian Central Time, known as WITA, is GMT+8 and covers all of Sulawesi, Bali, the Nusa Tenggara Islands and the east of Kalimantan. Indonesian Eastern Time, known as WIT, is GMT+9 and covers the Maluku Islands and West Papua.

TIPPING

In some restaurants and hotels, a service charge is added to your bill and thus tipping is not expected, whilst in others a service charge is not included though a tip is always appreciated. In many dive resorts, envelopes are provided for guests to leave tip money, which is distributed across the staff by the management. If you are not sure how the policy works, check with your operator.

VACCINATIONS

Recommendations vary from time to time, so check with your doctor around two months prior to departure for recommended vaccinations. Some parts of Indonesia are considered high-risk malaria areas.

VISAS AND PASSPORTS

Currently, citizens from the following 45 countries can enter Indonesia visa free for stays of up to 30 days: Singapore, Thailand, Myanmar, Brunei, Malaysia, Cambodia, Vietnam, Laos, Philippines, Chile, Morocco, Peru, Ecuador, Hong Kong, Macau, China, Russia, South Korea, Japan, United States, Canada, New Zealand, Mexico, United Kingdom, Germany, France, the Netherlands, Italy, Spain, Switzerland, Belgium, Sweden, Austria, Denmark, Norway, Finland, Poland, Hungary, Czech Republic, Qatar, United Arab Emirates, Kuwait, Bahrain, Oman, and South Africa. For visitors traveling from other countries, visas on arrival are available at all international Indonesian airports and cost USD35 for a 30 day tourist visa. If you are staying for longer than 30 days, a 60 day tourist visa is also available but must be purchased prior to entry from the Indonesian embassy in your home country.

When you enter Indonesia, make sure that you have at least one clean page in your passport and that your passport has at least six months' validity remaining on it. You may also be required to show your ticket for onward travel leaving Indonesia. You are advised to check on your foreign office website for up-to-date information.

WATER

Tap water in Indonesia is not drinkable. In many resorts, the tap water is potable but it is strongly recommended that you purchase bottled water. To save on plastic, it is a good idea to bring a refillable bottle with you, especially as many places offer free refills.

A visa is required for Indonesia. Check on your government website for up-to-date regulations.

Index

Photo Credits

All photos copyright Sarah Ann Wormald, except for those listed below:

Pages 1 © Ray Salm; **2 top left** © John Becker; **2 top middle** © Cornelis Opstal/Dreamstime.com; **3 top middle** © Manta Dive Gili Trewangan; **3 top right** © Courtesy of Indosiren; **4 top** ©Courtesy of Shakti Liveaboard; **5 top right** © Stubblefieldphoto/Dreamstime.com; **6 bottom** © Christian Nielsen; **7 top** © John Becker; **7 bottom** © Klaus Hollitzer/istockphoto.com; **9 top** © Rich Horner; **9 middle** © Image from Wikipedia; **11** © Ethan Daniels/Shutterstock.com; **12 bottom** © Brandelet/Shutterstock.com; **12 top left** © Mikhail Dudarev/Dreamstime.com, **12 top right** © John Becker; **13 top left** © Frhojdysz/Dreamstime.com; **13 top right** © John Becker; **18 bottom** © Howard Chew/Dreamstime.com; **19 above** © John A. Anderson/Shutterstock.com; **19 below** © John Becker; **20 top** © Courtesy of Aurora Liveaboard; **20 bottom** © John Becker; **21 bottom** © Paul Kennedy/Dreamstime.com; **22 top** © John Becker; **23 right** © John Chapman and World Diving Lembongan; **24 top** © Courtesy of Bali Scuba; **25 left and right** © Courtesy of Master Selam; **26 top** © John Becker; **26 below right** © John Becker; **26 bottom** © Rafał Cichawa/Dreamstime.com; **27** © Peter Manz; **28 top** ©Jeremy Brown/Dreamstime.com; **29 bottom** © John Becker; **30 top left** © John Becker; **30/31 top middle** © John Becker; 31 middle left © Jürgen Freund; **30/31 middle** © John Becker; **31 right bottom** © Teguh Tirtaputra/Dreamstime.com; **30 bottom** © John Anderson/Dreamstime.com; **32 top** © Teguh Hardi/Dreamstime.com; **33 top** © hkomala/Shutterstock.com; **35 bottom** © Christian Nielsen; **36 top** © Christian Nielsen; **36 bottom** © John Becker; **38 bottom** © Ziye/Dreamstime.com; **39 top** © John Becker; **40 above left** © Christian Nielsen; **40 below left** © John Becker; **40 below right** © Courtesy of Bali Scuba.jpg; **42 middle** © CHEN WS/Shutterstock.com; **43 top** © Edmund Lowe Photography/Shutterstock.com; **43 bottom** © Scott Fields/Dreamstime.com; **44 bottom** © Christian Nielsen; **45 below** © John Becker; **50 right** © Christian Nielsen; **51 top** © Christian Nielsen; **52 top** © John Becker; **54/55 top** © Christian Nielsen; **55 middle left** © Christian Nielsen; **55 middle right** © Patrick Compau; **55 bottom** © Christian Nielsen; **58 bottom** © Christian Nielsen; **59 top** © Patrick Compau; **60 above** © Jpiks1/Dreamstime.com; **60 below** © Trubavin/Dreamstime.com; **63 top** © Mikhail Dudarev/Dreamstime.com; **64 bottom** © Dirk-jan Mattaar/Dreamstime.com; **65 top** © Christian Nielsen; **66 below** © Christian Nielsen; **67 top** © Christian Nielsen; **67 bottom** © Dirk-jan Mattaar/Dreamstime.com; **68 left** © Mikhail Dudarev/Dreamstime.com; **69 top** © Dirk-jan Mattaar/Dreamstime.com; **69 bottom** © John Anderson/Dreamstime.com; **74 bottom** © John Chapman; **75 middle** © John Becker; **77 top** © John Becker, **78 bottom** © John Becker; **80 top** © John Becker; **82 top** © Shariff Che\'Lah/Dreamstime.com; 82 bottom © John Becker; **83 right** © John Becker; **85 below** © John Becker; **86 left** © John Becker; **86 right** © John Becker; **87 top** © John Becker; **88 top** © John Becker; **89 bottom** © John Becker; **91 middle** © John Becker; **91 bottom** © John Becker; **93 top** © Lembeh Resort; **96 bottom** ©Murex Dive; **97 left** © Two Fish Divers Resort Bunaken; **97 right** © Two Fish Divers Resort Bunaken; **98 top left** © John Becker; **98 top right** © John Becker; **98 bottom left** © John Anderson/Dreamstime.com; **98 bottom right** © John Becker; **100** © Joanna Perel; **101 below** © Kkg1/Dreamstime.com; **102 above** © John Becker; **103 above** © John Becker; **103 below** © Joanna Perel; **105** © Lembeh Resort; **106 top** © Lembeh Resort; **106 middle** © Patrick Van Moer; **108 top** © Stubblefield Photography/Shutterstock.com; **108 bottom** © John Becker; **110 above** © Juerg Kipfer; 110 below © Juerg Kipfer; **112 above** © Stubblefieldphoto/Dreamstime.com; **112 below** © Stubblefieldphoto/Dreamstime.com; **115 top** © John Becker; **115 bottom** © John Becker; **116 bottom** © Asiantraveler/Dreamstime.com; **117 top** © John Becker; **120 bottom** © Wakatobi/Dreamstime.com; **122 bottom** © John Becker; **123 top right** © Joanna Perel; **123 middle right** © Joanna Perel; **126 bottom** © John Becker; **128 bottom** © Joanna Perel; **129 bottom** © Black Marlin Dive Resort; **131 above** © Kristina Vackova/Shutterstock.com; **131 below** © John Becker;

Acknowledgments

To my family, with oceans of love and seas of gratitude

Also to Sue Beebe and John Chapman for their support, friendship and kindness. Thank you for everything and for being such wonderful people.

Many dive operators across Indonesia have contributed to this book and my thanks extend to all who have given up tanks, guides, time, knowledge and patience. Special thanks to:

Bali Scuba and Knut Hoff and Simon Gilbert for their time, resources and support. Black Marlin Togean and Crispin Gibbs for his assistance. Blue Marlin Komodo and Dai Lovell and Kim Guenier for ensuring I got to some of the best dive sites. Dive Alor Dive and Dive Kupang Dive and Donovan Whitford for some great dives and fun around the Alor archipelago. Divers Lodge Lembeh and Weda Bay Reef and Rainforest and Rob and Linda Sinke for their time and hospitality. Maluku Divers, Ambon, for their hospitality and for an incredible wreck dive. Misool Eco Resort and Marit and Andrew Miners for all that they have achieved in Misool and for allowing me to experience it. Murex Dive Resorts, critters@LembehResort and Lembeh Resort, thanks to Danny Charlton and Angelique Batuna. Papua-Diving and Max Ammer and his teams in Kri Eco Resort and Sorido Bay, thank you for sharing such a wonderful place with me. Selayar Dive Resort and Jochen Schultheis for his help, knowledge and support. Siladen Dive Resort for their assistance and knowledge of turtle hatcheries. Tauch Terminal Tulamben and Axel Schwan for his time, help and hospitality. Werner Lau Pemuteran for assisting me at the last minute in Pemuteran. World Diving Lembongan and John Chapman, Sue Beebe, Pak Nyoman, Putu Sri Widari, Nick Gaylarf and all WDL Divemasters, Instructors and Crew, thank you for being such a fantastic team to work with.

I would also like to sincerely thank the following: Eric Oey and June Chong at Periplus without whom this book would not have been possible. John Becker who has contributed numerous images and time at the drop of a hat. Rich Horner who has provided incredible images and helped with my technology issues. Joanna Perel for her research contributions and images for Lombok, North and Central Sulawesi and for being such good fun to work with. Christian Nielsen for stunning photographs from around Bali and Komodo. Patrick Compau for providing images and for accompanying me on numerous diving adventures in Indonesia. Jurg Kipfer for his Lembeh Strait images and for being a great dive buddy, and Peter Manz for his expert knowledge of recompression chambers in Indonesia.

Thank you to the following liveaboards that have also assisted in this project: Arenui, Aurora, Damai I and II, Ikan Biru, Indo Siren, Seven Seas, Shakti and Tambora.

I would also like to extend my thanks to every dive guide who has accompanied me during my research and to all other photographers who have generously provided photographs.

A final thanks goes to all dive guides, instructors, boat captains and crew who work in Indonesia and who strive to protect Indonesian reefs and marine life on a daily basis. The efforts that operators go to in order to conserve their reefs is nothing short of outstanding and I take my hat off to all of you. Dive safely my friends!

DIVE LOGS

DIVE LOG

DIVE #

DATE:

DIVE LOCATION:

DIVE SITE NAME:

TIME IN:　　　　TIME OUT:

BOTTOM TIME:

BAR / PSI IN:　　　BAR / PSI OUT:

MAX DEPTH:

WATER TEMP:

VISIBILITY:

AIR / NITROX:

COMMENTS:

DIVE BUDDY:

INSTRUCTOR

GUIDE:

OPERATOR'S STAMP:

DIVE LOG

DIVE #

DATE:

DIVE LOCATION:

DIVE SITE NAME:

TIME IN:　　　　TIME OUT:

BOTTOM TIME:

BAR / PSI IN:　　　BAR / PSI OUT:

MAX DEPTH:

WATER TEMP:

VISIBILITY:

AIR / NITROX:

COMMENTS:

DIVE BUDDY:

INSTRUCTOR

GUIDE:

OPERATOR'S STAMP:

DIVE LOG

DIVE #

DATE:

DIVE LOCATION:

DIVE SITE NAME:

TIME IN: TIME OUT:

BOTTOM TIME:

BAR / PSI IN: BAR / PSI OUT:

MAX DEPTH:

WATER TEMP:

VISIBILITY:

AIR / NITROX:

COMMENTS:

DIVE BUDDY:

INSTRUCTOR

GUIDE:

OPERATOR'S STAMP:

DIVE LOG

DIVE #

DATE:

DIVE LOCATION:

DIVE SITE NAME:

TIME IN: TIME OUT:

BOTTOM TIME:

BAR / PSI IN: BAR / PSI OUT:

MAX DEPTH:

WATER TEMP:

VISIBILITY:

AIR / NITROX:

COMMENTS:

DIVE BUDDY:

INSTRUCTOR

GUIDE:

OPERATOR'S STAMP:

DIVE LOG

DIVE #

DATE:

DIVE LOCATION:

DIVE SITE NAME:

TIME IN: TIME OUT:

BOTTOM TIME:

BAR / PSI IN: BAR / PSI OUT:

MAX DEPTH:

WATER TEMP:

VISIBILITY:

AIR / NITROX:

COMMENTS:

DIVE BUDDY:

INSTRUCTOR

GUIDE:

OPERATOR'S STAMP:

DIVE LOG

DIVE #

DATE:

DIVE LOCATION:

DIVE SITE NAME:

TIME IN: TIME OUT:

BOTTOM TIME:

BAR / PSI IN: BAR / PSI OUT:

MAX DEPTH:

WATER TEMP:

VISIBILITY:

AIR / NITROX:

COMMENTS:

DIVE BUDDY:

INSTRUCTOR

GUIDE:

OPERATOR'S STAMP:

DIVE LOG

DIVE #

DATE:

DIVE LOCATION:

DIVE SITE NAME:

TIME IN: TIME OUT:

BOTTOM TIME:

BAR / PSI IN: BAR / PSI OUT:

MAX DEPTH:

WATER TEMP:

VISIBILITY:

AIR / NITROX:

COMMENTS:

DIVE BUDDY:

INSTRUCTOR

GUIDE:

OPERATOR'S STAMP:

DIVE LOG

DIVE #

DATE:

DIVE LOCATION:

DIVE SITE NAME:

TIME IN: TIME OUT:

BOTTOM TIME:

BAR / PSI IN: BAR / PSI OUT:

MAX DEPTH:

WATER TEMP:

VISIBILITY:

AIR / NITROX:

COMMENTS:

DIVE BUDDY:

INSTRUCTOR

GUIDE:

OPERATOR'S STAMP:

DIVE LOG

DIVE #

DATE:

DIVE LOCATION:

DIVE SITE NAME:

TIME IN: TIME OUT:

BOTTOM TIME:

BAR / PSI IN: BAR / PSI OUT:

MAX DEPTH:

WATER TEMP:

VISIBILITY:

AIR / NITROX:

COMMENTS:

DIVE BUDDY:

INSTRUCTOR

GUIDE:

OPERATOR'S
STAMP:

DIVE LOG

DIVE #

DATE:

DIVE LOCATION:

DIVE SITE NAME:

TIME IN: TIME OUT:

BOTTOM TIME:

BAR / PSI IN: BAR / PSI OUT:

MAX DEPTH:

WATER TEMP:

VISIBILITY:

AIR / NITROX:

COMMENTS:

DIVE BUDDY:

INSTRUCTOR

GUIDE:

OPERATOR'S
STAMP:

DIVE LOG

DIVE #

DATE:

DIVE LOCATION:

DIVE SITE NAME:

TIME IN: TIME OUT:

BOTTOM TIME:

BAR / PSI IN: BAR / PSI OUT:

MAX DEPTH:

WATER TEMP:

VISIBILITY:

AIR / NITROX:

COMMENTS:

DIVE BUDDY:

INSTRUCTOR

GUIDE:

OPERATOR'S
STAMP:

DIVE LOG

DIVE #

DATE:

DIVE LOCATION:

DIVE SITE NAME:

TIME IN: TIME OUT:

BOTTOM TIME:

BAR / PSI IN: BAR / PSI OUT:

MAX DEPTH:

WATER TEMP:

VISIBILITY:

AIR / NITROX:

COMMENTS:

DIVE BUDDY:

INSTRUCTOR

OPERATOR'S
STAMP:

GUIDE:

DIVE LOG

DIVE #

DATE:

DIVE LOCATION:

DIVE SITE NAME:

TIME IN: TIME OUT:

BOTTOM TIME:

BAR / PSI IN: BAR / PSI OUT:

MAX DEPTH:

WATER TEMP:

VISIBILITY:

AIR / NITROX:

COMMENTS:

DIVE BUDDY:

INSTRUCTOR

OPERATOR'S
STAMP:

GUIDE:

DIVE LOG

DIVE #

DATE:

DIVE LOCATION:

DIVE SITE NAME:

TIME IN: TIME OUT:

BOTTOM TIME:

BAR / PSI IN: BAR / PSI OUT:

MAX DEPTH:

WATER TEMP:

VISIBILITY:

AIR / NITROX:

COMMENTS:

DIVE BUDDY:

INSTRUCTOR

OPERATOR'S
STAMP:

GUIDE:

DIVE LOG

DIVE #

DATE: _____

DIVE LOCATION: _____

DIVE SITE NAME: _____

TIME IN: _____ TIME OUT: _____

BOTTOM TIME: _____

BAR / PSI IN: _____ BAR / PSI OUT: _____

MAX DEPTH: _____

WATER TEMP: _____

VISIBILITY: _____

AIR / NITROX: _____

COMMENTS: _____

DIVE BUDDY: _____

INSTRUCTOR _____

GUIDE: _____

OPERATOR'S STAMP:

DIVE LOG

DIVE #

DATE: _____

DIVE LOCATION: _____

DIVE SITE NAME: _____

TIME IN: _____ TIME OUT: _____

BOTTOM TIME: _____

BAR / PSI IN: _____ BAR / PSI OUT: _____

MAX DEPTH: _____

WATER TEMP: _____

VISIBILITY: _____

AIR / NITROX: _____

COMMENTS: _____

DIVE BUDDY: _____

INSTRUCTOR _____

GUIDE: _____

OPERATOR'S STAMP:

DIVE LOG

DIVE #

DATE: _____

DIVE LOCATION: _____

DIVE SITE NAME: _____

TIME IN: _____ TIME OUT: _____

BOTTOM TIME: _____

BAR / PSI IN: _____ BAR / PSI OUT: _____

MAX DEPTH: _____

WATER TEMP: _____

VISIBILITY: _____

AIR / NITROX: _____

COMMENTS: _____

DIVE BUDDY: _____

INSTRUCTOR _____

GUIDE: _____

OPERATOR'S STAMP:

DIVE LOG

DIVE #

DATE:

DIVE LOCATION:

DIVE SITE NAME:

TIME IN: TIME OUT:

BOTTOM TIME:

BAR / PSI IN: BAR / PSI OUT:

MAX DEPTH:

WATER TEMP:

VISIBILITY:

AIR / NITROX:

COMMENTS:

DIVE BUDDY:

INSTRUCTOR

GUIDE:

OPERATOR'S
STAMP:

DIVE LOG

DIVE #

DATE:

DIVE LOCATION:

DIVE SITE NAME:

TIME IN: TIME OUT:

BOTTOM TIME:

BAR / PSI IN: BAR / PSI OUT:

MAX DEPTH:

WATER TEMP:

VISIBILITY:

AIR / NITROX:

COMMENTS:

DIVE BUDDY:

INSTRUCTOR

GUIDE:

OPERATOR'S
STAMP:

DIVE LOG

DIVE #

DATE:

DIVE LOCATION:

DIVE SITE NAME:

TIME IN: TIME OUT:

BOTTOM TIME:

BAR / PSI IN: BAR / PSI OUT:

MAX DEPTH:

WATER TEMP:

VISIBILITY:

AIR / NITROX:

COMMENTS:

DIVE BUDDY:

INSTRUCTOR

GUIDE:

OPERATOR'S
STAMP:

DIVE LOG

DIVE #

DATE:

DIVE LOCATION:

DIVE SITE NAME:

TIME IN: TIME OUT:

BOTTOM TIME:

BAR / PSI IN: BAR / PSI OUT:

MAX DEPTH:

WATER TEMP:

VISIBILITY:

AIR / NITROX:

COMMENTS:

DIVE BUDDY:

INSTRUCTOR

GUIDE:

OPERATOR'S
STAMP:

DIVE LOG

DIVE #

DATE:

DIVE LOCATION:

DIVE SITE NAME:

TIME IN: TIME OUT:

BOTTOM TIME:

BAR / PSI IN: BAR / PSI OUT:

MAX DEPTH:

WATER TEMP:

VISIBILITY:

AIR / NITROX:

COMMENTS:

DIVE BUDDY:

INSTRUCTOR

GUIDE:

OPERATOR'S
STAMP:

DIVE LOG

DIVE #

DATE:

DIVE LOCATION:

DIVE SITE NAME:

TIME IN: TIME OUT:

BOTTOM TIME:

BAR / PSI IN: BAR / PSI OUT:

MAX DEPTH:

WATER TEMP:

VISIBILITY:

AIR / NITROX:

COMMENTS:

DIVE BUDDY:

INSTRUCTOR

GUIDE:

OPERATOR'S
STAMP:

DIVE LOG

DIVE #

DATE: _____

DIVE LOCATION: _____

DIVE SITE NAME: _____

TIME IN: _____ TIME OUT: _____

BOTTOM TIME: _____

BAR / PSI IN: _____ BAR / PSI OUT: _____

MAX DEPTH: _____

WATER TEMP: _____

VISIBILITY: _____

AIR / NITROX: _____

COMMENTS: _____

_____

_____

_____

_____

DIVE BUDDY: _____

INSTRUCTOR _____

GUIDE: _____

OPERATOR'S STAMP:

DIVE LOG

DIVE #

DATE: _____

DIVE LOCATION: _____

DIVE SITE NAME: _____

TIME IN: _____ TIME OUT: _____

BOTTOM TIME: _____

BAR / PSI IN: _____ BAR / PSI OUT: _____

MAX DEPTH: _____

WATER TEMP: _____

VISIBILITY: _____

AIR / NITROX: _____

COMMENTS: _____

_____

_____

_____

_____

DIVE BUDDY: _____

INSTRUCTOR _____

GUIDE: _____

OPERATOR'S STAMP:

DIVE LOG

DIVE #

DATE: _____

DIVE LOCATION: _____

DIVE SITE NAME: _____

TIME IN: _____ TIME OUT: _____

BOTTOM TIME: _____

BAR / PSI IN: _____ BAR / PSI OUT: _____

MAX DEPTH: _____

WATER TEMP: _____

VISIBILITY: _____

AIR / NITROX: _____

COMMENTS: _____

_____

_____

_____

_____

DIVE BUDDY: _____

INSTRUCTOR _____

GUIDE: _____

OPERATOR'S STAMP:

DIVE LOG

DIVE #

DATE:

DIVE LOCATION:

DIVE SITE NAME:

TIME IN: TIME OUT:

BOTTOM TIME:

BAR / PSI IN: BAR / PSI OUT:

MAX DEPTH:

WATER TEMP:

VISIBILITY:

AIR / NITROX:

COMMENTS:

DIVE BUDDY:

INSTRUCTOR

OPERATOR'S
STAMP:

GUIDE:

DIVE LOG

DIVE #

DATE:

DIVE LOCATION:

DIVE SITE NAME:

TIME IN: TIME OUT:

BOTTOM TIME:

BAR / PSI IN: BAR / PSI OUT:

MAX DEPTH:

WATER TEMP:

VISIBILITY:

AIR / NITROX:

COMMENTS:

DIVE BUDDY:

INSTRUCTOR

OPERATOR'S
STAMP:

GUIDE:

DIVE LOG

DIVE #

DATE:

DIVE LOCATION:

DIVE SITE NAME:

TIME IN: TIME OUT:

BOTTOM TIME:

BAR / PSI IN: BAR / PSI OUT:

MAX DEPTH:

WATER TEMP:

VISIBILITY:

AIR / NITROX:

COMMENTS:

DIVE BUDDY:

INSTRUCTOR

OPERATOR'S
STAMP:

GUIDE:

DIVE LOG

DIVE #

DATE:

DIVE LOCATION:

DIVE SITE NAME:

TIME IN: TIME OUT:

BOTTOM TIME:

BAR / PSI IN: BAR / PSI OUT:

MAX DEPTH:

WATER TEMP:

VISIBILITY:

AIR / NITROX:

COMMENTS:

DIVE BUDDY:

INSTRUCTOR   OPERATOR'S
                           STAMP:

GUIDE:

DIVE LOG

DIVE #

DATE:

DIVE LOCATION:

DIVE SITE NAME:

TIME IN: TIME OUT:

BOTTOM TIME:

BAR / PSI IN: BAR / PSI OUT:

MAX DEPTH:

WATER TEMP:

VISIBILITY:

AIR / NITROX:

COMMENTS:

DIVE BUDDY:

INSTRUCTOR   OPERATOR'S
                           STAMP:

GUIDE:

DIVE LOG

DIVE #

DATE:

DIVE LOCATION:

DIVE SITE NAME:

TIME IN: TIME OUT:

BOTTOM TIME:

BAR / PSI IN: BAR / PSI OUT:

MAX DEPTH:

WATER TEMP:

VISIBILITY:

AIR / NITROX:

COMMENTS:

DIVE BUDDY:

INSTRUCTOR   OPERATOR'S
                           STAMP:

GUIDE:

DIVE LOG

DIVE #

DATE:

DIVE LOCATION:

DIVE SITE NAME:

TIME IN: TIME OUT:

BOTTOM TIME:

BAR / PSI IN: BAR / PSI OUT:

MAX DEPTH:

WATER TEMP:

VISIBILITY:

AIR / NITROX:

COMMENTS:

DIVE BUDDY:

INSTRUCTOR

GUIDE:

OPERATOR'S STAMP:

DIVE LOG

DIVE #

DATE:

DIVE LOCATION:

DIVE SITE NAME:

TIME IN: TIME OUT:

BOTTOM TIME:

BAR / PSI IN: BAR / PSI OUT:

MAX DEPTH:

WATER TEMP:

VISIBILITY:

AIR / NITROX:

COMMENTS:

DIVE BUDDY:

INSTRUCTOR

GUIDE:

OPERATOR'S STAMP:

DIVE LOG

DIVE #

DATE:

DIVE LOCATION:

DIVE SITE NAME:

TIME IN: TIME OUT:

BOTTOM TIME:

BAR / PSI IN: BAR / PSI OUT:

MAX DEPTH:

WATER TEMP:

VISIBILITY:

AIR / NITROX:

COMMENTS:

DIVE BUDDY:

INSTRUCTOR

GUIDE:

OPERATOR'S STAMP:

Published by Tuttle Publishing, an imprint of Periplus Editions (HK) Ltd

www.tuttlepublishing.com

Copyright © 2015 Periplus Editions (HK) Ltd

ISBN: 978-0-8048-4474-1

Distributed by

North America, Latin America & Europe
Tuttle Publishing
364 Innovation Drive
North Clarendon, VT 05759-9436 U.S.A.
Tel: 1 (802) 773-8930; Fax: 1 (802) 773-6993
info@tuttlepublishing.com
www.tuttlepublishing.com

Japan
Tuttle Publishing
Yaekari Building, 3rd Floor, 5-4-12 Osaki
Shinagawa-ku, Tokyo 141-0032
Tel: (81) 3 5437-0171; Fax: (81) 3 5437-0755
sales@tuttle.co.jp; www.tuttle.co.jp

Asia Pacific
Berkeley Books Pte. Ltd.
3 Kallang Sector, #04-01, Singapore 349278
Tel: (65) 67412178; Fax: (65) 67412179
inquiries@periplus.com.sg; www.periplus.com

Indonesia
PT Java Books Indonesia
Kawasan Industri Pulogadung
JI. Rawa Gelam IV No. 9, Jakarta 13930
Tel: (62) 21 4682-1088; Fax: (62) 21 461-0206
crm@periplus.co.id; www.periplus.com

21 20 19   10 9 8 7 6 5 4 3 2

Printed in China   1812CM

About Tuttle
"Books to Span the East and West"

Our core mission at Tuttle Publishing is to create books which bring people together one page at a time. Tuttle was founded in 1832 in the small New England town of Rutland, Vermont (USA). Our fundamental values remain as strong today as they were then—to publish best-in-class books informing the English-speaking world about the countries and peoples of Asia. The world has become a smaller place today and Asia's economic, cultural and political influence has expanded, yet the need for meaningful dialogue and information about this diverse region has never been greater. Since 1948, Tuttle has been a leader in publishing books on the cultures, arts, cuisines, languages and literatures of Asia. Our authors and photographers have won numerous awards and Tuttle has published thousands of books on subjects ranging from martial arts to paper crafts. We welcome you to explore the wealth of information available on Asia at **www.tuttlepublishing.com.**